Father Charles Connor's work studies the significant period of nearly five decades surrounding the American Civil War, which was so formative in the life of the American Catholic Church. He takes an in-depth look at these difficult years and paints a picture of how the Church, amidst widespread persecution, grew, developed, and contributed to the common good of our fractured nation. His work will prove an invaluable resource to those studying the contributions of the Church in the United States and its influence on our country at the most difficult time in our nation's history.

—Most Rev. William E. Lori, D.D., S.T.D.
Archbishop of Baltimore

Faith and Fury: The Rise of Catholicism during the Civil War is truly a remarkable work—a carefully researched and engaging study of nearly fifty years of the Catholic Church's growth, development, and contributions in the nineteenth century. I highly recommend this marvelous book. A monumental gift to the Church!

—Most Rev. Joseph C. Bambera, D.D., J.C.L.
Bishop of Scranton

Father Connor has once again proven that he is a master of Church history in the United States. In his book *Faith and Fury: The Rise of Catholicism during the Civil War*, he adeptly navigates a difficult period in American history and shows how the Church continued to grow and respond to her mission of proclaiming the Gospel. From the challenges of anti-Catholic bigotry and the contributions of great prelatic figures such as Archbishops Hughes and Kenrick, to the role of the Fighting 69th, and the Second Plenary Council of

Baltimore, this book gives a robust picture of the Catholic Church of the mid-nineteenth century. If you are interested in American Church history, or history in general, I highly recommend that you read this book.

—Rev. Msgr. Andrew R. Baker, S.T.D.
Rector, Mount Saint Mary's Seminary
Emmitsburg, Maryland

Father Connor's exceptional work brings to life the significant role the Catholic Church played during a particularly divisive period in our nation's history. Though marginalized by some, the Church helped ease the difficult transition of immigrants into our fledgling country and began a needed focus on the faithful education of children. As president of Mount Saint Mary's University, it makes me proud to read of the impact that graduates such as Archbishop Hughes, aka Dagger John, had on the development of our Church and other social systems in America.

—Timothy E. Trainor, Ph.D.,
U.S. Army Brigadier General (Retired)
President, Mount Saint Mary's University

∞

Faith and Fury

Also by Fr. Charles P. Connor:

Pioneer Priests and Makeshift Altars
A History of Catholicism in the Thirteen Colonies

Fr. Charles P. Connor, S.T.L., Ph.D.

FAITH AND FURY

THE RISE OF CATHOLICISM
DURING THE CIVIL WAR

EWTN PUBLISHING, INC.
Irondale, Alabama

EWTN Publishing, Inc.
5817 Old Leeds Road, Irondale, AL 35210

Distributed by Sophia Institute Press, Box 5284, Manchester, NH 03108.

Library of Congress Cataloging-in-Publication Data

Names: Connor, Charles P. (Charles Patrick), author.
Title: Faith and fury : the rise of Catholicism during the Civil War / Fr. Charles P. Connor, S.T.L., Ph.D.
Description: Irondale, Alabama : EWTN Publishing, Inc., 2019. Includes bibliographical references.
Identifiers: LCCN 2019017682 ISBN 9781682780664 (pbk. : alk. paper)
Subjects: LCSH: Catholic Church—United States—History—19th century.
Catholic Church—United States—History—Civil War, 1861-1865.
Classification: LCC BX1406.3 .C65 2019 DDC 282/.7309034—dc23 LC record available at https://lccn.loc.gov/2019017682

First printing

Contents

∞

Foreword

In his nearly three decades of priestly life, Father Charles P. Connor, professor of systematic theology and Church history at Mount Saint Mary's Seminary, Emmitsburg, Maryland, has served as a parish priest and rector of Saint Peter's Cathedral in his home diocese of Scranton, Pennsylvania, as well as producing, over the course of more than two decades, numerous series on Church history and Catholic spirituality for the Eternal Word Television Network. In his newest book, *Faith and Fury: The Rise of Catholicism during the Civil War*, he has substantially contributed to the literature of nineteenth-century United States Catholic history.

The prologue to the coming of the war (1828–1848) encompasses the growth of the Church under Her most remembered shepherds and set against the background of Jacksonian America. Manifest Destiny, and all that it meant to the rising tide of immigration, antagonized the nativist movement, which, in turn, produced literature, stump oratory, and even violence aimed at halting the growth of the Church, made up of a strong foreign element of Irish and German Catholics. The period of the war's coming (1848–1860) presented its own unique political landscape and politicians, many of whom played a role in the rise of Know-Nothingism, yet another manifestation of anti-Catholic bigotry. The Dred Scott decision handed down by the Catholic chief justice

Faith and Fury

Roger B. Taney, Taney's later thoughts on slavery, as well as those of Southern bishops, and the 1860 election of Abraham Lincoln (who had Catholic relatives), bring the period to a close.

Father Connor, whose doctoral thesis dealt with New York's archbishop John Hughes, concentrates much on the New York prelate's position on the peculiar institution of slavery, along with those of Archbishop Kenrick in Philadelphia, and Bishops John England in Charleston, Martin J. Spalding in Louisville, and Augustine Verot in Savannah. The work of religious communities of Black Sisters, the positions of lay Catholics on slavery, and the Catholic press's reaction to the Emancipation Proclamation are some of the areas studied.

The war years themselves (1861–1865) consider the political background of the period, and the fascinating correspondence between New York's Archbishop Hughes and Charleston's Bishop Patrick N. Lynch. Both natives of Ireland, both diplomatic representatives of their respective governments to European powers during the war, and both clearly emphasizing the respective theories of government upon which their nations were built, the prelates clearly underscore the fact that sectional divergence was no stranger to the Church, though Her unity of faith was never for a moment questioned. Contributions of scores of chaplains, from North and South, as well as the incredible works of mercy of religious Sisters to the wounded on the battlefield, and the brave gallantry of so many Irish, both immigrants and native born, all find their way into this narrative.

Another feature of American Catholicism was the question of Black evangelization, along with the plight of the freed former slaves after the war. This issue was hotly contested by the American bishops at the Second Plenary Council of Baltimore in 1866, and it was quickly discovered that unity of opinion would be very difficult to achieve. Archbishop John McCloskey of New York noted that "in no way was the conscience of the Bishops of the North burdened" when it came to the pastoral needs of African Americans. Bishop Augustin Verot of Savannah bemoaned the "hopeless situation" faced by many former slaves and urged strong action. An additional challenge pointed out by Bishop McGill of Richmond was the fact that the great majority of African Americans were non-Catholic. These three perspectives demonstrate that the social context of nineteenth-century America was both diverse and fluid, and once again, the situation of Catholics was no different as a result of waves of European immigration from east to west.

It has been argued that when the nation's bishops met again in Baltimore for the Third Plenary Council in 1884 to produce the *Baltimore Catechism* and create what became the magnificent parochial school system, they were merely building on the work of their predecessors in maintaining unity in the face of the considerable challenge of the years described aptly by Archbishop Hughes as the "melancholy strife." Father Connor's *Faith and Fury: The Rise of Catholicism during the Civil War* has decidedly underscored that work.

I highly recommend this book for students of the period, Civil War buffs, and all desirous of knowing more about the tremendous contributions of the Catholic Church in these years.

✚ Timothy Michael Cardinal Dolan
Archbishop of New York

∞

Faith and Fury

Chapter 1

Prologue to the Coming of the War: 1828–1848

Setting the Scene

Historians generally date the American Civil War era from the most tangible signs of the crisis of the Union in 1848 until the withdrawal of the final federal troops from the South and the implementation of Reconstruction in 1877. Any consideration of the history of the Catholic Church in the United States during these years must be concentrated in these years, but a tremendously important foundation had been laid in the two prior decades. This background, which will help us to appreciate better where the Church found Herself as the "melancholy strife" approached, is where we will begin.[1]

The Church had experienced significant growth in Her numbers and institutions in the decades leading up to the mid-nineteenth century. This was set against a background of political and social strife, including a virulent anti-Catholicism that found expression in literature, rhetoric, politics, and, in several instances, violence.

---

[1] The expression "melancholy strife" was used multiple times by New York's fourth bishop and first archbishop, John Hughes, in much of his correspondence, especially to his friend William H. Seward, Lincoln's secretary of state, as well as to other prominent friends in church and state. Hughes will be one of the most prominent players in the story of U.S. Catholicism in these years.

Faith and Fury

These incidents, along with those in the Colonial and Revolutionary periods, led the American historian Arthur Schlesinger Sr. to declare that anti-Catholicism was the deepest bias in the American people.

Amid challenging politics and social tides, the Church was gradually finding Her way in the early national period. The nation's premier Catholic see of Baltimore was divided in 1808 into the suffragan sees of New York, Philadelphia, Boston, and Bardstown, Kentucky.[2] It was an era when the Anglo-Catholicism associated with the Colonial and Revolutionary years was being replaced by the growth of cities teeming with immigrants, who eventually constituted the urban majority of American Catholicism. Alexis de Tocqueville, the French commentator on American culture and mores, opined that Catholics in the new nation were extremely devout in the practice of their Faith and were also the most independent of thinkers. This independence was reflected in a system of church governance, absorbed from American Protestantism, known as lay trusteeism. This system allowed lay parishioners, elected as trustees, to claim, on the basis of civil law, vast parochial and administrative powers, including the right to choose and dismiss pastors. In the Catholic context, it was often, essentially, a form of insubordination. Major lay-cleric conflicts occurred in cities such as Philadelphia, New York, Buffalo, and Norfolk, Virginia. Even after direct Vatican intervention, lay trusteeship continued to endure until its incompatibility with

---

[2]   The term "suffragan sees" refers to the relationship between dioceses with their bishops and metropolitan sees (archdioceses) with their archbishops. In these early years, Baltimore, which was raised to an archdiocese in 1808, would have been the metropolitan see, and its archbishop, the metropolitan. The actual authority a metropolitan has over his suffragan sees has shifted over the years but is generally minimal.

traditional Catholic church governance proved unsustainable, and it finally died off.

Baltimore was headed, until 1815, by Archbishop John Carroll, a member of the most prominent of Maryland Catholic families; he, in turn, was succeeded by a variety of shepherds, several of whom were major contributors to the Catholic history of their eras. Perhaps best known to this day is Philadelphia's John N. Neumann, who was celebrated then and now for his holiness of life and his exemplary priesthood. Born in the Czech Republic of a German-Bohemian background, he came to America, was ordained in St. Patrick's Old Cathedral in New York City, served parochial assignments, and eventually joined the Redemptorists, rising to become superior of the American congregation. Always more at home as an itinerant missionary and pastor of souls than in Philadelphia high society, this future saint built the Cathedral Basilica of Sts. Peter and Paul, established the Forty Hours devotion in the United States, founded a religious community of Sisters, and had to contend with anti-Catholic bigotry in the City of Brotherly Love. More than a century following his death, he was raised to the altars of sainthood.

Without a doubt the most recognized spokesman for Catholicism in America in the mid-nineteenth century, as well as the strongest fighter for Catholic rights, was John Joseph Hughes. Born in 1797 in County Tyrone, Ireland, he came to America with his family as a young man and settled in Chambersburg, Pennsylvania, where his father secured employment as a stone mason. He was employed as a gardener on the grounds of Mount St. Mary's Seminary in Emmitsburg, Maryland, and was later admitted there as a seminarian, at the urging of Mother Elizabeth Seton. The president and rector who accepted him, John Dubois, would one day become bishop of New York.

From his ordination and early years in Philadelphia, Hughes rose quickly to become coadjutor to Dubois and, in 1842, New

York's bishop. His career would involve him with politicians, city officials, fellow bishops from around the country, and adversaries of the Catholic Church, in whatever form they were found. His combative rhetoric made New York a significant bully pulpit for the Church. He was not a man to be crossed: James Gordon Bennett, editor of the *New York Herald* and one of Hughes's leading critics, in printing one of the bishop's statements, substituted a dagger for the traditional cross affixed to episcopal signatures. From this, the nickname "Dagger John" developed, and it is still used by historians for the formidable character who headed the New York Archdiocese for some two decades.

A glimpse of the Church's growth in these years is well captured by one of Her historians:

> Before the Civil War fifteen dioceses were established in the East. To the West, the most significant area for growth in the first quarter of the nineteenth century was the old Northwest Territory, bounded by the Mississippi and Ohio Rivers, and by the Great Lakes. Along the Southern border states of Kentucky and Tennessee, the See of Bardstown was moved to Louisville in 1841. By then, the real nucleus of Church development had shifted North across the Ohio to Cincinnati where the Dominican Edward Fenwick was Bishop, from 1821 through 1832, and John Baptist Purcell for the next half century.... German and Irish poured into Cincinnati, while French Canadian Catholics occupied trading posts from Detroit to Green Bay [to] Prairie du Chien. Ottawa and Chippewa Indians lived along Michigan's Saint Joseph River, and around the Straits of Mackinac.... Organization followed population growth: Detroit (1833), Vincennes (1834), Nashville in 1837, Chicago and Milwaukee, both in 1843.... The trans Mississippi West shared the development

of Saint Louis, the Gateway to the Great Plains, [which] became a diocese in 1826. The first bishop of Saint Louis was a Vincentian from Italy, Joseph Rosati. His successor, Irish born Peter Richard Kenrick, brother of the Archbishop of Baltimore, was to govern almost fifty years.[3]

Building Tensions

By the early decades of the nineteenth century, the sectionalism that would eventually divide the nation was mounting. The application by the Missouri Territory for slave statehood in 1817 initiated a new wave of tension. Slavery had been an accepted institution since the earliest English settlement at Jamestown in the seventeenth century. All the while, it disturbed consciences from one generation to the next. Up to the time of Missouri's request, Congress, by unwritten agreement, would admit one free state for every new slave state to maintain equality. Missouri would have changed the balance for the slave states, and there was no immediate prospect of a new free state applying for admission. As such, the slave states would control the Senate for an indefinite number of years.

Attempting to solve this difficulty, Congressman James Tallmadge of New York submitted an amendment that would grant freedom to slaves living in Missouri, permanently restrict the admission of new slaves, and grant freedom to all Black children upon reaching the age of twenty-five. Tallmadge's amendment was defeated upon reaching the Senate, only to be replaced by another one by Senator Jesse Thomas of Illinois. After negotiations with representatives from Massachusetts, the Bay State agreed to

---

[3] James Hennesey, S.J., *American Catholics* (New York: Oxford University Press, 1981), 110–112.

Faith and Fury

release its northern counties to become the state of Maine. The Thomas Amendment also called for a dividing line at 36 degrees 30 minutes latitude through the land of the Louisiana Purchase, along the southern border of Missouri. North of the line, slavery would be prohibited (except in the new state), and south of it, slavery would be permitted. "The Compromise was accepted and regarded as almost sacred," one source noted, "until the Mexican War, when the power of Congress to exclude slavery from the territories was again questioned."[4] At least one historian felt it defined Americans' self-understanding for decades to come:

> The whole nation had been shown that it must either accept the undemocratic dogma that the Negro had not been created the equal of the white man or else confess that something was seriously wrong with every part of its democratic structure. The Compromise intimated that the nation preferred the former of these alternatives.[5]

Another stressor was the Tariff of Abominations in 1828, which set the interests of the North, South, and an emerging West against one another. Southern states generally opposed tariffs, which protected Northern industries from foreign competition while raising expenses in its own agrarian economy. Meanwhile, the West desired across-the-board protectionism for its fledgling economy. Hoping to use these tensions for his own advantage, presidential hopeful Andrew Jackson and his supporters attempted to orchestrate a complicated legislative strategy that would result in a tariff bill unpalatable to both Northern industrial and Southern agrarian interests. The failure of the bill would please Jackson's southern

[4] Thomas C. Cochran, ed., *Concise Dictionary of American History* (New York: Charles Scribner's Sons, 1962), 620.
[5] George Dangerfield, *The Awakening of American Nationalism* (New York: Harper and Row, 1965), 139.

8

base, who would, in turn, blame the failure on intransigent New England business interests, thus uniting West and South and some border regions against the industrial North—and with the populist Jackson.

But the plan backfired spectacularly. In the end, enough Northern officials supported the tariff to pass into law the highest rates in American history. The South was especially furious that the plan had not materialized, prompting Vice President John C. Calhoun of South Carolina to write an anonymous states' rights pamphlet called *The South Carolina Exposition and Protest*. Here, he popularized the theory of nullification—that when a federal statute contradicts the law of a state, the state has the right to override the federal law—which became an essential part of the theoretical framework for secession.

Yet another example of emerging sectionalism was the celebrated debate between Senator Daniel Webster of Massachusetts and Senator Robert Hayne of South Carolina about a proposed bill that would restrict the sale of publicly owned lands in the West. One of the most vocal opponents of the bill was Senator Thomas Hart Benton of Missouri, who asserted that the North was plotting against the West because so much of its population was migrating there. Hayne proposed the South and the West form a political alliance of common interest: The South would vote with the West for cheap land if the West would oppose the North on tariffs. Webster contended the North was not plotting against anyone, but was working for the common good of the nation, adding that Hayne should rethink his parochialism and do the same. Hayne replied with a classic states' rights argument, asserting that the South's view of federal law was correct for everyone. Webster then took the floor, and, in what has been called his "Second Reply to Hayne," tore apart the states' rights theory of government. The national compact was, he argued, a compact of the people of America, not of thirteen states. This was the people's right, and the nation they formed was indissoluble.

South Carolina was at the center of much political and social activity in these early decades of the nineteenth century. What is less known is that it was a center of considerable Catholic activity as well. When the Diocese of Charleston was established in 1820, it included both Carolinas and Georgia. A priest named John England of the Diocese of Cork, Ireland, was chosen to head the new see. Ordained in 1809, Fr. England quickly became known for energetic apostolic activity, as well as his political agitation for Catholic emancipation in Ireland. Some Irish historians have suggested that his voice was second only to that of Daniel O'Connell in bringing about reform. Because he was as well known for the written word as the spoken, his rise in the Church was no surprise.

Upon arriving in America, he immediately declared his intention to apply for citizenship and, just as quickly, began ministering to the Irish immigrants as well as the many refugees from Santo Domingo found in Charleston. He led the life of an itinerant missionary, visiting any area where Catholics resided, teaching them the catechism and appointing others to continue his work before he moved on. He established parishes and preached in many cities in whatever venues presented themselves—quite often in Protestant churches at the invitation of their pastors. He founded the Philosophical and Classical Seminary of Charleston, a school where many of America's early priests were educated.

Fr. England's unique form of diocesan administration was based on the American bicameral system in Washington, with the House of Vestry corresponding to the U.S. Senate and consisting of two representatives from each parish in the diocese, and the House of Delegates based on proportional representation. England opened a school for free Black children in the city and, along with his sister

Joanna, began the nation's first Catholic newspaper, the *United States Catholic Miscellany*. He contributed much to the American Catholic position on slavery through his early writings, played a central role at the First Provincial Council of Baltimore, and did much to break down anti-Catholic prejudice in an area of the country where it was rampant. His desire to assimilate was well captured by one historian's observation:

> In Charleston he and his growing flock enjoyed liberties that Catholics in Ireland could only dream about. A close friend of his recorded that his greatest wish was to achieve "what might be called the 'naturalization' of Catholicity. He desired that it no longer be regarded as the religion of the stranger." On the contrary, he wanted it to be "American in principle, feeling and habit."[6]

In the 1830s, sectionalism became even more pronounced. Just one year into the decade, Nat Turner's Rebellion occurred in Southhampton County, Virginia. Turner, a Black preacher, led a group of slaves who killed more than fifty people, mostly White. The rebellion was put down within a matter of days, but Turner was not apprehended for two months. He and about twenty followers were executed after a series of trials. Throughout the South, slave codes "were tightened to curb the mobility of slaves …, prohibit their attendance at meetings, curtail their education, drastically restrict manumissions, and impose special disabilities on free Negroes."[7]

The protectionist tariff of 1832, introduced at the end of Andrew Jackson's first presidential term, did not win acceptance in

---

[6] David T. Gleeson, *The Irish in the South: 1815–1877* (Chapel Hill: University of North Carolina Press, 2001), 78.

[7] Richard B. Morris, ed., *Encyclopedia of American History* (New York: Harper and Row, 1965), 544.

the agrarian South. In response, South Carolina called a special convention, which issued the Ordinance of Nullification, declaring the tariff unconstitutional and noncollectible in the Palmetto State. Though South Carolina stood alone in its fierce opposition, it was not until the following year, when Henry Clay of Kentucky introduced a compromise bill lowering tariff rates over the next decade, that South Carolina acceded. Also introduced at President Jackson's behest was the Force Bill, which authorized the president to take coercive measures when a state refuses to comply with federal law.

New Year's Day 1831 witnessed the first issue of abolitionist William Lloyd Garrison's newspaper, the *Liberator*. Born in Newburyport, Massachusetts, Garrison had had a lengthy career in journalism, rising to become a nationally recognized speaker and publisher. Though never advocating violence in the pages of his paper, the intensity of his rhetoric and that of his contributors led many of his readers and supporters to believe otherwise—and to feel that Nat Turner's Rebellion, just seven months after the paper's founding, was a direct result. Garrison and a number of followers went on to establish the New England Anti-Slavery Society; as adherents and affiliated societies grew, the creation of the American Anti-Slavery Society soon followed. The purpose of these groups was to awaken the American consciousness to the moral evil of slavery, and how detestable it was in God's sight.

Also attracting national attention were the debates over slavery taking place at the Presbyterian Lane Theological Seminary in Cincinnati. Various groups of anti-slavery advocates gathered at the seminary in 1832, and when the school's board of trustees eventually voted to halt the disputations, much of the student body withdrew. The discussions moved to Oberlin College in Ohio, the first college in the country to admit women, and the place where Western abolitionism found a home. Events such as these played a direct role in the way the Catholic Church responded to American slavery: It turned out that American abolitionists, almost to a person, believed that the physical bondage of slavery was easily equated with the spiritual bondage in which Rome's doctrines kept Her members. The Church was not welcome in mainstream abolitionism and had to find her own way.

Tex-Mex Catholicism

In the 1840s, the annexation of Texas figured significantly in the future of Catholicism in this nation. Some Americans had always felt that Texas had rightfully been part of the United States since Thomas Jefferson's Louisiana Purchase. While this claim faded over the decades, many felt that the presidential election of 1844, which brought the expansionist James K. Polk to office, was a mandate for further American development. The departing president, John Tyler, felt that the Texas annexation treaty should be adopted by both houses of Congress on the grounds that a majority of states favored immediate annexation, and because American relations with Mexico were becoming more strained over time. It passed the House readily, but in the Senate, Missouri's Thomas Hart Benton posed the objection that Congress had no authorization to admit a state carved from foreign territory. To overcome this, an amendment was introduced that empowered the president to negotiate a new treaty that could either be ratified by the Senate or passed by a joint resolution. In this form, the Senate passed the treaty, which made no reference to securing the approval of the Mexican government. The resolution provided that

> Texas was to be admitted to statehood without a preliminary
> period of territorial status; that, with the consent of Texas,

no more than 4 additional states might be formed from its territory; that Texas was to retain her public lands, but pay her own debt; and that the Missouri Compromise line of 36 degrees 30 minutes was to be extended to Texas territory.[8]

Some influential people, such as editor John L. O'Sullivan, believed that certain foreign powers were attempting to block the annexation of Texas for fear that American power, influence, and territorial growth might become threatening. It was O'Sullivan, founder of the *United States Magazine and Democratic Review*, who coined the phrase "manifest destiny":

> After 200 years of westward expansion had brought them as far as Missouri and Iowa, Americans now suddenly perceived their destined goal. *The whole continent was to be theirs!* Theirs to exploit, but also theirs to make into one mighty nation, a refuge for the oppressed, a showcase to display the virtues of democratic institutions, living proof that Americans were indeed God's chosen people.... [O'Sullivan] now captured the new mood in a sentence. Nothing must interfere, he wrote in 1845, with "the fulfillment of our *manifest destiny* to overspread the continent allotted by Providence for the free development of our yearly multiplying millions."[9]

Closely aligned with the question of Texas was that of Oregon. President Polk, in his 1845 annual message to Congress, claimed the whole of the Oregon territory, terminating an existing Anglo-American convention that had established joint occupation of the area. Further, he called for U.S. jurisdiction over all settlers

8 Morris, *Encyclopedia of American History*, 191.
9 John A. Garrity, *The American Nation to 1877* (New York: Harper and Row, 1966), 1, 313.

in Oregon, military protection for the Oregon Trail,[10] and the opening of an Indian agency beyond the Rocky Mountains. Because the president's position was so unyielding on these points, a popular American rallying cry soon became "Fifty-four forty or fight!," referring to the northern latitude of the most extensive American claim, which would have been about half of the modern Canadian province of British Columbia. There were, as might be expected, British objections to the final draft, and after a series of negotiations, the president laid a final proposal before Congress. The resulting treaty relaxed the American claim, but the course of American expansion had been enhanced.[11]

The Mexican War would require its own multivolume story, but we will focus on just a few incidents. Well before hostilities ended, sectional division over the "peculiar institution"[12] again spiked. David Wilmot was a congressman from Northeastern Pennsylvania who was worried over the prospects of acquiring additional territory after the war's conclusion, specifically how the issue of slavery would figure into the discussions. In 1847, the congressman submitted an amendment to an appropriations bill that has come to be known as the Wilmot Proviso, which stated an "express and fundamental condition" for any territory acquired from Mexico:

[10] "The Oregon Trail began at the western border of Missouri, immediately beyond Independence, and followed the Kansas River, its tributary, the Little Blue, and then the perverse, muddy Platte ('a mile wide and six inches deep') past Fort Laramie to the Rockies. It crossed the Continental Divide by the relatively easy South Pass, veered south briefly to Fort Bridger, on Mexican soil, and then ran north and west through the valley of the Snake River and eventually, by way of the Columbia, to Fort Vancouver, a British post guarding the entrance to the Williamette Valley." Garrity, *American Nation*, 1, 313–314.

[11] For more detail, see Morris, *Encyclopedia of American History*, 195–196.

[12] A term popularly and often applied to the institution of slavery.

Faith and Fury

By virtue of any treaty which may be negotiated between them, and to the use by the Executive of the monies herein appropriated, neither slavery nor involuntary servitude shall ever exist in any part of said territory, except for crime, whereof the party shall first be duly convicted.[13]

The amendment was not adopted, but the controversy it raised further accelerated the sectionalism that would lead to war.

Finally, the 1848 Treaty of Guadalupe Hidalgo, which ended the Mexican War, would have great bearings on the Church's future in North America. By its terms, Mexico gave up all claims to Texas above the Rio Grande River and ceded New Mexico and California to the United States—the present-day states of Arizona, Nevada, California, Utah, and parts of New Mexico, Colorado, and Wyoming. In all, the treaty expanded American territory by well over one million square miles.

The idea of "manifest destiny" introduced by John O'Sullivan seemed to provide the rationale for nearly two decades of American expansionist policy. The concept included within it a certain notion of cultural superiority that was morally obligated to spread its ideals whenever and wherever possible. It was defined as:

Expansion, prearranged by Heaven, over an area not clearly defined. In some minds it meant expansion over the region to the Pacific; in others, over the North American Continent; in others, over the hemisphere.... It attracted enough persons by the mid 1840s to constitute a movement.... It was less acquisitive, more an opportunity for neighboring peoples to reach self-realization. It meant opportunity to gain admission to the American Union. Any neighboring peoples, established in self-government by compact or by

[13] Cited in Morris, *Encyclopedia of American History*, 202.

successful revolution, would be permitted to apply. If properly qualified, they would be admitted.[14]

Manifest destiny was both a challenge and an opportunity for the Church in the United States. On the one hand, the ideological underpinning of the concept was distinctly anti-Catholic, based on the expansion of a Protestant and liberal nation against the forces of tradition and "superstition." On the other hand, according to the dean of U.S. Catholic Historians:

> As the policy of Manifest Destiny sent Americans toward the Pacific and the Rio Grande, it must have seemed to them, if they adverted to it at all, that the Church had ever been before them in many areas for over two centuries. In the realm of the spirit none of the new settlers from the East felt more at home than the Catholics. Here old Catholic institutions of the Spanish and French regimes were links to bind them to their own past; the descendants of the *conquistadores* and the *coureurs de bois* fused with the newcomers to create an often strange amalgam of Catholic life on the distant American frontiers. The Holy See sometimes preceded government in looking to the needs of the settlers, as, for example, in California, where the first Bishop was appointed in April, 1840, eight years before the famous find at Sutter's Fort. In May, 1840, Father Pierre-Jean De Smet, S.J., left Saint Louis for the first of his journeys to the Indians of the Far Northwest, and a year and a half before John L. O'Sullivan's *Democratic Review* coined the phrase "manifest destiny," the Vicarate Apostolic of Oregon was erected in December, 1843. The same was true in the Southwest, where

[14] Frederick Merk, *Manifest Destiny and Mission in American History* (New York: Random House, 1963), 24.

a Bishop was appointed for Texas in July, 1841, four years in advance of its annexation to the United States. Nearly two years before the Gadsden Purchase, John M. Lamy, the principal character of Willa Cather's charming novel *Death Comes for the Archbishop*, arrived at Santa Fe to begin his almost forty years as a missionary Bishop in New Mexico.[15]

The Church responded gamely to these circumstances with an extraordinarily successful growth in her institutions in the new West and across the county. It wouldn't be too much to see the influence of the Holy Spirit in these events.

The Irish Issue

As inspiring as this sounds, the situation on the East Coast and in the Midwest, where large numbers of Irish and German Catholic immigrants had settled, was far different. The Irish, because of their superior numbers, occupied the greater portion of discussion. Reasons for this immigration varied: The Irish came to these shores primarily for economic reasons, the Germans for political reasons. The Irish did not have the language barrier the Germans faced, though their brogue clearly marked them out for ostracism and, in some cases, violence. Whatever his nationality, the Catholic immigrant had much to overcome before being socially accepted.

The story of the Irish in America was defined by a deep tension: They "were a rural people in Ireland, and became a city people in the United States."[16] They arrived in the Eastern port cities almost destitute and found manual jobs rather than attempting to till the

---

[15] John Tracy Ellis, *American Catholicism* (Chicago: University of Chicago Press, 1955), 78–79.

[16] William V. Shannon, *The American Irish: A Political and Social Portrait* (New York: Collier Macmillan, 1963), 27.

soil of America's frontier, a vastly different experience from working the small plots of largely uncultivated ground they had known in the old country. As one observer noted, "the Irish rejected the soil because the soil had rejected them."[17] In fact, they had endured a dozen crop failures over a thirty-year period.

> In 1846 there was a total failure [of the potato crop], with as much as 90 percent ... destroyed. The fear of misery and starvation spread across the land. The "death sign," as an Irish land agent put it, was the "fearful stench" of rotting potatoes, which "became almost unbearable." This same agent, having planted more than a hundred acres of potatoes, sadly wrote that "it had all passed away like a dream."[18]

Within two years, half the crop had been lost. The potato had originated in Peru and was introduced into Ireland in the sixteenth century. It soon became the staple crop in the Irish diet, especially for the poor. The British government at first did little to alleviate the problem of the dependence on the fickle potato, feeling that the Irish were inferior, a "nation of beggars," whose "leading defects were 'indolence, improvidence, disorder, and consequent destitution.'"[19]

How this economic blight occurred in Ireland has been the result of serious study for more than a century and a half. One of the most telling contemporary observations was that of New York's Bishop (later Archbishop) John Hughes. In March 1847, when the situation was at its worst, the prelate delivered a lecture on "The Antecedent Causes of the Irish Famine" in the city's Broadway Tabernacle. He began by listing the various reasons that

[17] Ibid.

[18] Jay P. Dolan, *The Irish Americans: A History* (New York: Bloomsbury Press, 2008), 67.

[19] Ibid., 71.

were widely discussed and then summarized the problem under the three headings of "incompleteness of conquest, bad government, [and] a defective or vicious system of social economy."[20] He traced his first point historically to the time of the Anglo-Norman King Henry II, toward the close of the twelfth century.

> They succeeded in effecting a partial conquest. The native population were driven out of that portion of the country which stretches along the east and southeastern coast, which afterwards became known in history as the English Pale. This portion of the kingdom, less than one third, may be considered as really conquered by the adventurers; but the rest of the island continued as before, under its ancient princes and proprietors.... Here is the real point in history, at which the fountain of Ireland's perennial calamities is to be placed.[21]

Hughes was not able to answer the question of why the English did what they did in piecemeal—perhaps it was weakness, or perhaps they were satisfied with what had been done and saw little need for anything more extensive. Regardless, the "calamities that have resulted to Ireland from that time until our own days, are but so many supplements, many of them bloody ones, to complete the volume."[22] One consequence was that every inch of Irish soil, divided into properties, had two owners—one by hereditary title, the other by "immemorial possession." If the king had thoroughly conquered the country at the outset, his land grants would have been an unquestioned reality throughout

---

[20] Lawrence Kehoe, *The Complete Works of the Most Rev. John Hughes, D.D., Archbishop of New York*, 2 vols. (New York: American News Company, 1864), 1, V, 33.

[21] Ibid., 34.

[22] Ibid., 35.

the land; instead, they were "simply as royal letters—patent, authorizing the iniquities and disorders of all kinds which make up the history of the relations between the Irish people and what was called the English Pale."[23]

Bad government, Hughes's second point, can be traced to the fall of the reign of terror of the Puritan Oliver Cromwell and the restoration of the Stuart Monarchy in 1660. English and Scottish loyalists had their property returned throughout the realm—except in Ireland, where, as a concession, Cromwell's virulently anti-Catholic followers maintained what they had claimed years earlier. After the Glorious Revolution of 1688 and the coming to power of William of Orange, still more difficulty awaited the Irish. By terms of the Treaty of Limerick, the inhabitants of Ireland were divided into two classes: those whose conscience would allow them to take the Oath of Supremacy affirming the preeminence of the king in religious matters, and those who would not. The overwhelming majority of Irish, staunchly Catholic, would not subscribe to the oath, and severe penalties in the form of penal laws were quickly enacted against them.

> This same system has been continued to the present day: as if some cruel law of destiny had determined that the Irish people should be kept at the starving point through all times; since the landlord, even now, claims the right and often uses it, of punishing the industry of his tenant, by increasing the rent in proportion to the improvement the tenant makes on his holding. If, then, it be true that the Irish are indolent, which I deny, the cause could be sufficiently explained by the penalties which a bad Government has inflicted upon them, in their own country for the crime of being industrious.[24]

[23] Ibid.
[24] Ibid., 39.

Finally, there was a defective or vicious system of social and political economy. By this term, Hughes meant "the effort of society, organized into a sovereign State, to accomplish the welfare of its members."[25] He admitted the ideal may not be fully realizable under any form of government, but it still should be kept in sight.

As might be expected, he felt the current system in Ireland had lost sight of this ideal of political and economic justice. England's free system had made it the richest country in the world, but how could that be reconciled with the tremendous poverty one found in Ireland, with anti-poverty measures going no further than Work Houses set up by the British Government to give Ireland a so-called economic boost? As presently constituted, Hughes felt the system was primarily an "element of pure selfishness."

> The true system, in my opinion, would regard the general interest first, as wholly paramount, and have faith enough to believe that individual interest would, in the long run, be best promoted by allowing it all possible scope for enterprise and activity within the general limits. Then individual welfare would be the result, and not the antecedent, as it is when the order is reversed. The assumption of our system is, that the healthy antagonisms of this self-interest, which, as applied to the working classes, its advocates sometimes designate pompously, "the sturdy self reliance of an operative," will result finally in the general good. I am willing to admit, that in the fallen condition of human nature, self-interest is the most powerful principle of our being, giving impulse and activity to all our individual undertakings, and in that way, to the general operations of life. But unfortunately this system leaves us at liberty to forget the interests of others.[26]

[25] Ibid., 41.
[26] Ibid., 42–43.

Direct as Hughes could be, he had to be somewhat diplomatic. He didn't want to directly accuse the British of religious prejudice against the one nation in the British Isles that had remained faithful to the Church of Rome. That allegiance would be readily apparent among those who emigrated to America to become laborers on the nation's canals, railroads, and, in certain areas, coal mines.

> Throughout the nineteenth century every successive railroad town — Albany, Buffalo, Cleveland, Chicago, Peoria, Omaha — became a center of Irish strength. Numbers of Irish also made the long voyage to California after 1849 to work in the goldfields. San Francisco from its earliest boom days had a sizeable Irish contingent, and from there they fanned inland to the mining cities of Butte, Denver and Virginia City.[27]

By mid-century, 26 percent of the population of the city of New York and one in five Bostonians had been born in Ireland. Philadelphia and Baltimore also showed sizeable increases in Irish denizens. Ralph Waldo Emerson wrote to his friend Henry David Thoreau expressing his surprise at seeing so many Irishmen working fifteen-hour days for fifty cents, and Theodore Parker, a Unitarian minister in Boston, observed that he rarely saw a "gray-haired Irishman."[28]

There seemed to be certain characteristics that singled out the Irishman and set him apart:

> He carried certain adamant convictions which strongly influenced his conduct. Foremost was his vindictive hatred for all things British. Most of his ideas on political or social questions were colored by their relationship with Britain.

[27] Shannon, *The American Irish*, 28.
[28] Ibid., 29.

Faith and Fury

If the British were anti-slavery, then the Irishman would be pro-slavery. If any American politician could be tagged with the pro-British stigma, he was anathema to the Irish. From the time the Irishman came to America, he allied himself politically with the Democratic party. He looked on the Whigs as the party which inherited the Federalist tradition and the Federalists had been responsible for the proscriptive alien and naturalization laws of President Adams's administration. Being largely of the laboring class, the Irish considered the Whig propertied interests their natural enemy. As time went on and the Whigs aligned themselves with nativist movements, the Irishman's fealty to the Democratic party was intensified. Numerically the bulk of the Irish immigrants were Roman Catholic in religion and loyalty to their church was a cardinal principal with the majority.[29]

Other historical commentators have offered different explanations for the Irishman's allegiance to the party of Jefferson and Jackson. It is true that anti-Catholicism was prevalent everywhere and that this influenced Irish-American politics, but some commentators have seen the party affiliation as an example of simple political pragmatism. Democratic bosses in the large cities "were the first to cultivate [the Irish], to see that they got jobs, and to help them when in trouble."[30] Still others felt that the average immigrant saw in the persons of Thomas Jefferson and Andrew Jackson great symbols of freedom, and exponents of the rights of

[29] Florence E. Gibson, *The Attitudes of the New York Irish toward State and National Affairs: 1848–1892* (New York: AMS Press, 1968), 13–14. The Adams whom the author mentions is John Adams, second president of the United States, during whose term of office the Alien and Sedition Acts were passed.
[30] Samuel Eliot Morison, *The Oxford History of the American People* (New York: New American Library, 1965), II, 229.

the common man, while Democratic party leaders early on saw the potential in the immigrant vote, and "outdid themselves to curry favor with the newcomers." In such an atmosphere, it was "only natural for the Whigs to seek what capital they could by marshalling under the Whig banner those alarmed by the foreign influx."[31]

America was indeed a Protestant nation, and the newly arriving immigrants would face great hostility in many forms. In November 1850, perhaps as a morale booster to the Catholic population, New York's Archbishop Hughes delivered a lecture in Saint Patrick's Cathedral on the city's Lower East Side titled "The Decline of Protestantism and Its Cause." After speaking of the growth of Protestantism in the sixteenth century, following the Reformation, he tried to show that God had given everyone two guiding principles: divine authority and human reason. To the Protestant charge that Catholics forfeit their reason by submitting to the Church's doctrines, Hughes replied that the very exercise of our reason leads

---

[31] Glyndon G. Van Deusen, *The Jacksonian Era: 1828–1848* (New York: Harper and Row, 1959), 16. Political conservatism was represented in the early national years by the Federalist Party, of which Alexander Hamilton was the leading thinker. After the demise of the party around 1815, National Republicans carried the banner until the formation of the Whigs in the 1830s, largely to oppose the policies of Andrew Jackson. They favored high protective tariffs, national banking, and federal aid for internal improvements. When the GOP, today's Republican Party, was formed shortly before the presidential election of 1856, it appeared liberal, at least socially, in many minds. It consisted of anti-slavery Whigs, conscience Democrats, Know-Nothings, Free Soilers, and so on. In later years, with the rise of industrialization, it began to take on many of the features of political conservatism one associates with it today. While, traditionally, Catholics in the United States allied themselves with the Democrats, they could be found in smaller numbers in each of the political expressions of conservatism throughout American history, and it would be a mistake to associate them completely with one political party.

us to the conclusion that God, having given us revelation, has appointed a Church to be the depository and witness of that truth in the world. Protestantism, by contrast, seeks not to build on this concept, but to dismiss it and, in the process, to tear down all that it considers unnecessary for a pure, undiluted Christianity. In so doing, the archbishop contended, it was destroying itself, step by step throughout the world. If any further proof was needed of this, the archbishop argued, one might only look at New England, where Puritanism had left a legacy of nineteenth-century secularism.

"Everybody should know we have for our mission to convert the world," said the prelate, "including the inhabitants of the United States, the people in the cities, and the people of the country, the officers of the Navy, and the marines, commanders of the army, the legislatures, the Senate, the Cabinet, the President and all!"[32] One wonders, though, how such extensive conversions could be carried out if Catholics, especially the Irish, did not associate with their separated brethren. Hughes apparently had a great fear that such mixing would bring about the abandoning of the Faith among Catholics, especially if immigrant populations moved from the Eastern cities to the Midwest, as many promoters of colonization schemes hoped.[33]

The archbishop's opposition to expanding Western colonization began when he read an article in a Buffalo newspaper proposing that Irish men of means buy up extensive land holdings in the West, and then sell lots to immigrant families. He later responded that the lot of the Irish in Eastern cities such as New York was hardly of a condition "more squalid than the Irish hovels from which many of them had been exterminated." Further, in *Reflections and Suggestions: The Catholic Press in the United States*, he made three

[32] Kehoe, *Complete Works of Hughes*, 11, 101.
[33] Gibson, *Attitudes of the New York Irish*, 12.

additional points: Life in the Ireland of old should not be overly romanticized; American life, hard as it might be on many of the immigrants, did at least offer a close proximity to churches and schools; and it was unrealistic to think that the life of a farmer in the Midwest was going to be in any way preferable to city life for those who might choose it.[34]

Then, in March 1857, a priest named Jeremiah Trecy, who was a determined advocate of colonization, addressed a large rally of Irish in New York's Broadway Tabernacle. Trecy painted a glorious picture of a colony in Nebraska named in honor of Saint John the Baptist, where the streets would be named after Irish towns and where hardworking Irish Catholics could raise their families in peace and tranquility. A gentleman bundled in a scarf and a long coat—Archbishop Hughes, who had dressed so as not to be recognized—then took the floor. Hughes had been through this sort of episode two years earlier, when General James Shields had spoken of a similar plan in Minnesota. When the archbishop objected, the general tried to engage him in debate. When this failed, Shields accused Hughes of not being able to "see beyond the length of his nose."

This time, Hughes was far more in control of the situation. He blamed the country's economic situation on a general feeling of depression, which could easily lend itself to the thought that life would be so much better in the West. What was actually needed were clear values, hard work, and an eye to the future.[35] It likely was a hard sell that evening, but at least the archbishop had the last word. Hughes's fear that the Faith might be abandoned in areas where Catholic churches, schools, and clergy were still scarce was

[34] John Loughery, *Dagger John: Archbishop John Hughes and the Making of Irish America* (Ithaca: Cornell University Press, 2018), 268–269.
[35] Ibid., 269–270.

coupled with anxiety that such westward expansion might fuel the flames of what is now called Nativism, a term that can be included within the larger concept of anti-Catholicism.

> [It] is not disagreement with what the Church believes and teaches, even when forcefully—or satirically—expressed. It is not heated theological disputes and expressions of negative judgments on Church activities or public positions. Anti-Catholicism ... is the blind use of negative generalizations, invented history, vicious stereotypes, appeals to shared prejudices, applications of underlying base motives without proof, misrepresentations of religious beliefs, all with the intent of ridiculing, dismissing, or publicly attacking Catholic positions or applications of belief in the public square without actively engaging the actual issues or positions involved.[36]

Popularizers of Anti-Catholicism

In the mid-nineteenth century and beyond, Catholicism was the faith of people whom the White Anglo-Saxon establishment in the United States deemed inferior. Catholics belonged to a Church intent on destroying individual freedom; they were thought to be anti-intellectual, filled with superstitious beliefs, and, on the whole, an alien and foreign presence, most disconcerting to Protestant America. True, many Protestants were of a broader mind, "yet even the most liberal, most indifferent dissenters had little use for Roman Catholics. English speaking peoples regarded Catholics as

[36] Robert P. Lockwood, "The Evolution of Anti-Catholicism in the United States," in Robert P. Lockwood, ed., *Anti-Catholicism in American Culture* (Huntington, IN: Our Sunday Visitor, 2000), 20.

… slavishly subservient to the Pope and his Jesuit minions, and treacherous allies of the country's enemies."[37]

This mind-set found expression in diverse ways through the nineteenth century, beginning as early as the 1830s with the writings of men such as Lyman Beecher, Samuel F. B. Morse, and Reverend William Craig Brownlee. Beecher, the father of *Uncle Tom's Cabin* author Harriet Beecher Stowe, was pastor of the Park Street Church in Boston and would later serve as president of Lane Theological Seminary in Cincinnati. In 1830, he began a series of anti-Catholic sermons showing the incompatibility of Catholicism with American democracy, specifically the connection between Catholicism and European despotism. Five years later, he preached an extremely powerful sermon, later published in book form as *A Plea for the West*. He insisted that the rapidly opening American West be safeguarded against Romanism and spelled out in detail the imagined specifics of a papal plot to gain control of Western territory and impose Catholicism's fearful doctrines.

Rivaling Beecher was Samuel F. B. Morse, best remembered as inventor of the telegraph. He was raised amid the anti-Catholicism of traditionally Congregationalist Massachusetts, and his opinions were confirmed by an episode that occurred while he was visiting Rome as a tourist in 1830:

> I was standing close to the side of the house when, in an instant, without the slightest notice, my hat was struck off to the distance of several yards by a soldier, or rather by a poltroon in a soldier's costume, and this courteous manoeuvre was performed with his gun and bayonet, accompanied with curses and taunts and the expression of a demon on his countenance. In cases like this there is no redress. The

[37] Cited in ibid., 23.

soldier receives his orders and the manner is left to his discretion.... The blame lies after all, not so much with the
pitiful wretch who perpetrates the outrage, as it does with
those who gave him such base and indiscriminate orders.[38]

Morse felt that his European experience gave him sufficient
expertise to write on the Romish conspiracy he felt certain was
a reality. In 1834, under the pen name Brutus, he published in
the *New York Observer* a series of twelve letters called "A Foreign
Conspiracy against the Liberties of the United States." They were
widely reprinted in nativistic publications and convinced many
in America of the link between immigration and the papal plot.
Encouraged by the success of these letters, Morse went on to publish a second series, "Imminent Dangers to the Free Institutions
of the United States through Foreign Immigration." These ran in
the *New York Journal of Commerce* in 1835 and were reprinted in
book form shortly after.

> The popular reception accorded the works of Beecher and
> Morse not only attracted attention to their arguments, but
> inspired a host of imitators, and the Catholic plot which they
> had sketched in outline was filled in by countless writers dur-
> ing the succeeding years.... The papal clergy, propagandists
> maintained, had been taught to keep no faith with heretics,
> and ordinary Catholics were being kept in ignorance until
> the time to strike, when they would be released from their
> oath of allegiance to the United States by the Pope, establish
> the Inquisition in America, and win converts to Catholicism
> by flame and sword. Already, it was claimed, the Papists were
> making plans for that day by building inquisitorial chambers

[38] Cited in Ray Allen Billington, *The Protestant Crusade: 1800–1860*
(Chicago: Quadrangle Books, 1964), 122–123.

beneath their churches and by arming their religious edifices for use in the final attack.[39]

One other writer of national note was Reverend William Craig Brownlee, pastor of New York City's Dutch Reformed Church and editor of *The Protestant*, the *American Protestant Vindicator*, and, more significantly in later years, the *New York Observer*. Brownlee was president of any number of Bible Societies and Protestant fraternal groups who felt they had a moral obligation to warn America of the impending dangers of Romanism. Brownlee's views were circulated only not through the printed word but also through lecturers whom he sent traveling around the country, giving popular speeches against the Catholic Church. He believed that "Popery ought always to be loathed and execrated, not only by all Christians, but also by every patriot and philanthropist." That this might be accomplished, "we shall endeavor to unfold its detestable impieties, corruptions and mischiefs."[40]

Anti-Catholic Violence on the Rise

These and similar fanatical diatribes were largely responsible for an episode in 1834, when an angry mob ransacked, robbed, and torched Mount Benedict Catholic girls school in Charlestown, Massachusetts, just across the Charles River from Boston. While there were no casualties, the fear inspired by the incident reached monumental proportions. Representatives from this mob had been allowed to search the building to see if any alleged "immoralities" were occurring, or if ammunition was being hoarded by Irishmen to work havoc in the city. Even when everything was discovered to be totally in order, the mob forged ahead, determined to destroy

[39] Ibid., 127.
[40] *American Protestant Vindicator*, August 20, 1834, cited in ibid., 93.

an imposing Catholic edifice. The mother superior had apparently even threatened the crowd that the bishop of Boston had twenty thousand Irishmen at his disposal, but it was to no avail. The mob wouldn't be denied.

Some of the rioters were brought to court in what has been described as a travesty of a trial. The state attorney general prosecuted the case, and he could not ask any of the potential jurors their views on Catholicism. On the other hand, defense counsel was perfectly free to query the bishop and mother superior about alleged immoral activities which were said to have taken place. Only one rioter was convicted, and he was quickly pardoned. The Massachusetts legislature then refused all pleas to compensate the Sisters for the loss of their property.

This is not to say, however, that all Protestants were totally unsympathetic to such gross injustice. There was sympathy among New England Unitarians, a sect whose view of Christianity included much theological latitude. Among its members was Caleb Stetson, a minister whose friends included Ralph Waldo Emerson and Bronson Alcott, father of Louisa May Alcott. Others such as Nathaniel Hawthorne, Horace Greeley of the *New York Tribune*, William Lloyd Garrison, and Elizabeth Cady Stanton, while no friends of Catholicism, would have more quickly perceived the injustice. In a Sunday sermon, Stetson expressed his amazement at the "delusion, as well as the wickedness of our fellow citizens," adding that "if an exasperated mob is allowed to supersede the laws ... [and] if unpopular persons or establishments may be destroyed without trial, or jury, or judge, there is an end of our civil and religious freedom."[41] Still another more liberal Protestant was Har-

---

[41] Caleb Stetson, A *Discourse on the Duty of Sustaining the Laws*, Occasioned by the Burning of the Ursuline Convent (Boston, 1834), cited in Maura Jane Farrelly, *Anti-Catholicism in America, 1620–1860* (Cambridge, UK: Cambridge University Press, 2018), 144.

rison Gray Otis, one of the last members of the Federalist Party, whose uncle James Otis had been one of the Revolutionary leaders in Massachusetts and whose aunt Mercy Otis Warren had written one of the earliest histories of the American Revolutionary War. He wondered, "Who among us is safe?" Those who favored no legal redress for injury to persons and property, Otis said, brought upon Boston society the "profoundest shame and humiliation."[42]

One historian has noted that the mainstream Protestant view was that "if Unitarianism was a virus that had given America a nasty cold and weakened the immune system of the country's soul, then Catholicism was a cancer—a growing cancer, thanks to immigration—that had the potential to capitalize on that weakness and destroy America's soul completely."[43] Two books released at this time bear this out: *The Awful Disclosures of Maria Monk* and Rebecca Reed's *Six Months in a Convent*.

In the first, the writer, Maria Monk, set out to expose conduct she claimed took place in the Hotel Dieu Nunnery in Montreal, Canada. She had been a convert to Catholicism who had attended the Hotel Dieu school and ended up entering its community of Sisters. She vacillated briefly, left, married, abandoned her husband, re-entered, and later gave her account of the years she spent in the convent, especially the sinful liaisons between priests and nuns, and the children born of their unions. According to Monk, they would immediately have these babies baptized and then strangled. She went on to recount the severe punishments inflicted on nuns who refused to give in to the sexual advances of priests. After the publication of the book, Maria Monk's mother, a Protestant living near Montreal, testified that her daughter had never been to the

---

[42] Nancy Lusignan Schultz, *Fire and Roses: The Burning of the Charlestown Convent* (Boston, 2000), cited in ibid., 144–145.
[43] Farrelly, *Anti-Catholicism in America*, 140.

Hotel Dieu Nunnery and that what was described in the book had been a complete fabrication, explainable as the result of a severe brain injury as a child.

Several investigations were made of the convent, including one by William L. Stone, editor of the *New York Commercial Advertiser*.

Stone was a Protestant who had interested himself mildly in the No-Popery crusade. He happened to be in Montreal during the fall of 1836 and sought for and secured permission to make a thorough investigation. He made his examination with Maria Monk's book in his hand, poking into every closet, climbing to a high window to see an unopened room, and smelling a row of jars in the basement which might have contained lime used in the disposal of the infants' bodies. He came away completely convinced and published an account which ended with the pronouncement "I most solemnly believe that the priests and nuns are innocent in this matter."[44]

Discredited as she was, three hundred thousand copies of her book were nonetheless sold prior to the Civil War, and afterward the book went into new printings. Rightly or wrongly, it has earned the title the "Uncle Tom's Cabin of Know-Nothingism."[45]

A less sensational story that nonetheless captured the imagination of American Protestantism was Rebecca Reed's *Six Months in a Convent*. Reed did indeed exist — she was an Episcopalian who briefly attended the same Canadian convent described in the work of Maria Monk — but her story was again a complete

[44] William L. Stone, *Maria Monk and the Nunnery of the Hotel Dieu: Being an Account of a Visit to the Convents of Montreal, and Refutation of the "Awful Disclosures"* (New York, 1836), cited in Billington, *The Protestant Crusade*, 105–106.

[45] Ibid., 108.

fabrication. Reed told the story of how she had been imprisoned after she tried to leave the school, which played into public curiosity because a young Sister had left the convent under a cloud of suspicion of malfeasance. That Sister was quick to return, and her reasons for leaving bore no relation to Reed's fabrications. Nonetheless, by the end of its first month in publication, the book had sold more than two hundred thousand copies, with many thinking it might well break record sales both in England and the United States.

> Rebecca Reed's work was important in the anti-Catholic movement, not because of its contents, however, but because of the controversy which it aroused. Soon after its appearance it was replied to by the Mother Superior of the Ursuline Convent, Sister Mary Edmund Saint George, in *An Answer to Six Months in a Convent Exposing its Falsehoods and Manifest Absurdities*. After a lengthy introduction attacking Miss Reed's character, the Mother Superior devoted most of her publication to a detailed attack on *Six Months in a Convent*, refuting its statements in a thorough, if dull manner. This was followed within a short time by *A Review of the Lady Superior's Reply to "Six Months in a Convent," Being a Vindication of Miss Reed*, in which an anonymous author not only attempted to prove the Mother Superior false but also attacked the whole Catholic system in the United States. The Committee on Publication which had sponsored, and probably prepared, *Six Months in a Convent* was ready with a second volume before the year was out, *A Supplement to "Six Months in a Convent," Confirming the Narrative of Rebecca Theresa Reed, by the Testimony of More Than 100 Witnesses*, in which were chronicled the events leading to the burning of the Ursuline convent, including

the escape of Elizabeth Harrison and the tortures inflicted upon her when she returned.[46]

The Problem of Education

In the 1840s, before additional notable uprisings and the formation of the Native American or American Republican Party, there was another curious episode in New York that had anti-Catholic elements. It involved an organization called the Free School Society, which disbursed public funds in order "to provide a free school for the education of children in the city who do not belong to, or are not provided for by, a religious denomination."[47] The group was a private corporation that interfaced with the government, and it was dominated by Protestants. State funds were given by the Society to both Protestant and Catholic schools, until it was discovered that one of the Protestant denominations was insisting that teachers in its schools kick back a portion of their salaries to church officials. At that point, the Free School Society stopped distribution of funds to all schools, and state education funds were instead handed over by the city's Common Council to a group called the Public School Society, which oversaw more than eighty public schools, while the city's Catholics had only seven. The move intentionally sidelined Catholic schools in favor of de facto Protestant public schools. Most Catholics had no desire to send their children to these schools, where the textbooks were full of

[46] Billington, *The Protestant Crusade*, 91. Elizabeth Harrison was the name by which Sister Mary Saint John was known in the world. Her departure and return had no bearing whatever on the scurrilous tales in Rebecca Reed's book.

[47] Edward Robb Ellis, *The Epic of New York City: A Narrative History* (New York: Kondansha International, 1997), 252.

anti-Catholic propaganda, and where it was not at all uncommon for teachers to ridicule the Church in front of students.

This situation caught the attention of William H. Seward, the upstate Whig who began his second term as Governor in 1840. In a message to the legislature he urged the establishment of schools in which foreigners' children "may be instructed by teachers speaking the same language with themselves and professing the same faith."[48]

Seward won many Catholic friends with his position, including Bishop John Hughes, with whom he would remain friends for over two decades. Bishop Hughes made two proposals to the city's common council requesting a share in educational funds for parochial schools, only to be rebuffed. On his second attempt, when he claimed that public schools were "poisoning the minds of Catholic children," the majority Protestant members of the Public School Society countered by claiming that, in fact, the real purpose of Catholic schools was "use of public funds to teach Catholicism not only to their own children but to Protestant children as well.... [If] Roman Catholic claims are admitted, all the other Christian denominations will urge similar claims."[49] An acrimonious dialogue ensued between Hughes and the Public School Society, including charges and countercharges. The bishop's next move was to approach the state legislature in Albany.

A state election was approaching in the Fall of 1841, and two state senators and thirteen state assemblymen were to be elected from the city. Just days before the election, the bishop convened a mass rally at which he told hundreds of attendees that, since both the Whigs and the Democrats opposed any change in the existing

[48] Ibid.
[49] Ibid., 253.

system of public funding of education, it was time for Catholics to form their own political party of candidates who could be relied on to support Catholic claims. The evening produced a movement that has since been referred to as the Carroll Hall Party, named for the venue of the rally, with its slate of candidates, both Democrat and Whig.[50]

Not a single candidate of the Carroll Hall slate was elected, but the ticket split the Democrats so that the Whigs were elected by a slight margin in the state election. The legislature went on to pass a bill denying state funds to any school in which any religious doctrine was taught. The bill was thought to be a compromise but really pleased neither side. On the evening of its passage, "New York City gangsters beat up Irishmen, stoned the Bishop's home on Mulberry Street, and broke windows in old Saint Patrick's Cathedral. Other Catholic churches were saved from destruction only by prompt action by the militia."[51]

Third Party Rising

With events like this becoming more numerous, it is not surprising that anti-Catholic bigotry translated into political activism. Many native-born Americans viewed the influx of immigrants as a serious threat that demanded concerted government action. These citizens believed that the country's naturalization laws were not effective and that the traditional five-year probationary period before one

---

[50] Carroll Hall, named for America's first bishop, John Carroll, was located at the site of the present Saint Andrew's Church, behind City Hall in Manhattan. The church was long known for its 2:30 a.m. Sunday Mass for printers working for the many New York newspapers and was also just doors from the birthplace of Patrick Cardinal Hayes, New York's fourth archbishop.

[51] Ellis, *The Epic of New York City*, 254.

could apply for citizenship was not long enough. They argued that this relatively lax requirement was put in place as a sop specifically to French and Irish immigrants, who had made significant contributions to the American Revolutionary War—but that era was over. More than anything, anti-immigrant activists worried that newcomers were depriving native-born citizens of jobs and depressing wages, content as they were to work for meager salaries.

Neither major political party satisfied those whose anti-Catholicism was rising to a fever pitch. The Democrats had sold their heritage, the activists argued, to win foreign votes; the Whigs, while politically more conservative and occasionally flirting with nativist ideas, never brought significant anti-immigration proposals into the political arena. It seemed that a new entity, dedicated specifically to the anti-immigration cause, was needed. It took form in the American Republican Party, which, after 1845, became known as the Native American Party.

These events were set against the presidential election of 1844, pitting the Democrat James Knox Polk and his running mate, George Dallas, against the Whig nominee, Henry Clay, who ran with New Jersey's Theodore Frelinghuysen. Frelinghuysen's association with evangelical and Bible associations was especially satisfying to nativists, and, though Henry Clay had many Catholic connections and regarded the Church well, the Whigs were keen to reach out to nativists, promising to help many of their candidates in local elections in return for support of the national ticket. The party did particularly well in New York City and Philadelphia, and its platform, wherever in the country it could draw strength, was uniform:

> In its public documents the party adhered to three major
> objectives: (1) to change the naturalization laws in such a
> way that foreigners would have to dwell in the United States

twenty-one years before being naturalized, (2) to restrict authority over naturalization to the federal courts, and (3) to reform the gross abuses arising from party corruption. In addition to these principal aims a number of minor reforms were agitated: a restriction of public office holding to natives, a continuation of the Bible as a schoolbook, the prevention of all union between Church and state, a lessening of the number of street riots and election disorders, a guarantee of a right to "worship the God of our fathers according to the dictates of our own consciences, without the restraints of a Romish priest, or the threats of a Hellish Inquisition."[52]

Unsurprisingly, the rise of a full political party dedicated to these aims was followed by a series of violent episodes. The worst by far occurred in Pennsylvania's City of Brotherly Love, founded by benevolent Quakers who deeply prized religious toleration. The Kensington Riots began with a simple request from Philadelphia's Catholic bishop—Irish-born Francis Patrick Kenrick—to the city's Board of Controllers: that Catholic children in the city's public schools be allowed to read a Catholic Bible and be excused from distinctly Protestant religious exercises. The Board of Controllers quickly granted the request, to the dissatisfaction of much of the city's Protestant establishment, who argued that Catholics were surreptitiously trying to eliminate the Bible from public schools—a scurrilous and unsupported claim.

Tensions were growing by April 1844, especially in the city's Kensington section, where many Irish laborers lived. Nativists called for a public meeting on the issue right in the heart of the Irish quarter; resentment of this provocation was so pronounced that Irish leaders let it be known that if such a meeting went forward,

[52] Billington, *The Protestant Crusade*, 203.

the venue would be burned. The nativists were undeterred and went ahead with the gathering; true to form, the Irish routed them, driving them from their designated place. They quickly reconvened nearby, passed a series of resolutions, and scheduled yet another session, publicly advertised as such:

NATIVE AMERICANS

The American Republicans of the city and county of Philadelphia, who are determined to support the NATIVE AMERICANS in their Constitutional Rights of peaceably assembling to express their opinions on any question of Public Policy and to *Sustain them against the assaults of aliens and Foreigners* are requested to assemble on *THIS AFTERNOON* May 6, 1844, at 4 o'clock at the corner of Master and Second Streets, Kensington, to express their indignation at the outrage on Friday evening last, and to take the necessary steps to prevent a repetition of it. *Natives be punctual and resolved to sustain your rights as Americans, firmly but moderately.*[53]

Several thousand attended this meeting on a rainy evening. As they entered the hall, shots rang out, coming either from the nativist mob or from the Hibernia Hose Company, a strong Irish bastion. One of the participants, a Protestant named George Schliffer, was killed and was quickly carried from the hall amid mass confusion in the streets. Later the same evening, many Irish homes were attacked by nativists in retaliation. The following day, the activists reassembled in the statehouse yard and listened to speakers strongly caution against the use of violence — but the mob would hear none of it. Once again, a series of resolutions was passed, and straightaway the marchers took to Kensington and demolished the

---

[53] *Native American*, May 6, 1844, cited in ibid., 223.

Faith and Fury

Hibernia Hose Company building; by the end of the day, more than thirty Irish homes had been burned to the ground. By the third day, angry Protestant mobs continued chanting against the pope and demanding revenge — and once again, rows of Irish homes were pillaged and destroyed. The militia seemed to be powerless, and a public letter by Bishop Kenrick forbidding Catholics to participate in any violence had little, if any, effect.

Rioters torched Saint Michael's Church and then moved on to Saint Augustine's, where they destroyed not only the church but the library of the Augustinian Fathers, which contained hundreds of priceless volumes. Even after the deaths of at least twenty Philadelphians, two months later violence commenced again:

> The excitement of the Independence Day celebration led to a renewal of mob rule a day later. A clash between Irish laborers and a group of American Republicans, together with widespread rumors that arms were being smuggled into the Church of Saint Philip de Neri in Southwark, another suburb, attracted a turbulent group of natives to that Catholic edifice by nightfall on July 5. Fortunately no attack was made until the sheriff could arrive; the crowd then demanded that he search the church for arms. Twelve muskets were found and exhibited to the rioters, who, unappeased, demanded a second investigation, this time by a group of twenty men from their own ranks. This search disclosed seventy-five more guns with a quantity of ammunition, supplies probably stored there by an ill-advised pastor as a precautionary measure during the earlier period of church burning. Wise counsel prevailed among members of the searching party, and they kept all knowledge of their find to themselves, fearing violence should the mob learn of the firearms.... By the following morning news of the committee's find had

leaked out, and at nine o'clock a crowd gathered around the church. All that day they milled about, checked from violent action only by a large force of the militia who were ranged before the church doors. By night the mob was pressing so close upon the militiamen that orders were given to fire.... [The] order to fire had its effect, and the crowd broke up without further delay.[54]

Other serious episodes continued at Saint Philip Neri throughout the next day but ended quietly—though not without much fear and trepidation on all sides. It was said that priests and religious Sisters throughout the city feared for their lives.

The Catholic Voice

Such violence necessarily attracted national press attention. Nativist and even many mainstream newspapers reacted as would be expected. But the Catholic press, by now a growing journalistic force, was anything but silent:

> The Catholic editors' analysis of the causes of the riots was relatively simple and consistent and colored not only the Catholic attitude toward them but also toward the wider problem of adjustment to American society. The predominant interpretation said that religious bigotry motivated the turmoil. The nativist political party, despite denials by its defenders, came in for a full share of the blame because of the anti-Catholic diatribes in its newspapers and its provocative street meetings. The *Freeman's Journal* contended that "the soul and animus of the Native American party is hostility to the Catholic citizens, whether of native or

[54] Ibid., 227–228.

foreign birth.... The *Pilot* observed that Native Americans were "about nine-tenths sectarian, and one tenth purely political." Catholic commentators also apportioned part of the guilt to the anti-Catholic harangues of Protestant clergymen in Philadelphia, so prevalent in the months preceding the outbreaks of violence.[55]

The writer Orestes Brownson had been a prime catch for the Church when he converted to Catholicism in 1844. Though often a thorn in the side of members of the American hierarchy, especially the archbishop of New York,[56] Brownson brought tremendous intellectual abilities to his newly adopted Faith, even if he didn't always have great sympathy for the Church's quickly expanding immigrant population. He did agree, in the pages of *Brownson's Quarterly Review*, that nativism contained elements of historical, political, and economic hostility to the foreign born, but then concluded:

> The Native American party is not a party against admitting a certain class of foreigners.... It is really opposed only to *Catholic* foreigners. The party is truly an anti-Catholic party, because a majority of the emigrants to this country

[55] Robert Francis Hueston, *The Catholic Press and Nativism: 1840–1860* (New York: Arno Press, 1976), 80–81. The *Freeman's Journal* was a Catholic publication in New York for several decades. From time to time, archbishops of New York used it as their official organ. It was edited for several years by the convert James Alphonsus McMaster, a staunch foe of the Lincoln administration and its policies. The *Pilot* was published in Boston, and, as of this writing, is the oldest continuously publishing Catholic paper in the United States.

[56] On the Bronx, New York, campus of Fordham University are to be found two statues—one of the school's founder, Archbishop John Hughes, the other of Brownson. The monuments face in opposite directions, and local lore has always contended that this was on purpose.

are probably from Ireland, and the greater part of these are Catholics.[57]

Brownson sharply criticized the Irish for their clannishness, which he believed provoked Americans' suspicion, leading to the conclusion that they were "a separate people, incapable even in their political and social duties of fraternizing, so to speak, with their Protestant fellow citizens. Here is the first and immediate cause of the opposition they experienced."[58]

As might be expected, most Catholic editors refused to blame their coreligionists in the Philadelphia riots. Though they couldn't get around the fact that the first episode of violence occurred when the Catholic Irish disrupted the nativist meeting in Kensington, they asserted that this was nonetheless not sufficient cause for the Protestant retaliation that went on for three days. Further, the presence of Northern Scotch-Irish Presbyterians reinforced the view that Catholics had tremendous opposition arrayed against them long before the Philadelphia riots broke out—and that this hostility was only looking for an occasion to break into violence.[59]

Northern Irish were conspicuous as members of the Native American Party and as participants in the riots. Most of the inhabitants of Kensington, where the trouble began, had either emigrated from Northern Ireland or descended from such immigrants; fights between the Catholic and Protestant elements in this area occurred regularly. After the May riots the *Freeman's Journal* observed, "The most active, though

---

[57] "Native Americanism," *Brownson's Quarterly Review* 11(1845): 85, cited in Hueston, *The Catholic Press and Nativism*, 81–82.

[58] Ibid.

[59] Scotch-Irish is a term applied to Scotch Protestants (usually Presbyterian) who settled in Ulster, the province containing nine Northern Irish counties, and later emigrated to the United States.

not the most prominent, of the Native Americans in New York, and probably in Philadelphia also, have been Irish Orangemen. They alone have been capable of furnishing the anti-social virus with which our young Natives have been inoculated. The *Catholic Telegraph* of Cincinnati reported that Orangemen were the "master spirits" of the May mob and merited as much "or perhaps more" criticism than native Americans.[60]

Dagger John

Though similar violence was averted in New York in the same year, events in that city did become colorful. John Hughes had only recently succeeded John Dubois as ordinary, and his confrontation with nativists was one of the early opportunities he had to show his force of character. The Native Americans had succeeded in electing one of their own, James Harper, as mayor; this victory no doubt increased their confidence in putting down Catholic foreigners. Few historians would disagree that it was the strength of New York's bishop that ensured that the city would remain calm. Bishop Hughes famously and publicly asserted that if one Catholic church were attacked, the city would "become a second Moscow."[61] He was quick to blame Catholics in Philadelphia for not adequately defending their churches, since the public authorities appeared unwilling to do it for them.

On May 7, 1844, in the immediate aftermath of the Kensington Riots, New York natives called for a rally to denounce Catholic aggression and to reward those who had captured Irish rioters.

---

[60] Hueston, *The Catholic Press and Nativism*, 85–86.

[61] This threat referred to the Russian "*scorched* earth" tactics in advance of the arrival of Napoleon's army.

Another call was then issued for a similar meeting in Central Park two nights later. Fearing the very real danger that could materialize, Hughes asked city authorities for assistance and was told that the city was not obligated to help defend Catholic churches—Catholics would have to do it for themselves. The bishop hurriedly surrounded each of the city's churches with between one and two thousand men fully armed, mostly members of the Ancient Order of Hibernians, an Irish Catholic fraternal group. As a result, public posters began to appear around the city announcing that the Central Park rally had been canceled because of the "existing tension and danger of rioting."[62] One of the more recognized historians of American nativism has observed that Hughes's position, while seemingly belligerent, "was necessary, for only through open threats could bloodshed have been averted in New York in those troubled days."[63]

Archbishop Hughes's earliest biographer felt that it was a "remarkable proof of the influence he had acquired over [his flock], that in the midst of so much excitement his warnings were strictly obeyed."[64] More than 140 years later, yet another observer referred to Hughes as a "pugnacious Irishman" who was "the personification

[62] Billington, *The Protestant Crusade*, 232. To this day, a plaque on the front of Saint Patrick's Old Cathedral, Mott and Pearl Streets on the city's Lower East Side reads "Erected to the Memory of the Members of the Ancient Order of Hibernians of the City of New York Who Like Their Irish Fathers of Old Were Ready to Sacrifice Their Lives for Religious Freedom and the Right to Worship God as Their Consciences Dictated and Who In ... 1844 at the Call of the Most Reverend John Hughes First Archbishop of New York Rallied to the Defense of This Cathedral When It Was Threatened with Destruction by the Forces of Bigotry and Intolerance"

[63] Ibid.

[64] John R. G. Hassard, *Life of the Most Rev. John Hughes, D.D., First Archbishop of New York* (New York: D. Appleton, 1866), 276.

of a militant Catholicism fighting to gain its rightful place in Protestant America."[65] In many ways, he was the man for the times.

Religiously, socially, and politically, Catholics were the newcomers in America in the two decades prior to the Civil War era. That Catholics had been here since 1634 in Colonial Maryland and in other colonies, or that they had contributed bravely to the American War of Independence, meant little to the native American mind of the nineteenth century. As their numbers increased, they were seen only as the strange Catholic foreigners whose ecclesial body was set upon depriving America of her rights and liberties, and whose pope was all too ready to assume command either from Rome or perhaps from America's own shores.

Despite all the invective thrown at Catholics and the violence they encountered, they continued to do what they had done since arriving in their new country—growing in numbers, developing institutions, and producing notable bishops, priests, religious, and laity. With the passage of time, they would encounter much more hostility, but at the same time, they would have many opportunities to prove their patriotism, and to share in the American dream. By 1848, the story had well begun and was about to become more dynamic.

[65] Dolan, *Irish Americans,* 132.

Chapter 2

⚮

The Coming of the Civil War: 1848–1860

Church and State at Mid-Century

The period of the war's coming, beginning thirteen years before the actual outbreak of hostilities, saw heightened sectional divisions, strongly (and sometimes violently) debated political events, and very significant growth in the Catholic presence in America. This era began with the signing of the Treaty of Guadalupe Hidalgo, ending the Mexican War, and gaining for the United States vast territories that included all or part the present-day states of California, Nevada, Arizona, New Mexico, Wyoming, and Colorado. Like so many other developments in the American Church, this expansion proved to be both a significant challenge and a great opportunity, especially in terms of the growth in buildings and institutions it required the Church to undertake.

While the war progressed from 1846 to 1848, a Democratic congressman from Pennsylvania, David Wilmot, offered several times his Wilmot Proviso, which would have prohibited slavery in any lands acquired from Mexico. Though it never passed, the question of whether slavery would be allowed in these lands roiled the nation.

The year 1848 also brought another presidential election. Zachary Taylor, a Mexican War general from Louisiana, was the candidate of the Whigs. Michigan's Senator Lewis Cass represented the

Faith and Fury

Democrats, and former president Martin Van Buren represented the "Free Soil Party," which was dedicated to keeping slavery out of the Western territories. Taylor, the winning candidate, had attempted to stay neutral on the slavery issue, fearing he would offend either pro- or anti-slavery factions of the Whigs. Cass, on the other hand, developed the concept of popular sovereignty, in which the question of slavery in the new territories would be left to the vote of the people.

Senator Henry Clay of Kentucky, one of the towering figures of the mid-nineteenth century,[66] attempted to solve the question of slavery in the territories when he introduced his Compromise of 1850. The bill had five parts, each of which was debated and passed separately: admit California as a free state (its population had been considerably swelled by the 1849 gold rush); prohibit the slave trade — that is, the buying and selling of slaves, but not slavery itself — in the District of Columbia; enact a strong fugitive slave law empowering federal marshals to catch runaway slaves and return them to their owners; organize the territories of Utah and New Mexico with popular sovereignty determining the future of slavery; and pay Texas $10 million to settle its debts and resolve its border dispute with New Mexico.

President Taylor said he opposed the Compromise and would veto it, but his untimely death in July 1850 made that a moot point. The bills were passed through both Houses of Congress by the efforts of Illinois Senator Stephen A. Douglas, Abraham Lincoln's future presidential opponent. The Compromise lasted only a bit more than four years due to the deaths of Clay, Calhoun, and Webster; the reluctance of the North to enforce the Fugitive Slave Act; and the growing influence of the abolitionist movement.

[66] Along with Massachusetts's Daniel Webster and South Carolina's John C. Calhoun.

During these years, the Church hosted the First Plenary Council of Baltimore in 1852. Three such sessions were eventually held in the nation's premier see, each a gathering of all the bishops of the dioceses then extant in America. The first council's primary concern was the establishment of parish schools and provision for competent teachers to staff them. As a result, the parish school became a fixture throughout the nation, "even if the ideal of a Catholic school for every Catholic child was never fully realized."[67] Without a doubt, the chief proponent of this measure in the hierarchy was Philadelphia's John N. Neumann, who was canonized in 1977.

Yet another very significant event, one that polarized the country, was the 1852 publication of *Uncle Tom's Cabin* by Harriet Beecher Stowe. The daughter of Lyman Beecher, one of the fiercest anti-Catholic speakers and writers of his time, she had been born in Connecticut and moved to Cincinnati in 1832. She began developing anti-slavery sympathies as a young woman, and her marriage to Calvin Stowe, professor of biblical literature at Cincinnati's Lane Theological Seminary, further cemented both spouses' convictions. She eventually left the Midwest when her husband became president of Bowdoin College in Maine. The agitation over the Fugitive Slave Act inspired her to write the work, which "was universally read, 100,000 copies being sold within two months, and 300,000 within a year."[68] The South considered the book to be a travesty, nothing less than an abolitionist tract.

The book was written hastily, and its popularity had little to do with its literary merit; Stowe was, at least in the view of one historian, a second-rate writer. But the story explained the abolitionists' cause with narrative better than they could with argument:

[67] Hennesey, *American Catholics*, 109–110.
[68] J. G. Randall, *The Civil War and Reconstruction* (Boston: D.C. Heath, 1937), 169.

Her approach to the subject explains the book's success. This tale of the pious, patient slave Uncle Tom, the saintly White child Eva, and the callous slave driver Simon Legree appealed to an audience far wider than that reached by the abolitionists. It avoided the vindictive and self-righteous tone found in most abolitionist tracts and was thus infinitively more persuasive.[69]

It was a book that touched the hearts of millions; some became abolitionists, and others, while hesitant to take a public or vocal stand, at least began to question the justice of the slavery system. Despite its enormous influence, "it would be wrong ... to conclude that in the early fifties most Americans were ready to break up the union over slavery. The overwhelming majority was not."[70]

Congress next took up the question of slavery, particularly in the territories, in the form of the Kansas-Nebraska Act. Stephen A. Douglas, in attempting to facilitate the building of a railroad to the Pacific, proposed organizing lands west of the Mississippi River as the territories of Kansas and Nebraska. In his plan, the Missouri Compromise would be repealed and popular sovereignty would decide the status of slavery in both areas. The law passed along sectional lines, resulting in a full party realignment. Opponents of the Kansas-Nebraska plan formed the Republican Party, gathering anti-slavery elements of the Northern Democratic and Whig parties. It emphasized a free-soil platform—the acceptance of slavery where it existed and opposition to its expansion into the territories—and attracted a significant number of abolitionists, as well as nativist Know-Nothings.

Anti-slavery groups began organizing migration to Kansas to balance the pro-slavery settlers from Missouri for the purpose of

[69] Garraty, op. cit., 379.
[70] Ibid.

tilting the popular sovereignty vote against slavery when the territory applied for statehood. The rivalry intensified between the factions, leading to what became known as "Bleeding Kansas." The crisis worsened when each side elected a government they claimed spoke for all of the territory. In 1856, the city of Lawrence was sacked by pro-slavery advocates from Missouri, who burned stores, robbed homes, and destroyed printing presses. The abolitionist John Brown made his first significant appearance when he led a night raid during which he executed pro-slavery men, known as the Pottawatomie Massacre.

Meanwhile, in Washington, D.C., Massachusetts Senator Charles Sumner, an avowed abolitionist, delivered a speech called "The Crime against Kansas." In retaliation, South Carolina Congressman Preston Brooks crossed the aisle and beat Sumner over the head with his cane, severely injuring the senator. The psychological effects were devastating on the country.

Finally, in 1856, experienced diplomat James Buchanan of Pennsylvania defeated the Republican Party's first candidate for president, John C. Fremont. Buchanan advanced popular sovereignty as a solution to the slavery question, while his Republican opponent favored free-soil opposition to slavery's expansion. The Whig Party, with no presidential candidate to run, became defunct on the national level, and its Northern and Southern members drifted to either of the two existing national parties.

"I Know Nothing"

The 1850s brought a familiar but evolving form of anti-Catholicism with the birth of the Know-Nothing Party. As a political entity, it was short-lived, originating in 1854 and suffering a quick demise after the presidential election of 1856. It was the brainchild of Charles B. Allen of New York, who had begun a secret patriotic society called the Order of the Star Spangled Banner, targeting immigrants in general and Catholics in particular. It appears to have been a reasonably complex fraternity, much like the Ku Klux Klan of later years.

Aside from its opposition to Catholics, the party was divided along sectional lines, just like the Republicans and Democrats. Southern Know-Nothings, for example, favored territorial expansion into areas where slavery could expand; their Northern counterparts were opposed. Southern elements favored a low tariff, whereas the Northern element felt that American labor should be protected from competition by high rates. Northern Know-Nothings favored a homestead bill much like the one Lincoln would introduce some years later, but their Southern brethren felt that public lands should not be simply given away. Northerners tended to favor Henry Clay's idea of internal improvements, whereas Southerners were opposed to it. "Only one force held the members of the Know-Nothing Party together," it has been observed, "their hatred for the Catholic Church."[71]

With many of these sectional differences either temporarily settled or on hold by mid-century, people were only too happy to turn to their long-standing fear of Catholicism:

> Why did hundreds of thousands of Americans desert the well-established parties and support this intolerant organization which promised war on Catholics and foreigners? Three forces were operating that together accounted for the rise of Know-Nothingism: the confusion of party alignments, the slavery controversy, and the growth of a sincere nativistic sentiment.[72]

---

[71] Billington, *The Protestant Crusade*, 387.
[72] Ibid., 389–390.

Still, the appeal of Know-Nothingism was stronger in some regions than in others. The Northwest seemed to be arid ground for Know-Nothings, mostly because citizens of that region were in daily contact with foreigners and realized that they were not the notorious enemies they were portrayed to be. The Northeast and the border states, on the other hand, were ripe for the message of bigotry, mostly because of the effectiveness of anti-Catholic propaganda.

In many ways, the Know-Nothings echoed their counterparts of a decade earlier:

> The Know-Nothings pledged to prohibit the introduction into the United States of the physically and morally unfit, and to seek a twenty-one year probationary period before the naturalization of aliens; offered a platform attractive to eastern laborers, southern planters, and western farmers as well as to avowed nativists. All of these groups believed that their political or economic welfare would suffer from a continued alien influx.[73]

One of their chief opportunities to be heard came in 1853 with the arrival of a papal diplomat, Archbishop Gaetano Bedini. His celebrated tour of the United States was billed as a mere courtesy call on America en route to Brazil to take up his position as nuncio at the court of Emperor Dom Pedro II. In fact, he was sent by the Vatican to study carefully the question of lay trusteeism, which had haunted the Church in several large cities, where boards of trustees had attempted to seize control of parish properties, to have a greater say in the appointment of pastors, and to usurp proper clerical authority in other ways. Though these outrages had mostly

[73] Ibid., 410.

occurred some years earlier, vestiges of them remained, and, in some instances, the fires had yet to be extinguished.

Bedini was also to investigate the possibility of inaugurating diplomatic relations with the United States in the form of a papal nuncio (or ambassador), a counterpart to the American minister already in place in Rome. The archbishop's visit began successfully enough: He visited with President Franklin Pierce, toured several East Coast cities, and headed for the Midwest. But there, problems immediately began to emerge. Allesandro Gavazzi, an Italian ex-priest and a popular lecturer on the anti-Catholic circuit, charged that Bedini, as papal governor of Bologna,[74] had been responsible for certain executions performed by Austrian military authorities. This was all the American public needed to hear. Mobs began to gather in city after city protesting his appearance, and protestors converged on the cathedrals of Cincinnati and Wheeling decrying the "Butcher of Bologna." In addition, a group of Know-Nothings converged on the Washington Monument, then under construction in the nation's capital; they seized a slab of Italian Carrara marble brought by Bedini as a personal gift from Pope Pius IX to be inserted into the monument and, by some accounts, dumped it into the Potomac River. The archbishop finally had to be smuggled onto a steamer in New York harbor and transported out of the country. This series of events was considered by the Know-Nothings and their sympathizers to have been a shining hour.

A more serious confrontation occurred in Louisville, Kentucky, in 1855, in what has become known as "Bloody Monday." Stirred up by an anti-Catholic lecturer and the recent election of a Know-Nothing mayor, a riot broke out on August 6: "Over twenty

[74] At this point in history, the pope was still a temporal as well as spiritual ruler. Bedini would have been the Holy Father's personal political representative in Bologna.

were killed, three-quarters of them 'foreigners,' and hundreds lay wounded. The city's Catholic Bishop, Martin J. Spalding, whose first American ancestor had landed in Maryland in 1657, pleaded for calm.... Privately, he confided to the Archbishop of Baltimore 'we have just passed through a reign of terror surpassed only by the Philadelphia riots.'"[75]

Perhaps the single greatest triumph of the short-lived political party was their ability to nominate a presidential candidate in the 1856 presidential election: New York's Millard Fillmore, who had served as Zachary Taylor's vice president until Taylor's death in July 1850 and assumed the presidency until Franklin Pierce was elected in 1852.

Fillmore's rhetoric during the campaign was not a barrage of anti-Catholicism: He made a few references to the dangers of unrestricted foreign immigration, but the bulk of his message was the preservation of the Union. Curiously, he carried the electoral votes of only one state—Maryland, where Catholics had first arrived in 1634. The party was already practically a nonentity by 1856, and this campaign was its last stand. The country was quickly heading for the bloodiest conflagration it had known, and, though anti-Catholic bigotry would raise its head several times again, national preoccupation was shifting in a different direction. As one leading student of the movement has observed:

> Know-Nothingism had nothing permanent to offer. Its principles were inimical to those on which the American nation had been founded; its demands were of a sort that could never be realized in a country constituted as was the United States. Thus the party's success contributed to its failure, for its leaders, once in power, were helpless, and the people,

[75] Hennesey, *American Catholics*, 125–126.

realizing this, began to desert the organization as quickly as they had joined.[76]

A Potpourri of No-Popery

The Catholic press, as might be expected, had its own take on the origin and objectives of the Know-Nothings. Many Catholic newspapers saw the religious bigotry of the 1850s as merely an intensification of what had been occurring in the country since colonial days. Numerous Protestant sects were blamed for fueling the flames, and some Catholic editors felt that the tremendous growth of the Church so scared WASP America that the WASPs were lashing back as strongly as they could. The Catholic press also averred that religiously bigoted American nativists had joined forces with other anti-Catholic immigrant groups:

All Englishmen, Germans (provided they be Protestants, or at least infidels and Sabbath-breakers), Italians too (provided they know how to curse the Pope …), even Irishmen, if they are Protestants, are regarded with the greatest favor and welcomed into the Nativist ranks as brothers. We suppose no sensible man will venture to deny that Irish Orangemen constituted full one-half of the Nativist rioters in Philadelphia during 1844, or that the editors of the New York papers under their control are all, or nearly all foreigners, Englishmen, Welchmen, &c., as are also the street-preachers hired by the faction to promote popular excitement and religious riot. Is it not clear, then, that this whole Native American movement is, at bottom, a mere modern improvement on the old No-Popery cries; a movement directed not against

[76] Billington, *The Protestant Crusade*, 417.

foreigners in general, not even against Irishmen as such, but against the Catholic religion?[77]

Orestes Brownson, an astute if not uncontroversial observer, had difficulty believing that the Know-Nothing movement was of native origin; rather, he argued its source was "Irish Orangemen, German radicalism, French socialism, and Italian astuteness and hate."[78]

The *Pittsburgh Catholic* was even more explicit:

> Not from the heroes of 76 do the Know-Nothings borrow their ideas, but from the Irish Orangemen. Know-Noth-ingism is in reality, only an American development of that ruffian Irish society.... It is a well-known fact that from the beginning the Orangemen fraternized with the Know-Nothings, and were considered qualified to become members of the new order. Itinerant anti-Catholic lecturers from England, Ireland and Scotland were its first apostles.... At the late election, in this State at least, the greatest strong-holds of the Know-Nothings were those places where north of Ireland Protestants or their descendants predominated.[79]

Others felt that the no-Popery crusade was not strong enough in itself to explain the success of the nativist movement. The free-soil anti-Catholic character of the Know-Nothings, Orestes Brownson believed, found its deeper origins in England, along with the growing anti-slavery movement. England was only too happy

---

[77] *United States Catholic Miscellany* XXXIII (January 28, 1854): 222, cited in Hueston, *The Catholic Press and Nativism*, 230–231.

[78] "The Know–Nothings," *Brownson's Quarterly Review*, 3rd series, II (1854): 458, cited in Hueston, *The Catholic Press and Nativism*, 213.

[79] *Pittsburgh Catholic*, December 23, 1854, 334, cited in Hueston, *The Catholic Press and Nativism*, 232.

to sow internal dissent in the United States, many believed, so as to avoid a war between the two nations, which many considered a real possibility during the 1850s.

Brownson ignited a firestorm in the July 1854 issue of his *Review* when he drew a sharp distinction between anti-Catholicism and native-Americanism. Catholics, and especially the Irish, had been in part responsible for nativism, he argued, by isolating themselves and failing to accept the fact that Anglo-Saxon Protestantism was the dominant force in the United States. They had therefore incurred the not-unearned wrath of the majority, and "true Americans" were thus only too happy to join forces with anti-Catholicism, especially the Know-Nothings. Brownson seemed to agree with the native-American sentiment that opposed Irish clannishness; he believed citizenship was the "gift" of the host nation and that immigrants coming to American shores should approach the matter discreetly. While Brownson felt that many native Americans had distorted what real Americanism was about, as far as the Irish were concerned, though he was an enthusiastic convert to Catholicism, he showed his true native colors.

A somewhat distinctive feature of mid-century anti-Catholicism was the emergence of street preachers.

Sidewalk oratory attracted many outlandish figures such as John S. Orr, who called himself the "Angel Gabriel" because he appeared in seraphic robes and summoned his audience by blowing a trumpet. (Catholics accepted an account which declared that he was a Scotchman whose real name was Sandy McSwish). Such characters generally attracted a turbulent crowd of listeners, and, when a few tipsy Irishmen stood in the gathering, violence often resulted.[80]

---

[80] Hueston, *The Catholic Press and Nativism*, 270–271.

By 1854, street preaching and its related violence had largely abated, due to a combination of factors: "ample preparation of authorities to prevent disturbance, cooler counsel of the leaders of the Know-Nothings, and the work of ... the Roman Catholic clergy in entreating their people to refrain from acts of violence."[81]

Meanwhile, Horace Greeley's *New York Tribune* was never to be found on the side of the Know-Nothings, but even this publication turned a suspicious eye on the waves of immigrants sweeping across the East Coast:

> [We] have never denied the great provocations to Nativism in this country, and, unless these can be put aside, we expect to witness occasional outbursts of anti-foreign excitement. Our immigrant population is deplorably clannish, misguided, and prone to violence. We never saw a party of American-born approach a peaceable poll with weapons in their hands; we *have* seen Irish bands of two or three hundred, armed with heavy clubs, traversing the streets on election day clearly provoking a fight; we have known such beat a peaceful opponent for no fault—twenty falling on one—until his life was in danger. We have seen men taken to courts to be naturalized and put through like a sheep-washing, when they did not know what they swore or were in no condition to take on the responsibilities of citizenship. We have seen the public advertisements of party Naturalization Committees offering to grind out voters *gratis*, in order to swell the votes for their party; and we thought adopted Citizens who *are* Citizens ought to interfere with this scandalous business, which casts reproach on their whole body; but they said nothing and seemed to take it quite as a matter of course.[82]

---

[81] Gibson, *Attitudes of the New York Irish*, 81.
[82] *New York Tribune*, June 15, 1854, cited in ibid.

Faith and Fury

There was also a spiritual rebuttal to anti-Catholic bigotry put forward by the Catholic press, which argued that the entire movement of hostility would fall in on itself because of Christ's words that the gates of Hell would never prevail against His Church. In fact, these voices claimed, the Church would experience a greater unity, attract many curiosity seekers to look more closely at the truth of Catholicism, and, in the end, win many converts to the Faith. While this result was not clearly discernable on any large scale, the argument could by no means be dismissed out of hand. The New York *Freeman's Journal*, insisting on the compatibility of Catholicism and the American spirit, "envisioned a day when Catholicism would win the allegiance of most Americans and renovate the country socially and morally."[83] Such was in accord with the thinking of the famed convert Father Isaac Hecker, founder of the Paulists, whose congregation was established on such a hope and achieved great success for decades. A more recent historical study, however, may well have captured the true relationship between America and the Church:

> Rome's 19th century course, as shaped, in reaction to France's revolution and continental liberalism, did not facilitate the task. American ideas and concerns did not always translate easily into European idiom and were frequently misunderstood by those whose horizons were bounded by the Adriatic and Tyrhennian seas. On the American side of the water, ancestral memories from two continents mingled: of English and colonial penal laws which ostracized Catholic forebears and of Louis XIV's persecution of Huguenots; of Protestant martyrs at Smithfield under Bloody Mary and Catholic martyrs on the Tyburn gallows under her successors; of Cromwell's

---

[83] Hueston, *The Catholic Press and Nativism*, 274.

massacre of the Irish at Drogheda and the Indian massacre of New Englanders at Deerfield. Evangelical sympathy to the Whore of Babylon was alive and well and heartily reciprocated. American civil religion, grounded in a curious inversion of Calvinism and heavily colored by the Enlightenment, would always be a difficult bedfellow for Christians in communion with the bishop and the church of Rome.[84]

A Growing Church

In such a climate, it is not surprising that plans would emerge to attract immigrants to leave the teeming cities of the eastern seaboard and settle in the West. At least two such ventures were discussed very publicly—one involving territory in Iowa, and another a specific colony in honor of Saint Patrick to be established in Nebraska with towns and streets named after those in Ireland. The idea seems to have originated among editors such as Thomas D'Arcy McGee of the *American Celt*, Patrick Donohue of the *Boston Pilot*, and a number of Western bishops and priests. An immigrant aid convention was held in Buffalo in February 1856, at which an organization was officially established to promote, develop, and carry out a Western venture. One of the main supporters among the hierarchy was Bishop Mathias Loras of Dubuque, Iowa, a Frenchman who, in seminary days, had been a classmate of St. John Vianney, the Curé of Ars.

Shortly after the Buffalo Convention, Loras held a similar meeting in Dubuque, at which delegates passed several resolutions, including statements to the effect that "we heartily approve of the action of the Catholic Convention recently held at Buffalo, New York, for the formation of Catholic settlements in the interior;

---

[84] Hennesey, *American Catholics*, 126–127.

Faith and Fury

[further] resolved that Catholic societies be formed throughout
the state of Iowa for the promotion of the above object, subject
to the directions of the Supreme Directory created by the Buffalo
Convention; [and] resolved that the Catholics of Dubuque now
form themselves into a Society of the character named above."[85]

Colonization projects, even when they were carried out, met
with limited success. On other fronts, however, much progress was
taking place — including receptions into the Church, which were
common through the 1850s. A notable case was that of Eliza Allen
Starr, a woman of Unitarian background whose ancestry on both
sides traced back to colonial America. Miss Allen's cousin, George
Allen, was a professor of Greek and Latin at the University of
Pennsylvania; he and his wife and children were received in 1847
by Philadelphia's Catholic bishop, Francis Patrick Kenrick, who
had guided their conversion. Miss Starr was influenced by Bishop
Kenrick and Bishop John Bernard Fitzpatrick of Boston and went
on to write poetry and popular essays, receiving Notre Dame's
prestigious Laetare Medal in 1885.[86]

Protestant ministers came to Rome, including James Roosevelt
Bayley, the nephew of St. Elizabeth Seton, who would be ordained
a priest and become bishop of Newark and later archbishop of
Baltimore. Two other notable conversions were those of Thomas
S. Preston and Levi Silliman Ives, the first Anglican bishop to
enter the Church since the Reformation. Although the numbers
of converts in the United States were significant, they did not approach those of the Oxford movement in England.

---

[85] John Tracy Ellis, *Documents of American Catholic History* (Milwaukee: Bruce, 1956), 321–322.
[86] James J. McGovern, ed., *The Life and Letters of Eliza Allen Starr*
(Chicago: Lakeside Press, 1905), 63–66; 67–68, cited in Ellis, *Documents*, 314–315.

Just as indicative of the growing prestige of American Catholicism was the foundation of two major American seminaries in Europe, first at the University of Louvain in Belgium in 1857 and two years later in the Eternal City of Rome. Talk began about the first seminary while some of the American bishops were gathered in Rome for the promulgation in 1854 of the doctrine of the Immaculate Conception of the Blessed Virgin Mary. Baltimore's Archbishop Kenrick was one of the chief proponents, as was the coadjutor bishop of Detroit, Peter P. Lefevere. One of Lefevere's Detroit priests, Peter Kindekens, was on mission to Rome for his ordinary shortly thereafter and was asked to look more deeply into the matter. The political situation in Rome at the time was not auspicious, but Kindekens, a native of Belgium, found much better prospects there. Upon his return, he sent a letter to the American hierarchy proposing the idea of an American College at Louvain, then one of the finest centers for Catholic study in Europe. He noted the enthusiastic approval of the cardinal archbishop of Malines, Engelbert Sterckx, and clearly stated that the object of the Belgian seminary would be

> to serve as a nursery of properly educated and tried clergymen for our missions; and ... to provide the American Bishops with a college to which some at least of their students might be sent to acquire a superior ecclesiastical instruction and a solid clerical training, without much expense, as the College will require no other Professors than those for the English and German languages.[87]

The American College at Rome would be founded just two years later. At the time of its inception, there were more than sixteen hundred priests, both diocesan and religious, serving in the United States. The Church in America by now had nearly

---

[87] Cited in Ellis, *Documents*, 324.

thirty domestic seminaries, and a large number of the young men studying in them were foreign born. Baltimore's Kenrick, Hughes of New York, and Bishop Michael O'Connor of Pittsburgh appear to have been the prelates most interested in the establishment of the Roman seminary. O'Connor acted as delegate to Rome on the matter and returned to tell his fellow bishops that Pope Pius IX had great hopes that the seminary could be opened soon. It became a reality on December 7, 1859, when the North American College opened with twelve students in a former convent of Visitation Nuns on the Via dell'Umiltà. After nearly a century in that location, updated and expanded facilities were needed, and so, in 1953, a new college on the Janiculum Hill was dedicated. The original building became the Casa Santa Maria, a center for graduate study for American priests working on advanced degrees.

Bishop O'Connor was quite explicit as to the seminary's purposes, in a pastoral letter he wrote to Catholics in the Diocese of Pittsburgh:

> That an American College in Rome is necessary to impart a sound ecclesiastical education to our clergy, or to maintain our union with the Holy See, no one will pretend. [It] will greatly promote the higher ecclesiastical studies among them, and add new grace to our National Church. The clergy and people of the United States yield to no others, in their loving attachment to Rome; and are second to none, in their zeal for the promotion of ecclesiastical and secular learning. [A] National College at Rome will, it must be presumed, very much augment the number of the learned among our clergy, and prove a powerful means, under God, of perpetuating the orthodoxy of our young Church, which no taint of heresy has, thus far, touched.[88]

[88] Cited in ibid., 347.

The Catholic Justice Taney

One of the monumental events leading to the Civil War was the decision rendered in the *Dred Scott* case in 1857. It is particularly significant in American Catholic history because the Chief Justice who wrote the brief and handed down the decision was a practicing Roman Catholic, Roger Brooke Taney of Maryland.

The Taneys were an English family, as were the judge's maternal ancestors, the Brookes. Both had come to the Maryland Colony in the seventeenth century—the Taneys to Calvert County, the Brookes to Delabrooke, across the Patuxent River from what would become the Taney estate. Both families were members of the Church of England but converted to Catholicism. In the case of the Taneys:

> They did so in spite of legislation which deprived them of political rights, limited their privileges of worship, and prohibited the establishment and maintenance of Catholic Schools. Whether the change was made as an incident to marriage into a Catholic family is not clear, or whether it represented a step upward socially—since many of the more prominent people were Catholics, who adhered to their faith in spite of persistent governmental discrimination against them. The Brooke family, too, sometime within the same period, underwent the same transition.[89]

Since Catholic higher education was prohibited by law in Maryland, many of the wealthier families sent their sons to Europe, specifically to the College of the English Jesuits at St. Omer in French Flanders. The Carrolls, Maryland's first family, were conspicuous for this, and some of Judge Taney's forbearers had matriculated there.

---

[89] Carl B. Swisher, *Roger B. Taney* (Hamden, CT: Archon Books, 1961), 8.

For Roger, born on March 17, 1777, it was still financially possible, but other family concerns made it not feasible. Instead, at age fifteen, he was sent to Dickinson College in Carlisle, Pennsylvania, a center of Scotch-Irish Presbyterians, who were "for the most part strict … shrewd in things political as well as religious, and who had opened the school in the 1780s for the purpose of perpetuating their influence."[90] Later, at the age of nineteen, Taney was sent to Annapolis to read law in the office of Jeremiah Townley.

The Taneys had long been affiliated with the Federalist Party, which was synonymous with political conservatism. As Roger advanced in his legal career, though, the party was waning. The young jurist affiliated with the Democratic Republicans and later became a Jacksonian Democrat, due, in part, to his growing distrust of power concentrated in the national government, which, he felt, was inimical to individual liberty. In his later career as chief justice, his judicial philosophy stood in marked contrast to that of his predecessor, John Marshall, who was a strong judicial nationalist. Taney, on the other hand, would assume the position that, in the absence of strong evidence, the expressed, enumerated, delegated, or implied powers of the federal government should be operative, and the liberties of individual states to enact their own laws should be preserved.

Taney practiced law in his hometown of Frederick, Maryland, and rose, under Andrew Jackson, to become attorney general, secretary of the treasury, and secretary of war. He had also been a member of the president's "Kitchen Cabinet" who particularly helped Jackson in his fight against the Bank of the United States. Jackson appointed him Chief Justice in 1836, and he remained in office until his death on October 12, 1864.

Taney was a parishioner at the venerable Saint John's Church in Frederick, where he could often be seen in line for Confession.

[90] Ibid., 16.

In 1806, he had married Anne Key, the sister of Francis Scott Key, writer of the "The Star Spangled Banner." The Keys were a prominent Episcopalian family in Frederick, and a story has long prevailed that, although they were married in the Catholic Church, the couple had made an agreement that all boys born of their union would be raised Catholics, while the girls would be Protestant. As it happened, they became the parents of six girls, and only one, quite late in life, converted to Catholicism. Taney's biographer notes that "Catholics have been reluctant to believe that Taney would make such an agreement," adding that when one of his relatives had asked him if such were the case, "he replied that he could not have done so as a Catholic." The biographer concluded that "the reply indicates nothing definite except his unwillingness to discuss the matter."[91]

His adherence to Catholicism seems to have been deeply interiorized, rather than merely an intellectual, creedal adherence. Following the death of his wife in 1855, he confided his terrible anguish to his cousin Ethelbert Taney, to whom he described his inability to fully regain his personal composure to attend to judicial business. On a trip to Baltimore, he was accompanied by a priest, to whom he confided that before he could engage in any official business, his first stop must be at the cathedral to attend Mass and receive Holy Communion, in order to resign himself fully to God's Holy Will in Anne's death.

At the same time, he had opposed attempts of his coreligionists to try to convert his wife or daughters, including a priest dinner guest who carried on at length about the glories of the true Faith, strongly encouraging them to consider conversion. Taney was quick to remind his guest that such topics were not discussed at his dinner table.

[91] Ibid., 50.

Faith and Fury

His attitude toward their religion is not easy to discover. In view of his devotion to them and of his firm belief in a future life it seems clear that he could have been happy in the belief that they, by their separate religious paths, would arrive at the same goal as he. If holding such a belief constituted in any sense disloyalty to his own church, it seems probable that to this extent he was disloyal.[92]

Taney is surely best remembered for his decision in the case of *Scott vs. Sandford*, better known as the *Dred Scott* case. Scott was an illiterate Black slave owned by Doctor John Emerson in St. Louis, Missouri. In 1834, the doctor left St. Louis for Illinois, taking Scott with him. Scott married on the trip and had a child. In 1838, the army, for whom Doctor Emerson was working, sent him back to St. Louis, and he returned with Scott and his new family. Six years later, Emerson died, leaving Scott to his daughter, who was not yet of age. An executor, John Sandford, took responsibility for Scott, and, at this point, a number of abolitionists took interest in the case. Trying to ascertain whether Scott might be considered a free man because he had lived in the free territory of Illinois, they hired lawyers to argue the case to the Missouri state courts. The first of those judicial bodies replied that he was, but on appeal to the Missouri State Supreme Court, the judgment was reversed. On further appeal, the U.S. Federal District Court for Missouri failed to render a verdict as to whether Scott was free, or, for that matter, a citizen. At this point, the case was appealed to the judicial authority of last resort, the United States Supreme Court.

Taney delivered a long, detailed decision, beginning with the judgment that the lower court should have dismissed the case because Scott had no constitutional right to sue in a federal court.

[92] Ibid., 470.

His argument can be boiled down to three seemingly simple points: (1) Negroes, having been regarded as persons of an inferior order at the time when the Constitution was adopted, and not as "citizens," were not intended to be included in the term "citizen" as used in the Constitution, and were not included when the Constitution gave to citizens of different states the right to sue in federal courts. (2) Apart from the question as to whether *any* negro could be a citizen in the constitutional sense, it was obvious that no slave could be such a citizen. It was admitted on the record that Dred Scott had been taken from Missouri as a slave. He had not become free by virtue of residence in territory covered by the Missouri Compromise, since the Missouri Compromise was unconstitutional, so that unless he had some other claim to freedom he was still a slave, not a citizen, and not entitled to sue in a federal court. (3) Whatever the temporary effect of Dred Scott's residence in Illinois, he had returned to Missouri, where his status was determined by Missouri law. The Missouri courts had held that he was a slave. Therefore he was not a citizen and could not sue.[93]

As might be expected, the chief justice and all but two of his sssociates who concurred were bitterly castigated by many, especially abolitionists, while they found great support among the Southern slaveholding classes.

---

[93] Ibid., 505–506. Taney's argument in *Dred Scott* that the Missouri Compromise, with its limits on slavery in the territories, was unconstitutional was only the second time in U.S. history that a federal law was struck down by the Supreme Court, the first being in *Marbury v. Madison* in 1803. Taney argued that the Missouri Compromise had not entitled Dred Scott to his freedom because Congress had no power to prohibit slavery in the territories.

Faith and Fury

Some months after the judgment was rendered, Massachusetts Congregationalist minister Reverend Samuel Nott sent Taney a pamphlet he had written on slavery, in which he included an analysis of the *Dred Scott* decision. Taney's reply is indicative of his conservative Southern mind, and, though some would strongly disagree, demonstrates a fairness of mind that went beyond the blind racial prejudice frequently found in his era.

The chief justice argued that those raised in slaveholding states had a factual knowledge that Northern abolitionists did not always have. In both Maryland and Virginia, Taney went on, many opportunities for emancipation were offered to slaves, and freed Blacks were allowed to remain in these states and pursue any occupation they might have a talent for. These manumissions were based on the kindness of many owners, but in many cases these decisions were made with little thought for the freedman's ability to handle his new life of liberty. Very often, Taney asserted, the manumitted slave had "brought upon himself privations and sufferings which he would not have been called upon to endure in a state of slavery."[94]

He then spoke of the kind relations that allegedly often existed between master and slave, the fact that the bondsman was cared for from the cradle to the grave, given work, properly fed, taken care of in sickness, and so on. He was quick to admit, however, that "there are indeed exceptions—painful exceptions. But this will always be the case, where power combined with bad passions or a mercenary spirit is on one side, and weakness on the other."[95]

Taney believed that slaveowners had a strict obligation to raise their slaves with proper moral and spiritual education; he no doubt had in mind the truths of the Catholic Faith. Meanwhile, the spread of abolitionism, according to Taney, strained the relationship

[94] Ellis, *Documents*, 331.
[95] Ibid., 332.

72

between master and slave at least in part because the slaves were "for the most part weak, credulous, and easily misled by stronger minds."[96] Thus, anti-slavery ideas might rouse in the enslaved desires and notions that would make them less content in their station.

Taney respectfully requested that his minister correspondent not allow his response to appear in print. He felt the *Dred Scott* decision should stand for itself without any further comments from him—but, even more important, members of the supreme judiciary should not be seen or heard to be sympathizing with any social or political or religious opinions beyond the particulars of judicial interpretation in cases brought before them. In closing, the chief justice noted that he was not a slaveowner:

> More than thirty years ago I manumitted every slave I ever owned, except two, who were too old, when they became my property, to provide for themselves. These two I supported in comfort as long as they lived. And I am glad to say that none of those whom I manumitted disappointed my expectations, but have shown by their conduct that they were worthy of freedom; and know how to use it.[97]

President Lincoln, only six months before his own death and along with three of the members of his cabinet, attended a memorial service for Taney following his death at the age of eighty-seven. There followed a Requiem Mass at Saint John's, Frederick, after which Taney was laid to rest next to his mother in Saint John's Cemetery. Whatever may be said of his judicial positions, few would argue the sincerity of his Catholic faith. Writing in another letter to Ethelbert Taney, he wrote:

[96] Ibid.
[97] Ibid., 333.

Faith and Fury

Most thankful I am, that the reading, reflection, studies and experience of a long life have strengthened and confirmed my faith in the Catholic Church, which has never ceased to teach her children how they should live and how they should die.[98]

The Faith among the Enslaved

The question of the education of slaves was discussed in the Church many years before the Civil War began. One of the main partici-pants in these conversations was the Bishop of Natchez, Mississippi: William Henry Elder. Elder hailed from an old Maryland Catholic family who came to Southern Maryland in colonial days, later migrated to the Frederick County hamlet of Emmitsburg (later home of Elizabeth Ann Seton), and also lived for some time in Baltimore. In all this, he was well positioned to see the institution of slavery firsthand and to conclude what practical pastoral steps had to be taken to ensure that slaves remained faithful to the faith into which they had been born.

Bishop Elder's diocese contained about ten thousand Catholics out of a state population of over six hundred thousand. More than half of the state of Mississippi's population was enslaved:

These poor Negroes form in some respects my chief anxiety. I believe they are generally well cared for, so far as health and the necessaries of life are concerned. But for learning & practicing religion, they have at present very little op-portunity indeed. Commonly their masters are well disposed to allow them religious instruction, & sometimes they pay Ministers to come & preach on the plantation. They do not

[98] Swisher, *Roger B. Taney*, 470.

like to let the Negroes go to a public church, because there is danger of their misbehaving when they are away from home, & out of sight of the Overseer; & because various inconveniences result from the servants of one plantation mingling with those of another.... Some masters indeed object to having a Minister come to preach to their slaves, & they rather encourage some one of the blacks themselves to become a preacher for the rest.[99]

Elder went on in this letter, written to the Society for the Propagation of the Faith, to lament that all the priests he had in his diocese were very much tied to their parish assignments. What he needed was a band of traveling missionaries who would move from plantation to plantation, searching out the scattered Catholics one was bound to find who had had no access to priestly ministrations, sometimes for many years. Because the slaves had so little of this world's goods, the bishop felt that they were more inclined to think about and hope for the things of eternity. All his evidence indicated that when put in contact with a priest who would patiently explain the Faith, they were quite open to listening. At the same time, he wrote, "they are so entirely animal in their inclinations, so engrossed with the senses, that they have no regard for anything above the gratifications of the body."[100] This sensuality arose, he felt, not from malice or animosity to the spiritual life, but from their complete deprivation. There was a hunger for truth in many of them, said Elder, but at the same time years of gratifying their sensuality had left so many of them weak willed in the face of temptation:

The humility of their condition & the docility of their character take away many of the ordinary obstacles to the

99 Ellis, *Documents*, 335.
100 Ibid., 336.

workings of grace; & where other circumstances are favorable, these lowly ones in the eyes of the world sometimes rise very high in the favor of God.... Oh! what a harvest of souls among these 310,000 negroes: every one of them immortal, made to the image & likeness of God, redeemed by the Precious Blood of the Son of God! Oh! What frightful havoc Satan is making among them![101]

The Rise of Lincoln

In the same year as *Dred Scott*, a North Carolina farmer named Hinton R. Helper wrote a book called *The Impending Crisis*. Using census data, he contrasted Northern and Southern states to show that the South, with its slave labor, was unable to keep pace with the North in population, agriculture, commerce, and industry. The book had an immense and immediate psychological impact and was well-circulated by abolitionists and anti-slavery advocates in both major political parties. The idea that these two regions were diverging unstoppably was becoming more and more the conventional wisdom.

An even more compelling view of the division of the country could be found in the Lincoln-Douglas debates in the Illinois senatorial race of 1858. The young representative from Springfield, who had been born in Harden County, Kentucky, spent time in Indiana, and finally settled on the Illinois prairie, was challenging U.S. Senator Stephen A. Douglas, who had become one of the major power players in the Democratic Party. Lincoln, a former Whig, had joined the newly formed Republicans. There were seven debates in all, held in towns where canals allowed for convenient transportation access.[102]

[101] Ibid., 337.
[102] The debates were held in Ottawa, Freeport, Charleston, Galesburg, Jonesboro, Quincy, and Alton, Illinois.

The Coming of the Civil War: 1848–1860

Upon accepting the Republican nomination, Lincoln gave his famous "House Divided" speech, in which he contended that a nation that was half slave and half free was not sustainable. During the debates, he did not strongly commit himself to a position on slavery, declaring his opposition when in the northern part of Illinois and giving a quite different view when in the southern part of the state. (In the era before mass communications, these inconsistencies would be hard to pin down.) Douglas, known for bombastic rhetoric, usually got carried away, while Lincoln got excellent response from his crowds. Though the incumbent Senator was reelected, the rail splitter had made a decisive mark.

Of even more interest to Catholics, though, were Lincoln's views on religion. Some years earlier, in response to a question about his political views, he replied that he thought he was a Whig, but under no circumstances was he a Know-Nothing. In an often-quoted statement he said:

> How could I be? How can anyone who abhors the oppression of Negroes be in favor of degrading classes of white people? Our progress in degeneracy appears to me to be pretty rapid. As a nation, we began by declaring that "*all men are created equal.*" We now practically read it "all men are created equal, *except Negroes.*" When the Know-Nothings get control it will read "all men are created equal, except Negroes, *and foreigners and catholics.*" When it comes to this I should prefer emigrating to some country where they make no pretense of loving liberty—to Russia, for instance, where despotism can be taken pure, and without the base alloy of hypocrisy.[103]

---

[103] Lincoln to Joshua F. Speed, Springfield, August 24, 1855, in Roy P. Basler, ed., *The Collected Works of Abraham Lincoln* (New Brunswick, 1953), 11, 322–323, cited in Ellis, *Documents*, 84.

In fact, Lincoln had rather close Catholic ties. His father's brother, Mordecai, entered the Church and began a Catholic branch of the Lincolns. Mordecai converted upon his marriage to Mary Mudd, daughter of Luke Mudd of an old Southern Maryland Catholic family who had emigrated to Kentucky. Their marriage was witnessed by Father William de Rohan and was recorded in the old Catholic city of Bardstown, Kentucky. From their union came six children, all first cousins of the sixteenth president: Abraham, James, Mordecai Jr., Elizabeth, Mary Rowena, and Martha. These Kentucky Lincolns, like their famous cousin, settled on the Illinois prairie, lured by the Military Bounty Land Tract set aside for veterans of the War of 1812. Fifteen years after the close of the war, in 1830, these Lincolns arrived at Fountain Green, in the west central portion of the state, and were soon followed by many other Kentucky Catholic families. These families produced one of the earliest pockets of Midwestern Catholics and were responsible for the construction of a church dedicated to Saint Simon the apostle, which James Lincoln and his nephew Robert helped to build. Attached to the church is a period cemetery where one may still relive a bygone era.

Prior to the church's completion in 1837, Catholics were often visited by a missionary priest, Irenaeus St. Cyr, known for searching out scattered flocks along the Mississippi valley from St. Louis to Chicago. St. Cyr noted that the Lincolns were not well instructed in their Faith but were strong and sincere in their profession of it; he often said Mass in their home. Nicolay and Hay, President Lincoln's private secretaries, who compiled ten volumes on the slain chief executive, often commented on the physical characteristics the Lincolns of Fountain Green shared with their cousin in the White House. Another early-twentieth-century biographer of Lincoln, William E. Barton, noted that they were subject to the same emotional moods as their cousin, going from boisterous mirth one moment to the depths of despair the next.

The Coming of the Civil War: 1848–1860

As a young congressman, Abraham Lincoln often visited his Catholic relatives, who happened to live within his district. By the time he achieved national prominence, his male first cousins had died, but their children, some fourteen strong, actively supported his presidential campaign, and were strong devotees of the Union cause—proved in part by their numerous enlistments.[104]

The year 1859 witnessed John Brown's raid on the federal arsenal at Harpers Ferry, Virginia (now West Virginia). Brown hoped to secure weapons from the arsenal and then to begin a slave rebellion by freeing and arming local bondsmen and marching them south. He was quickly apprehended, arrested, tried, convicted of treason against the state of Virginia, and sentenced to be executed. Brown was celebrated as a martyr for the abolitionist cause—but to Southern slaveowners, his actions were seen as nothing less than a failed plan to incite racial war in the country.

By 1860, the slave population had exceeded four million. It was imperative that both political parties speak clearly to the issue in their platforms. President James Buchanan had been largely unable to hold his Democratic coalition together and, like his predecessor, Franklin Pierce of New Hampshire, was thought to be a "doughface"—a Northerner sympathetic to the Southern point of view. That year, the Republicans convened in Chicago, and their logical candidate seemed to be William Henry Seward, U.S. senator and former governor of New York. But the Republicans realized that they needed Know-Nothing support, and Seward had favored financial aid to Catholic schools in New York years earlier. Thus, his appeal waned. On the third ballot, the convention nominated

[104]References to the Catholic Lincolns can be found in David Herbert Donald, *Lincoln* (New York: Simon and Schuster, 2011); Ida Tarbell, *The Early Life of Abraham Lincoln* (New York: S. S. McClure, 1896); J. Henry Lea and John R. Hutchinson, *The Ancestry of Abraham Lincoln* (Boston: Houghton Mifflin, 1909).

Faith and Fury

Abraham Lincoln, who had risen to national attention two years earlier during his celebrated campaign against Douglas.

The GOP platform was free soil, pledging to leave slavery alone in the South while prohibiting its introduction in the territories.[105] They also supported free land for homesteaders, the admission of Kansas as a free state, a transcontinental railroad subsidized by the federal government, tariff reform, and an end to the practice of polygamy (an issue raised by the emergence of the Mormon sect). The Democrats met in Charleston and experienced deep division. A Northern wing of the party went on to nominate Stephen A. Douglas, who had supported popular sovereignty in the territories, and the Southern wing nominated the current vice president, John C. Breckenridge, who pledged the protection of slavery. Southern members of the now defunct Whig Party came together and formed the Constitutional Union Party, choosing former Tennessee senator John Bell as their candidate.

With four major candidates, it was one of the most complex and tempestuous presidential campaigns in American history. Breckinridge carried most of the Southern states, but Bell tallied close to 40 percent of the Southern vote and won three states of the Upper South. Lincoln defeated Douglas in the free states, winning 54 percent of the Northern popular vote while carrying every county in New England and a majority in the Old Northwest. Lincoln was not even on the ballot in many of the Southern states. He polled fairly well in the border states of Delaware and Missouri, but in the other border states of Maryland, Kentucky, and Virginia, he received no more than 3 percent. Lincoln's popular-vote total, though, was significantly higher than that of the first Republican

[105] Prior to the convention, Lincoln made his well-remembered Cooper Union speech in New York, telling the Young Men's Republican Union that the Founding Fathers gave the federal government the constitutional authority to restrict slavery in the territories.

candidate four years earlier, John C. Fremont, and his sweep of the Northern states assured him victory in the Electoral College. As one commentator has noted, "If the electoral votes for Bell, Breckinridge and Douglas had been united in a single candidate, Lincoln would still have been elected."[106]

With the news of Lincoln's election, South Carolina immediately voted to secede from the Union.[107] A final attempt to stop secession was introduced in Congress by Senator John Crittenden of Kentucky; it was known as the Crittenden Compromise. The measure called for constitutional amendments to protect slavery where it existed and an extension of the Missouri Compromise line of 36 degrees, 30 minutes all the way to California, with slavery prohibited in the territories north of the line and permitted in those territories south of it. It was quickly rejected by Republicans who feared the expansion of slavery in any possible future conquests in Latin America.

On December 3, 1860, President Buchanan sent a message to Congress denying the right of the federal government to coerce a state to remain in the Union, and so, when South Carolina seceded, the administration did nothing. Likewise, when forts, arsenals, post offices, and federal buildings in the South were seized by the Southern states, the administration made no response. On January 9, 1861, the first firing on the United States flag occurred at Fort Sumter in the harbor of Charleston, and again there was no retaliation. By March 4, 1861, the mood of the country was so intense that after the new president's train ride from the Midwest,

[106] Eric Foner, *The Fiery Trial: Abraham Lincoln and American Slavery* (New York: W. W. Norton, 2010), 144.

[107] The Confederate States of America, as finally constituted, consisted of: South Carolina, Mississippi, Florida, Alabama, Georgia, Louisiana, Texas, Virginia (minus the new state of West Virginia), Arkansas, Tennessee, and North Carolina.

Abraham Lincoln had to be smuggled, with the aid of Pinkerton detectives, from Harrisburg into the nation's capital in order to take the oath of office.

The Civil War had, in effect, begun. It was to be the bloodiest conflagration in the country's history to that time. The North and South were deeply divided over the constitutional powers of the federal government versus those of individual states, and, of course, the most serious manifestation of that constitutional crisis was the question of slavery. This was also a question that the Church would have to confront, speak to, and, in many lamentable cases, divide over. Church teaching had addressed slavery for centuries; now, in the unique circumstances of America, She would address it again.

Chapter 3

The Church and Slavery

Papal Pronouncements

In the post–Civil War decades, many Northern historians were quick to identify slavery as the primary, if not exclusive, cause of the war. James Ford Rhodes, who was preeminent in this school, once noted that at the time of the foundation of the republic, both North and South looked on slavery as a moral, social, and religious evil that needed to be eradicated. Only in later years, with the invention of the cotton gin, did the Southern mentality begin to change. Slavery became economically profitable, given the Southern soil's suitability to growing cotton. From being economically profitable, the peculiar institution was soon seen as indispensable to the South's future. After some generations of this mentality, only extraordinary concessions or moral conversions might have succeeded in avoiding the inevitable:

> The Civil War might have been averted had the North yielded to the South and in the words of Lincoln ceased references to "slavery as in any way wrong" and regarded it "as one of the common matters of property" speaking "of negroes as we do our horses and cattle." In other words, the North must repress its own enlightened sentiment regarding slavery.... Or, on the other hand, the war might have

been prevented had the Southerners had a change of heart, reverted to the sentiment of the founders of the republic that slavery was an evil and agreed to limit its extension. The logical result would have been gradual abolition and the North stood ready to bear her share in compensating the owners of slaves. But anybody who should have promulgated such a doctrine in the South in 1861 would have been laughed at, hooted and mobbed.[108]

While succeeding generations of historians from different regions and backgrounds added some nuance, there can be no question that slavery was the core of the political, social, and moral division between the North and South. And, indeed, slavery had been a subject of Catholic teaching for centuries: Popes had condemned it many times—a fact apparently lost on many American Catholics in the mid-nineteenth century.[109]

In the early decades of the fifteenth century, Spain and Portugal led the way in opening the Age of Discovery. In their various colonizing expeditions, it quickly became accepted practice to force native peoples into servitude—even when the purpose of colonization was supposed to be the spread of the gospel. Such servitude was inflicted on peoples not because "they were prisoners of war or criminals or indentured servants or born into servitude, but rather

---

[108] James Ford Rhodes, *Lectures on the American Civil War* (New York: Macmillan, 1913), 2–16, 76–77, cited in Kenneth M. Stamp, ed., *The Causes of the Civil War* (New York: Simon and Schuster, 1991), 155–158.

[109] The study finds one of its most thorough treatments in Joel S. Panzer, *The Popes and Slavery* (New York: Alba House, 1996). Panzer lists Popes Eugene IV, Pius II, Paul III, Gregory XIV, Urban VIII, Innocent XI, Benedict XIV, Pius VII, Gregory XVI, and Leo XIII as condemning either the slave trade or the institution of slavery itself.

was enforced on people out of an immoral desire for cheap human labor."[110] These practices were strongly condemned by Pope Eugene IV in 1435 in the Papal Bull *Sicut Dudum*, in which he invoked the Blood of Christ, shed for all, to beg His subjects to "desist from [such] aforementioned deeds, cause those subject to them to desist from them, and restrain them vigorously."[111]

In the sixteenth century, Pope Paul III issued several such condemnations, the best remembered being *Sublimis Deus* in 1537. Paul stressed that all Christians are equal because of their calling, and as such are not "to be deprived of their liberty or their possessions. Rather, they are to be able to use and enjoy this liberty and this ownership of property freely and licitly, and are not to be reduced to slavery."[112]

Though several other exhortations were to follow, perhaps the most stinging condemnation came in the late nineteenth century from Pope Leo XIII in *Catholicae Ecclesiae*, in which he added to the arguments from eternal salvation and the universal call to the true faith, the reason of "the unity of human origins."[113] That is, rather than just talking about the spiritual good of colonizers and colonized, Leo specifically refuted a common argument among American slavers that the enslaved were not, properly speaking, human beings. But as applied to the United States, at least one writer felt it was too little, too late:

> Clearly, this was already about one hundred years too late to be of any effective value in the antislavery campaigns and civil wars and revolutions of the nineteenth century; the lay reformers and abolitionists had won their campaigns without

[110] Ibid., 4–5.
[111] Cited in ibid., 8.
[112] Cited in ibid., 64.
[113] Ibid., 65.

much effective help or moral leadership from the teaching authority of the Catholic Church which had hitherto consistently refused to condemn the institution of slavery or the practice of slave trading as such.[114]

This claim that the Church had failed to condemn slavery has been shown to be incorrect—but when the time came for American bishops to assert this teaching, to a man they accepted existing social mores: While they condemned the slave trade, they were equally strident in their opposition to abolitionism and its anti-Catholic overtones.

Ministering on the Margins

Nonetheless, in early decades of the nineteenth century, there was much good done in the Church for American slaves. In 1805, Father Stephen Badin, the "Apostle of Kentucky," was already hard at work evangelizing on the frontier. Father Badin was a French émigré from the revolution. He came as a young man to the United States, entered Saint Mary's Sulpician Seminary in Baltimore, and has the distinction of being the first priest ordained in the United States, with all major orders taken here as well. Bishop John Carroll assigned him to the Kentucky frontier, where he more than distinguished himself for his missionary efforts. He went on to do similar work in Tennessee, Ohio, Indiana, Illinois, and Michigan. In a letter to the Congregation for the Propagation of the Faith in Rome, he observed:

> The population of Kentucky is at least 220,000 souls counting the Negroes who are slaves, and who [are] scarcely less

---

[114]John F. Maxwell, *Slavery and the Catholic Church* (Chichester, UK: Ross, 1975), 119.

numerous than the whites. One could very well ask how the people who follow the principles of [John] Calvin, which predominate here, and who profess to put all men on the same level, can reconcile these without embarrassment, with the traffic in Negroes whom they treat almost like animals; whose services they receive every day of every year without giving them either instruction or compensation, whom they feed with course food and dress meagerly. In fact several masters do not furnish even a measure of cloth for the children until they reach the age of ten, twelve or more years.[115]

By 1815, another great American Catholic, Saint Elizabeth Seton, was established in the hamlet of Emmitsburg, Maryland. She noted in her diary that "so many ... mountain children and poor Blacks came today for First Communion instructions. They were told from the pulpit all to repair to the [Convent] so they came, as for a novelty, but we will try our best to fix them."[116]

A very significant milestone was the foundation of the first community of Black women, the Oblate Sisters of Providence, in Baltimore in 1829. Begun by four Black women under the leadership of Elizabeth Lange,[117] the women had been teaching Black children

---

[115] Sr. M. Ramona Mattingly, *The Catholic Church on the Kentucky Frontier, 1785–1812* (Washington, D.C.: Catholic University of America Press, 1936), 173, cited in Kenneth J. Zanca, Ph.D., ed., *American Catholics and Slavery: An Anthology of Primary Documents* (New York: University Press of America, 1994), 171.

[116] Cited in Zanca, *American Catholics*, 143. The date of Mother Seton's entry is June 10, 1815.

[117] The others were Marie Balas, Marie Rose Boegue, and Therese Duchemin Maxis. All had been teaching in the West Indies prior to their arrival in Baltimore. Therese Duchemin Maxis would eventually leave to join another religious community.

of the city in a private home. They were introduced to a French émigré Sulpician, James Joubert, who had taught classes of Black children in the basement of Saint Mary's Seminary Chapel and had the idea of forming a religious community of women dedicated solely to this purpose. Their initial focus was on young Black girls, and they opened their first school, Saint Francis Academy, in 1829 with twenty students. All the bishops gathered for Baltimore's First Provincial Council in 1829 visited the school, and within a few years, an adjacent chapel was constructed, built solely for the use of Black Catholics throughout the city. Pope Gregory XVI officially recognized the community of oblates in 1831.

The death of Father Joubert was a major setback for the community. The Sulpicians withdrew their support, and the Sisters had to secure the help of confessors and spiritual directors wherever they could find them. They began taking in poor Black children, often the children of slaves, and educating them free of charge. To sustain themselves, they made vestments, took in laundry, and begged among the general Catholic populace. Only when the Redemptorist Fathers, at the direction of the vice provincial, John N. Neumann, intervened did the fortunes of the Sisters improve. As the Civil War neared, they were attached to Baltimore's Jesuit parish of Saint Ignatius; the chapel of this parish was dedicated to Saint Peter Claver and was the nucleus for the first Black parish in the United States. During the war years, the Sisters opened a school for Black women and children in Philadelphia and an additional school in Baltimore.

The bishop of Charleston, South Carolina, the Irish-born John England, had also begun a school for free Blacks in 1829, which he was ultimately forced to close.[118] He saw this sad result as the fault

---

[118] England, as noted, came from County Cork, where he once served as rector of the seminary in his diocese. Besides starting the first

not of Southern slaveholding interests, however, but of meddling abolitionists, as he expressed in a letter to the rector of the Irish College in Rome, Paul Cullen, a future archbishop of Dublin. He told Cullen that the States and territories where slavery existed were found in the Dioceses of Baltimore, Bardstown, St. Louis, Charleston, New Orleans, and Mobile, and that if there were any interference from any other diocese in which slavery did not exist, it would have been considered treason. For some years, England asserted, fanatical Calvinists in New England and New York had been "forming associations to procure, if possible, the abolition of slavery in the South. The South was exasperated, and looked upon this as a malicious and outrageous insult; and the Southerners are a high, proud and chivalrous people." "Northern fanatics," according to the prelate, had done a tremendously effective job in circulating pamphlets to stigmatize slavery, and to incite insurrection among the slaves. Those who circulated these views posed as "preachers, peddlers, or doctors or land speculators." As to conditions in his see, the bishop was even more explicit:

> In Charleston, we are not permitted to teach the slaves to read. The law does not permit the education of free Negroes. I found that most of our free Negroes were drawn from the Church by being educated in sectarian schools. Whites only are allowed to be teachers, and the children of Negroes or mulattoes are not permitted to be taught in the schools of

---

Catholic newspaper in the United States, he was a man well respected by the Protestant elite of his time. He was a scholar of Church history, a talented theologian, a prolific writer, and a careful thinker. He played a pivotal role in Baltimore's provincial councils of 1833, 1837, and 1840, writing the pastoral letters for each of these gatherings. He consistently upheld the slaveholding South in his writings and would write one of the definitive justifications of slavery for American Catholics.

white children. I established a school for the free children of color, and I got two of my students to teach the boys, and two of the Sisters to have care of the girls. On account of the superior instruction, numbers of children attended, and their parents began to come to our church. As soon as this new excitement concerning the [abolitionist] tracts arose, the sectarian papers denounced us for our extensive literary education of the Blacks.

As to the school's closing:

[Mobs] were organized in Charleston; and at night they surrounded the Post-office and forcibly entered, took out of the mailbags the tracts and pamphlets upon Abolition which had been sent by the office from New York, directed not only to this city but to Georgia, Alabama and Florida; they reserved them to the next night and burned them publicly in the square under the guns of the citadel.[119]

England went on to relate to Cullen that a few Catholics overheard some talk that as soon as they finished at the post office, the mob would come to the diocesan seminary where the bishop lived, give him the benefit of "Lynch's Law," and then proceed to tear down the buildings. A guard was kept for two nights, the bishop reported, but no attempt was made on him or his buildings. England was informed by many of the city's most distinguished citizens that immediate assistance would be provided if needed. A committee then called on England, though, and respectfully asked him if he would discontinue the school, since it had been and would likely continue to be a danger. His response would be compliance, he said,

[119] *Records of the American Catholic Historical Society of Philadelphia* 8 (June 1897): 215–233, cited in Zanca, *American Catholics and Slavery,* 147–148.

provided that such a request was made of all other denominational schools in Charleston.[120]

Prior to the outbreak of hostilities in 1861, New Orleans was home to the largest number of black Catholics in the United States, where Jesuits, Capuchins, and Ursuline Sisters ministered to them. Though more Blacks were baptized Catholic there than in any other city, the percentage who remained with the Faith throughout their lives was comparatively small; masters did not want their slaves to be married, and very few encouraged the fervent practice of the Faith or the reception of the sacraments.

Many free creoles and mulattoes also lived in the city, known generally as *les gens libres de couleur* ("free people of color"). The best remembered among them was a laywoman, Henriette Delille, foundress of the Sisters of the Holy Family. She had been born to a free woman of color and a wealthy French father; because of Louisiana law at the time, her parents were not permitted to marry. Nonetheless, she was financially well off through her upbringing and would have been expected to assume a position of mistress to a White patron when she came of age. Experiences doing social work among poor Blacks in New Orleans, however, changed her thinking. Along with two like-minded women, Julietta Gaudin and Josephine Charles, she sought admission to various religious communities, though racial prohibitions seemed to exclude them wherever they tried. With the help of a wealthy patron, they sought Church approval to organize a community of their own, and the city's bishop, Anthony Blanc,[121] gave permission to form a pious

[120] Ibid., 148.

[121] Anthony Blanc (1792–1860) was the fifth bishop and first archbishop of New Orleans. Born and ordained a priest in Lyon, France, he volunteered for the American mission and arrived in Annapolis, Maryland, in 1817. He eventually accompanied Bishop Louis William Dubourg to New Orleans and led the very arduous life of a

society without any formal vows. Within a decade, they received canonical status as a congregation of Black women religious, the second to be founded in the United States, devoted to teaching Black children.

Finally, the work of the Sisters of Saint Joseph in the city of Saint Augustine, Florida, was deeply significant. Bishop Augustin Verot[122] recognized the need to evangelize the newly freed slaves less than one year after the war ended in 1865. He visited his home region of LePuy, France, hoping to find another community of religious women who could assist the Sisters of Mercy, whom he had brought to Florida half a dozen years earlier. Some sixty Sisters of Saint Joseph volunteered, and eight were chosen. These religious women began learning English on the steamer bringing them to

---

missionary in the Mississippi valley. Appointed vicar-general of New Orleans, he became bishop of the Diocese in 1835, hugely built up the physical plant, introduced numerous orders of religious men and women to the city, and became its first archbishop in 1850.

[122] Augustin Verot (1804–1876) was born in LePuy, France, studied at the seminary of Saint Sulpice in Paris, and was ordained in 1828. He came to Baltimore in 1830 to teach at Saint Mary's Sulpician Seminary, served as pastor of Saint Paul's Parish, Ellicott City, Maryland, and was ultimately named vicar apostolic for Florida. In 1861 he became bishop of Savannah, Georgia, but retained his administration over Florida. He secured the services of numerous orders of priests and sisters to work in the Florida mission, many of them coming from his native France. He was particularly conspicuous for his response to President James Buchanan's call for a national day of fasting and prayer to be observed on January 4, 1861; he delivered a sermon defending Southern rights and slavery's legal basis, and his sermon, circulated throughout the South, soon became a Confederate tract. His pastoral letter against abolitionism was just as widely circulated. He is also remembered for his devotion to Florida's early martyrs, Spanish as well as French. In 1870, he became St. Augustine's first bishop.

Savannah and then set to work immediately to instruct Black children in the Faith and in all aspects of a Catholic education.

Treating Slaves as Human Beings

Another area of the Church's concern was the manumission of slaves owned by Her members, lay and clergy. Stories are told of Jesuits in Maryland manumitting slaves, and Charles Carroll of Carrollton manumitted significant numbers of his slaves who had worked and lived at his Doughoregan Manor near Ellicott City, Maryland. Notable, too, was an entry in the last will and testament of Archbishop John Carroll of Baltimore:

> Moreover, I bequeath to him [Daniel Brent, nephew] my Black servant Charles, to be however manumitted within twelve months after my decease, unless I should do so previously thereto; and it is more over my will and desire, that after he shall be set at liberty, he settle in, or near his friends in the city of Washington, and make a prudent use of his emancipation; and I charge on my personal estate or wardrobe the sum of fifty dollars to be given to my servant Charles in testimony of his faithful services.[123]

Of special interest is the story of Judge William J. Gaston of North Carolina, a devout Catholic and the first student to be enrolled in Georgetown Academy shortly after its establishment by Bishop Carroll.[124] In his many years as a jurist, Gaston's views on

---

[123] Cited in Zanca, *American Catholics and Slavery*, 233.

[124] William J. Gaston (1778–1844) was born in New Bern, North Carolina, to a Protestant father and a devout Catholic mother. After Georgetown, he received more education in North Carolina, went to Princeton University, where he studied law, and was admitted to the bar in 1798. He was a member of the North Carolina General

slavery became well known. In one address to many of the state's prominent citizens, he declared:

> On you too, will devolve the duty which has been too long neglected but which cannot, with impunity, be neglected much longer of providing for the mitigation and (is it too much to hope for in North Carolina) for the ultimate extirpation of the worst evil that afflicts the Southern part of our Confederacy. Full well do you know to what I refer, for on this subject there is with all of us a morbid sensitiveness which gives warning to even an approach to it.... Disguise the truth as we may and throw the blame where we will, it is slavery which, more than any other cause, keeps us back in the career of improvement. It stifles industry and suppresses enterprise; it is fatal to economy and prudence; it discourages skill, impairs our strength as a community, and poisons morals at the fountain head.[125]

Assembly and served in the State House of Commons, including in the role of speaker for a time. He was elected to Congress as a Federalist in 1813 and reelected in 1815. While in Congress, he obtained a federal charter for Georgetown University. During these years, he was elected to membership in the American Antiquarian Society. Gaston returned to the North Carolina House of Commons and is especially remembered for a commencement address he gave at the University of North Carolina in 1832, encouraging its graduates to take action against slavery. He was appointed judge of the North Carolina Supreme Court the following year, and in 1840 he declined a nomination to the U.S. Senate. Gaston was elected multiple times, despite a prohibition in the North Carolina State Constitution on Catholics holding elective office. He was largely responsible, as a member of the North Carolina Constitutional Convention in 1835, for removing official discrimination against Catholics from state law.
[125]Record in the Georgetown University Archives, September 1, 1824, cited in J. Herman Schauinger, *William Gaston, Carolinian* (Milwaukee: Bruce, 1949), 165–166.

Judge Gaston had the advantage of the North Carolina climate in which he had been born and raised. Though Catholics were a small minority and anti-Catholic legislation had been the norm, as it had been in nearly all the original thirteen states, nonetheless North Carolina had a long tradition of anti-slavery sentiment; the political atmosphere was milder than in the deep South. Court decisions and laws involving slaves and slavery traditionally took a gentler tone, even showing a certain respect for the life of the Black slave.

During the North Carolina Constitutional Convention of 1835, Gaston opposed a provision depriving Black freeholders of the right to vote for members of the State Senate and House of Commons. He noted that Blacks were "part of the body politic, and they will feel an attachment to the form of government and have a fixed interest in the prosperity of the community, and will exercise an important influence on the slaves."[126]

The judge's greatest contribution was the decision he rendered in the case *State v. Will*, which came before him shortly after he had taken his seat on the bench. The slave Will had fatally injured his overseer in an attempt to save himself from a brutal attack. On the evidence, Gaston contended that Will was guilty of manslaughter — a lesser charge — rather than murder. Malice, said the judge, was not present in those situations where the slave was "excited into unlawful violence, by the inhumanity of his master or temporary owner, or one clothed with the master's authority."[127] In other words, the severity of Will's actions was mitigated because they were an attempt to defend his life against the unlawful attempt of his master to take it.

He made another significant judgment in 1840, in *State v. Jarrott*. Gaston reversed the decision of a lower court that had

---

[126] Madeline Hooke Rice, *American Catholic Opinion in the Slavery Controversy* (New York: Columbia University Press, 1944), 135.
[127] Ibid.

convicted a slave of the murder of a White man in a quarrel. The judge argued that an initial assault from a White man other than his master meant that the slave's actions to defend himself could not be murder, but were rather simple homicide:

> [The] law would be savage if it made no allowance for passion. He may have been disciplined into perfect obedience to the will of his master, and, therefore, habitually patient under his correction; but he cannot but feel a sense of wrong when authority is wantonly usurped by a stranger, and exercised with cruelty. There is therefore no difficulty in laying it down that a battery which endangers his life or great bodily harm—proceeding from one who has no authority over him—will amount to such a provocation.[128]

Judge Gaston's mother was descended from one of the earliest Catholic families to settle in North Carolina, and she rooted her son in the fundamentals of Catholicism to such an extent that his Faith played a fundamental role in his personal life and his judicial career. One proof of this is in the church register of Saint Paul's, New Bern, which attests that all slaves owned by the judge were baptized.[129] And yet, of course, this leaves us with the truth that, in spite of everything, Judge Gaston still owned slaves, so embedded into the Southern psyche was the institution.

Silence and the Status Quo: The Bishops Speak

For this reason, even Catholic prelates in the North, who looked to the country as a whole, sensed that any word from them in

---

[128] Ibid., 136.

[129] Schauinger, *William Gaston, Carolinian*, 166. See pages 200–209 for a thorough discussion of Gaston's Catholic roots, personal upbringing, and faith influence throughout his career.

opposition to or in favor of American chattel slavery could cause unrest—if not worse. As a result, one historian noted, "Antebellum American Bishops chose not to publish any collective statement on the legitimacy of domestic slavery. Catholic slaveowners in the South neither heard nor read any clear instruction from their hierarchy commanding or recommending general manumission, much less abolition."[130]

What a number of Church leaders did, however, was make abstract theological statements on the topic, finding scriptural justifications both for and against slavery. The first example occurred in 1840, when Bishop John England in Charleston wrote a series of letters to John Forsyth, secretary of state in the administration of Martin Van Buren. Forsyth had been governor of Georgia and was in the South in 1840 campaigning for the president in his reelection bid against the Whig candidate, William Henry Harrison. In the course of his campaign remarks, Forsyth had made reference to an 1839 encyclical of Pope Gregory XVI, *In Supremo Apostolatus*, yet another papal condemnation of, as many thought, both the slave trade and the institution of slavery itself. Forsyth argued that the pope was, at least in sentiment, an abolitionist. England felt compelled to answer this assertion, and he set out his view of the Catholic position:

> Respecting domestic slavery, we distinguish it from the compulsory slavery of an invaded people in its several degrees.... The first is "voluntary"; that which exists among us is not of that description, though I know very many instances where I have found it to be so; but I regard not the cases of individuals, I look to the class. In examining the lawfulness of voluntary slavery, we shall test a principle against which

---

[130] C. R. Heisser and Stephen J. White Sr., *Patrick N. Lynch: 1817–1882* (Columbia, SC: University of South Carolina Press, 2015), 57.

abolitionists contend. They assert, generally, that slavery is contrary to the natural law. The soundness of their position will be tried by inquiring into the lawfulness of holding in slavery a person, who has voluntarily sold himself. Our theological authors lay down a principle, that man in his natural state is master of his own liberty, and may dispose of it as he sees proper.... [The] natural law does not prohibit a man from bartering his liberty and his services to save his life, to provide for his sustenance, to secure other enjoyments which he prefers to that freedom, and to that right to his own labor, which he gives for exchange for life and protection. Nor does the natural law prohibit another man from procuring and bestowing upon him those advantages, in return for which he has agreed to bind himself to that other man's service, provided he takes no unjust advantage in the bargain.... We may say that the natural law does not establish slavery, but it does not forbid it.[131]

The bishop then went on to argue that the divine sanction for slavery could be seen in many instances in both the Old and New Testaments. The "Divine legislator of Christianity," England claimed, "made no special law, either to repeal or to modify the former and still subsisting right [to slavery]; but He enforced principles that, by their necessary operation and gradual influence, produced an extensive amelioration."[132]

In 1843, Bishop Francis Patrick Kenrick of Philadelphia, a noted moralist who would later become Archbishop of Baltimore, published a three-volume study, *Theologia Moralis*, in which he also

[131] Ignatius Reynolds, ed., *The Works of the Right Reverend John England, III* (Baltimore: John Murphy, 1849), 106–131, cited in Zanca, *American Catholics and Slavery*, 191–199.
[132] Ibid.

set forth Church teaching for Catholics and all interested readers of the day.[133] He regretted that

> [in] the present fullness of liberty in which all glory, there should be so many slaves, and that to guard against their movements, it has been necessary to pass laws prohibiting their education and in some places greatly restricting their exercise of religion. Nevertheless, since this is the state of things, nothing should be attempted against the laws nor anything to be done or said that would make them bear their yoke unwillingly.[134]

As the war was beginning in 1861, New York's archbishop, John Hughes, penned some thoughts on slavery as a sort of working paper. He more or less reiterated the position of Kenrick, but he added:

---

[133] Francis P. Kenrick (1796–1863) was born in Dublin, Ireland, and after ordination, was sent to teach in Saint Thomas Seminary, Bardstown, Kentucky. He served as a peritus, or theological adviser, to the bishops at Baltimore's First Provincial Council of 1829, and in 1832 went to Philadelphia as its Ordinary. He founded Saint Charles Borromeo Seminary, ended the trustee controversies that had disrupted several Philadelphia parishes, and was celebrated for his level-headed handling of the nativist riots that broke out in the City of Brotherly Love. He was the author of several of the letters of Baltimore's provincial councils and was known as a prolific scholar, producing ten studies on the Old Testament and a four-volume work on dogmatic theology in addition to his contribution to moral theology. He had enormous influence on the thinking of the Catholic Church in the United States on slavery. He was the brother of Peter Richard Kenrick, who would serve as archbishop of St. Louis for over four decades.

[134] "The Catholic Church and the Question of Slavery," *Metropolitan Magazine* (June 1955): 267ff., cited in Zanca, *American Catholics and Slavery*, 200.

[If] heaven had permitted me to have been born in Africa as in America, as the son of an African slave, I confess that I should sooner remain in Southern bondage than avail my- self of the opportunity of Northern freedom. In the South, I should know my place. I should bend to it.... I should bow my head to that providence of God which had placed me in that position. I should be faithful to the master, and under the laws ... in all humility endeavor to comply in my condition to the requirements of God's will.[135]

Martin J. Spalding was archbishop of Baltimore for only the final year of the war. Prior to his coming to the premier see, he had served as bishop of Louisville, where he produced a *Dissertation on the American Civil War*.[136] Spalding began by reiterating

---

[135] Ibid., 214. For additional thoughts of Archbishop Hughes on the question of slavery see Hassard, *Life of Most Rev. John Hughes*, 42, 216, 434.

[136] Martin J. Spalding (1810–1872) was of English Catholic heritage. His ancestors had come to Southern Maryland in the seventeenth century and generations later joined the Catholic migration to Kentucky. There, he was born into a slaveholding family. Ordained in 1834, he began his priestly service in Bardstown, edited the Catholic newspaper, and became vicar-general and finally bishop of Louisville in 1848, succeeding Benedict Flaget. He was a prolific writer and lecturer, helped establish the American College in Louvain as well as the North American College in Rome, presided over the Second Plenary Council of Baltimore in 1866, and at- tended the First Vatican Council in 1869–1870. As a Kentucky native, he strongly favored the Confederacy and sent a copy of his *Dissertation* to Rome to present the Southern case, and to try to offset the work of the Purcells of Cincinnati as they advanced their strong anti-slavery position. As Archbishop of Baltimore, he brought the Josephite Fathers to the city to work with and for Black Catholics.

the Church's condemnation of the slave trade—a position, he felt, on which all fair-minded men would agree. He also felt that slavery must be considered a social evil "left to us as a sad heritage by Protestant England."

> But how can we free ourselves of it without ruining our country and causing injury to the poor slaves themselves? What can be done to free them in such a way as not to worsen their sad condition?... This is the real problem for which a wise and *practical* solution is very difficult: because then the Catholic religion, according to its spirit and its practice in times past, would first be able gradually to better their condition, instructing them in their Christian duties and at the same time inclining the hearts of their masters to compassion; and if they were sufficiently prepared for freedom, to emancipate them with the consent of their masters, at least without doing them violent wrong.

Then, perhaps in response to the anti-Catholic feeling so prevalent in the country, Spalding added:

> But where the dominant religion is Protestant it becomes very difficult in practice to decide how the slaves can be emancipated to their spiritual and also temporal profit. Almost all the Catholics who are Negroes are found in the states of the South, and those who are emancipated and go to the states of the North become almost all, at least their children, within a short time Protestants, or else indifferent and infidel. In my diocese, for example, there are from two to three thousand such Catholic negroes, who are among the best and most devout of my flock. Now I am convinced that if these were suddenly emancipated in the present circumstances of violence and war, they would all be lost to

Faith and Fury

the Church and to heaven; and so would also be the sad result with the others.[137]

The Church's Slaves

Given the guidance of the shepherds, it's easy to see why most Catholics had little difficulty with the existence of slavery in their midst. In an era when obedience to the Church's lawful authority was paramount in their minds and hearts, the Church had clearly spoken to them. And, indeed, the actions of churchmen often spoke just as loudly as their words.

By the mid-eighteenth century, the Maryland Jesuits owned several plantations and a goodly number of slaves. They preferred the terms "servant man" and "servant woman" to "slave," and these were categorized as laborers or working hands. Due to their humane treatment relative to prevailing norms, contemporary observers thought that these Jesuits got far less out of their slaves than most masters. One Jesuit, Father George Hunter, during a retreat, preached to fellow members of the Society that "charity to Negroes is due from all, particularly their masters. As they are members of Jesus Christ, redeemed by His precious blood, they are to be dealt with in a charitable, Christian, paternal manner; which is at the same time a great means to bring them to do their duty to God, and therefore to gain their souls."[138] Later in the nineteenth

[137] David Spalding, "Martin J. Spalding's 'Dissertation on the American Civil War,'" *Catholic Historical Review* 52 (April 1966): 66–85, cited in Zanca, *American Catholics and Slavery*, 210–213.
[138] Thomas Hughes, *The History of the Society of Jesus in North America: Colonial and Federal Periods*, vol. 1, pt. 1 (London: Longmans, Green, 1917), 288–297, cited in Zanca, *American Catholics and Slavery*, 153.

century, records confirm the buying and selling of slaves by Maryland Jesuits to prevent the breakup of slave families.

Mother Hyacinth of the Daughters of the Cross in northern Louisiana presents yet another case of Catholic acceptance of slavery. She and other members of her community had come from France to teach in the parishes of Louisiana, where they founded the first school of their order, Presentation Academy for Girls in Cocoville, in 1856. At first, Mother was stridently anti-slavery, but she came around to a grudging acceptance of it so that they might have workers to cultivate the land and to do necessary chores around the convent mission. Much like the Jesuits, she was charitable to the slaves on their property—though she had to participate in the practice of buying and selling, which greatly disturbed her conscience. She paints a vivid portrait in a letter to her brother in France:

> [We] have twenty-four acres of land here, but we cannot cultivate it ourselves. The population is composed of white and black people, or Negroes. There are also some mulattos.... [The] white people do not work. They have a certain number of Negroes to do the work on the farms or plantations that produce cotton, sugar, rice and corn. These poor Negroes are *really* slaves. They are absolutely sold or bought like the beasts or animals in Europe. How sad this is, my poor brother! This fearful condition! The first time I saw a rational human being exposed "For Sale" in New Orleans, I was seized with horror. The Bishop proposed that we buy one slave. I showed my repugnance, and he did not insist! These poor Negroes are not well fed, nor well clothed. They work only with a stick over their heads. They do not live in the master's house. They are degraded. They have their own huts, shanties, built not far from the master's house.

Faith and Fury

They receive no attention nor care. They are treated like beasts with little pity. And yet, they are children of God![139]

Bishop Patrick N. Lynch of Charleston represents yet another study in Catholic slaveholding.[140] Prior to the Civil War, he had not made any public statements about the legality and morality of slavery. His two predecessors, John England and Ignatius Reynolds, had also both owned slaves: Bishop England purchased a man named Joseph for $450, not for himself, but for work on the grounds of the Ursuline Sisters Convent in Charleston. Bishop Reynolds owned a man named Thornton, a Black preacher in his younger days, who became a Catholic and, before his death, willed the diocese his entire life savings for the use of the cathedral building fund. One of Bishop Lynch's biographers described the Southern family from which he emerged:

> Patrick Lynch was brought up in a slaveholding family. His close familiarity with the institution convinced him to regard it as workable, fundamental and essential to Southern society, and even as benign. According to census records, the Bishop's father, Conlaw Lynch had two slaves in 1830 and seven from 1840 to 1860. Dr. John Lynch, the Bishop's

[139] Sr. Dorothea O. McCants, *They Came to Louisiana: Letters of a Catholic Mission 1854–1882* (Baton Rouge: LSU Press, 1970), cited in Zanca, *American Catholics and Slavery*, 160.

[140] Patrick Neeson Lynch (1817–1882) was born in Clones, County Fermanagh, Ireland, where his family had settled in the mid-seventeenth century. He and his parents came to Cheraw, South Carolina, in 1819, where a number of other siblings were born. His priestly studies were taken in Rome, and he was ordained a priest of the Charleston Diocese in 1840. He became Charleston's third bishop in 1858 and would ultimately undertake an unsuccessful diplomatic mission for President Jefferson Davis to attempt to secure Vatican recognition of the Confederate States of America.

brother, owned three slaves in 1850 and twenty-eight in 1860. The third son, Francis Lynch, a Cheraw storekeeper and manufacturer of leather footwear, had ten slaves in 1850 and twenty-two in 1860 and purchased at least a dozen more during the war. Two of Bishop Lynch's sisters married slaveowners. The Lynches appear to have been benign masters by the light of their day.[141]

Through the years, the bishop acquired a large number of slaves, primarily from estates willed to him and the diocese. The largest number came from the estate of William McKenna, a native of County Donegal and an exceptionally devout Catholic who had once studied for the priesthood in his native Ireland but then became successful in business; he was said to be the wealthiest Catholic in South Carolina at the time of his death in 1859. His estate, in excess of $250,000, was left to the bishop for a boys orphanage, as well as to the Sisters of Our Lady of Mercy for their work in the Diocese.

Bishop Lynch's slaveholding can be viewed from several angles. The prevailing American Catholic opinion before the Civil War was that slavery was a licit, if not desirable practice. During the war all Southern Bishops were loyal to the Confederacy. The Bishop of Charleston was in line with fellow members of the Catholic hierarchy in his defense of slavery, although he went further than they in his acquisition of a significant number of slaves. He displayed ingenuity in devising a plan that combined practical and humanitarian motifs: protecting the church's considerable financial interest, while safeguarding the unity of Black Catholic families. William McKenna's will dictated that, with few exceptions,

[141] Heisser and White, *Patrick N. Lynch*, 59.

all his slaves were to be sold, so the Bishop's options were to take the church's portion of the estate in the form of real and chattel property, to take it in cash, or a combination of the two. He opted to accept a large part of the legacy in the form of slaves. Had he not done so, the families might well have been broken up and sold, and some would most likely have fallen into the hands of owners less benign than the Bishop. By the late antebellum period South Carolina laws severely restricted manumission. One might well ask what would have befallen these people had Bishop Lynch not acquired them. Seen in retrospect, the Bishop's large investment in slave property was doomed, but in the heady days that followed secession, most white South Carolinians were confident of achieving independence and of ensuring the continuation of servitude.[142]

At a certain point during the war years, Bishop Lynch penned what appears to be a working paper titled *A Few Words on the Domestic Slavery in the Confederate States of America*. He informed his readers that it was not meant to be a defense of slavery, for "to say that freedom is better than slavery is to my mind very much like saying that health is better than sickness."[143] It was rather to be a "diagnosis of slavery," after which the reader was apparently meant to make up his or her own mind on the institution.

He was convinced that the "novelists, philanthropists, and fanatics" painted a wholly unrealistic picture of slavery for the rest of the country, and it took a conscientious native Southerner to set the record straight. He estimated that the South consisted of eight million White inhabitants of European heritage and some

[142] Ibid., 71.
[143] Dr. William G. Peters, *The Catholic Bishops in the Confederacy* (Chattanooga: C.S. Printing Office, 2016), 55.

four million Blacks of African origin, most of whom lived in a state of servitude. Many of these slaves "work in the erection of the earthen fortifications, which throughout the Confederacy, protect every railway bridge, and every pass, that engineers think may, in the course of the war, become of importance. The great mass have desired and desire nothing more than to be left quietly at home pursuing as their fathers did, the easy cultivation of the fields, under the guidance and discipline of their masters."[144]

The bishop distinguished between the slave trade and domestic slavery. The former he defined as "that commerce in which merchants visiting chiefly the coast of Africa purchased there from African princes or their agents, negroes as slaves, and transporting them to other countries, sold them to continue as slaves." Lynch was quick to point out that this slave trade had not existed in the Southern states since 1807, when it was suppressed. Domestic slavery, on the other hand, was "the continued retention in slavery of the descendants of those who were originally brought in by the slave trade."[145]

After tracing the introduction of slavery to colonial America, as well as papal pronouncements condemning both the trade and the institution itself, Lynch summarized what he claimed were Southern efforts to restrict if not abolish the system in the eighteenth century. The bishop then castigated his Northern neighbors:

> We feel indignant, when the Northerners boast of their own fancied enlightenment, and declaim with vituperation against the horrors of Southern Slavery. For we remember how, in the Convention of 1787, they opposed the immediate suppression of the traffic, how they engaged largely in it until 1808, and how even since then, vessels have gone

[144] Ibid., 58.
[145] Ibid., 60.

forth from the Northern ports to transport slaves cruelly and illegally from Africa to Brazil and Cuba, whilst their owners at home talked pharasaically of Emancipation. Had they legitimately freed all their own Negro slaves—we might respect their sincerity. But as long as it was pecuniarily profitable for them to hold slaves, there was not a word among them of Emancipation.[146]

Domestic slavery, said the bishop, was to be found in three categories: the house servants, those who hired their own time, and the agricultural laborers. The first group did not differ, on his account, from house servants in any other country, though Lynch did not think much of their work abilities. Those who hired themselves paid a small sum each month to their master and then lived and worked and earned for themselves as much or little as they pleased; in this, it could be said they enjoyed a certain degree of freedom. The vast majority worked on the plantations, and especially the rice plantations, where, according to Bishop Lynch, their African constitution made them far more fit for the intense heat than White workers would be. Most slaves lived in small houses not far from the manor house, had a small garden, and had their daily tasks assigned based on their age, usually beginning at fourteen.

Lynch continued by observing how most state laws forbade the education of slaves, though often favored ones would be taught to read and write by the owner's children. There were no schools for their education, and, naturally, vast numbers had no opportunity for any education whatsoever. Religiously, they were free to associate with any denomination, and it seemed that Methodists and Baptists had a goodly number. Many (because of their African temperament, Lynch editorialized) often rose during church services

[146]Ibid., 65.

to "preach a ludicrous exhortation, or to scream forth a wild, un-
tutored extempore prayer, as often blasphemous in its phraseology,
as it is hypocritical in its meaning."[147]

The real difficulty, as Bishop Lynch saw it, was the incompatibility between the slaves' religious fervor and the immoral lifestyle
many of them led. They believed firmly in the divinity of Christ,
preferred Baptism by total immersion, and frequently asked God's
pardon of their sins. But this supplication, Lynch thought, would
have been more effective and prized more highly "if they proceeded
from humble and penitent hearts. But unfortunately this is seldom
the case. The usual characteristics of a religious Negro are spiritual
pride, and very often, hypocrisy. So long as he stands well in the
Church, he is sure of heaven."[148]

The bishop did notice a significant difference in many of the
slaves who had been raised with the fullness of Catholic Faith and
had practiced it sincerely throughout their lives. These testimonies
came from "men of distinction, even Protestant judges on the
bench," who witnessed to "the superiority and exalted character of
Catholic Negros over others."[149] The difficulty, Lynch had to confess, was the paucity of Black Catholics. While there was a certain
hope in such statements, the bishop could not foresee a significant
increase in Catholic identification occurring any time soon. The
only exceptions were to be found in Maryland and Louisiana, where
substantial Catholic populations were found. But even in those
areas, few priests meant infrequent visitations, and thus little opportunity for the type of catechesis a missionary would hope for.

Regarding the future of slavery, the bishop felt that any plan
that would emancipate the slaves quickly would be disastrous — not

[147] Ibid., 76.
[148] Ibid., 77–78.
[149] Ibid., 78.

primarily to the Southern economy, but to the freedmen as human beings. Colonization schemes that would transport them to an African nation seemed more realistic to him, but which nation? Further, the development of such a plan would be so complex that it might be workable only in the far distant future. In the 1860s, in the Southern states comprising the Confederacy, according to Bishop Lynch:

> [The] Negros are well provided and well cared for, happy and content. I know of no condition in which the Abolitionists would place them, in which they would be equally so. I see clearly that most of the plans they advocate would lead to internecine war of the most atrocious character, and would end either in the bloody enslavement of the Negroes, or more probably in their utter extinction.[150]

Slaves Tell Their Stories

Bishop Lynch was convinced that slaves who were permitted by their masters to be instructed in the Catholic Faith were better for it — not just spiritually, but in their comportment toward their work and their masters. And, indeed, many Catholic slaves passed on the truths of the Faith to their own families; to this day, many Black Catholics can trace their heritage to their enslaved Catholic forbearers. But the Faith did not always stick, given the instability of chattel life, as the recollections of certain freed Blacks attest.

For instance, we have the account of one Henri Necaise, a slave in Mississippi who was not expansively educated but was able to read and to write his memories. He never knew his mother: she

---

[150]Ibid., 99.

had been sold and thus separated from him and his siblings when he was only a few months old.

> My marster was a Catholic. One thing I can thank dem godly white folks for, dey raise me right. Dey taught me out of God's word. "Our Father, Which are in heaven," Everybody ought-a know dat prayer. I was raised a Catholic, but when I come here 'tweren't no [Catholic] church and I joined de Baptists and was baptized.... I was thirty one years old when I was set free. My marster didn't tell us about bein' free. Dey way I found it out, he started to whip me once, and the young marster up and says: You ain't got no right to whip him now; he's free. Den Marster turn me loose.[151]

Another such testimony was that of Pierre Landry, who had been a slave in Louisiana, and was raised by a conscientious master who saw to it he was trained in the Faith and received the sacraments. Sometime before the Civil War, he bought his freedom and later joined the Methodist Episcopal church, in which he eventually became a preacher.

> My early religious training was in the Roman Catholic Church at Donaldsonville. I was prepared for first communion in a large class of both white and colored youths. The sacrament was administered on an Easter Sunday morning, and I shall never forget the impressiveness of the services of that day. The august presence of the bishop [who confirmed the class] was to me typical of extraordinary grandeur and power, and when it came my turn to kiss the signet ring of His grace, the jewel appeared to me as a blazing torch in

[151] Norman R. Yetman, ed., *Voices from Slavery* (New York: Holt Rinehart, 1970), 237–238, cited in Zanca, *American Catholics and Slavery*, 165.

Faith and Fury

which were reflected the burning candles of the resplendent altar. It was then that I first learned to respect the priesthood and the ministry of God.[152]

Overturning Slavery

The inherent inhumaneness of slavery took its toll on the country in many ways well before the outbreak of hostilities in 1861. Anti-slavery arguments continued to gain traction, and the cruelty of the institution became less and less deniable. The entire gospel ethic militated against its existence — and yet progress in overturning the existing social order was decidedly slow.

One inspiring life story that demonstrates overcoming the enormous barriers imposed by racial hierarchy was that of James Augustine Healy. Born in Georgia in 1830, he was the son of an Irish Protestant immigrant named Michael and his common-law slave wife, who bore him ten children. State law specified that all offspring of such unions were slaves, and so his father took several of his children north and enrolled them in Quaker schools in New York and New Jersey. On a ferry crossing in the course of this trip, by chance Healy made the acquaintance of the bishop of Boston, John B. Fitzpatrick. The bishop took much interest in the elder Healy's story and had his boys enrolled in Holy Cross College; their sister, also on the journey, was placed in a convent school in Boston. The boys were instructed in the Catholic Faith, and in 1844 formally converted and were baptized in the same ceremony in which the sons of the famed convert Orestes Brownson were received.

[152] Pierre Landry, *From Slavery to Freedom* (unpublished memoirs) in Charles B. Rousseve, *The Negro in Louisiana* (New Orleans: Xavier University Press, 1937), 39, cited in Zanca, *American Catholics and Slavery*, 165.

Remarkable stories like this are unfortunately few and far between. Centuries of social mores take a long time to dismantle. Even the president, who set so much in motion with his Emancipation Proclamation in the Fall of 1862, came to his position slowly. In his 1858 debates with Stephen A. Douglas, Lincoln referred to slavery as a "monstrous injustice"—but regarding its future, he admitted his own uncertainty:

> If all earthly power were given me, I should not know what to do, as to the existing institution. My first impulse would be to free all the slaves and send them to Liberia—to their own native land. But a moment's reflection would convince me, that whatever of high hope (as I think there is) there may be in this, in the long run, its sudden execution is impossible.... What then? Free them all, and keep them among us as underlings? Is it quite certain that this betters their condition? Free them, and make them politically and socially our equals? My own feelings will not admit of this; and if mine would, we well know that those of the great mass of white people will not.[153]

While in office, Lincoln responded to a famous editorial written by Horace Greeley of the *New York Tribune*, "The Prayer of Twenty Millions," which was a plea to the president to act swiftly on complete emancipation for all slaves. In what could have been taken as an affront to Greeley, the president chose to respond in the pages of the Washington *National Intelligencer*:

> I would save the Union. I would save it in the shortest way under the Constitution.... My paramount object in this struggle is to save the Union, and is *not* either to save or destroy

---

[153] Foner, *The Fiery Trial*, 67.

slavery. If I could save the Union without freeing *any* slave I would do it, and if I could save it by freeing *all* the slaves I would do that. What I do about slavery, and the colored race, I do because I believe it helps to save the Union.... I have here stated my purpose according to my view of official duty; and I intend no modification of my oft-expressed personal wish that all men everywhere could be free.[154]

His ideal, though it had not yet come to complete fruition, had established itself strongly in his mind, according to one notable Civil War author:

He believed that it was a moral wrong; he had not come to believe that it was a legal wrong, though he believed that too would be clarified in time. The words of his mouth came like meditations from his heart: "Slavery is founded in the selfishness of man's nature, opposition to it in his love of justice. These principles are an eternal antagonism, and when brought into collision so fiercely as slavery extension brings them, shocks and throes and convulsions must ceaselessly follow. Repeal the Missouri Compromise, repeal all compromises; repeal the Declaration of Independence, repeal all past history — you still cannot repeal human nature. It still will be the abundance of man's heart that slavery extension is wrong, and out of the abundance of his heart, his mouth will continue to speak."[155]

The abolitionist movement had preceded the war by three decades. In that time, anti-slavery advocates had done their job well.

[154]Ibid., 228. The editorial and Lincoln's reply occurred in August 1862.
[155]Shelby Foote, *The Civil War: A Narrative* (New York: Random House, 2011), 1, 27–28.

This humanitarianism found a home among certain segments of American Protestantism, most notably the Quakers. Their broadmindedness in toleration, from which Catholics had also profited since colonial days, came to the forefront in the years leading up to the war. William Lloyd Garrison had broken from them because of what he perceived as a lack of fervor, but in fact, the Friends, stressing the "inner light" in all human beings, saw the divine likeness in everyone and were quick to form the core of the first national organization dedicated to emancipation: the Pennsylvania Abolition Society (PAS), dating from way back in 1775.

> Led by elite philanthropists, the PAS favored a strategy of petitioning the government against slavery, giving legal aid to African Americans (such as free blacks who had been fraudulently seized by slaveholders), and sending itinerant preachers into slave states like Delaware, Virginia and North Carolina to plead with slaveholders to release their bondspeople. While Philadelphia was the center of Quaker life, the Friends established communities within slave states such as Maryland, Virginia and North Carolina. The Quaker community in Loudon County, Virginia, for example, dated back to the 1720's and was home to anti-slavery minister Samuel Janney … [who] worked with other Virginia Quakers to found a benevolent society in Alexandria to rescue free blacks who were illegally captured by slave traders, wrote anti-slavery essays for the *Alexandria Gazette*, and coauthored a petition to Congress asking for the abolition of slavery in the District of Columbia.[156]

[156]Elizabeth R. Varon, *Disunion! The Coming of the American Civil War: 1789–1859* (Chapel Hill: University of North Carolina Press, 2008), 71–72.

Faith and Fury

As moderate as they could be in their approach, the Quakers were eminently realistic: They knew it would take a great deal of time before anything they were advancing would become reality. This was, of course, an eminently commendable cause, true to Quaker beliefs over the centuries—but it was a cause that Catholics, even if sympathetic, were loath to participate in.

Against the Abolitionists

As the presidential election of 1860 drew nearer, some abolitionists criticized Lincoln's position on issues such as suffrage and other rights for freed Blacks. One went so far as to declare that no candidate "is entitled to the sympathy of anti-slavery men, unless the party is willing to extend to the black man all the rights of a citizen."[157] Others within the abolitionist movement were optimistic about Lincoln's candidacy, however, feeling that his victory would strengthen the anti-slavery position within the new political party—even if it wouldn't bring everything they wanted immediately. Lydia Maria Child, an anti-slavery author, wrote that she trusted Lincoln because of a statement he made during his senate debates with Stephen A. Douglas that the Black man was his equal, every bit as good as himself. Given the strong pro-slavery sentiments in Illinois, she felt it demonstrated honest bravery. And, though Frederick Douglas could not bring himself to vote for Lincoln, he described the candidate as "a man of will and nerve."[158]

One contemporary historian had this to say about the 1860 campaign:

> After the northern faction of an irrevocably divided Democratic Party nominated Stephen A. Douglas, Republicans not

[157] Foner, *The Fiery Trial*, 141–142.
[158] Ibid., 142.

only tried to beef up Lincoln's spiritual credentials, but also plied evangelical voters with tales of the Little Giant's drinking and ties to Catholicism. In fact, Catholic support for the Democrats seemed more sustained than in any previous election campaign. Yet Catholic confidence in both Democrats and Douglas wavered during the summer — in part owing to reports that supporters of southern Democratic candidate John C. Breckinridge were attacking Douglas, Archbishop John Hughes, and the Pope to woo anti-Catholic voters.[159]

Though Lincoln's election gave many abolitionists hope, it is quite certain that most Catholics did not cast their ballots for him and were growing ever more distrustful of the anti-Catholic elements in abolitionist movement. The most stinging indictment of the movement up to this point came in an 1861 pastoral letter from Augustin Verot, bishop of Savannah and vicar apostolic of Florida. He preached this message first as a sermon in the church of Saint Augustine on January 4, 1861 — the day set aside by outgoing President James Buchanan as a day of public humiliation, fasting, and prayer.

At the outset, Verot was very clear about his purpose in what was a lengthy discourse to sit through:

I wish to show on the one side, how unjust, iniquitous, unscriptural, and unreasonable is the assertion of Abolitionists,

---

[159] George C. Rable, *God's Almost Chosen Peoples: A Religious History of the American Civil War* (Chapel Hill: University of North Carolina Press, 2010), 34. Douglas, though a believer in God, never identified himself with any particular church. Following the death of his first wife in 1853, in 1856 he married Adele Cutts, a great-niece of President James Madison and a member of a Maryland Catholic family. She and Douglas had two sons, both of whom were raised in their mother's Catholic Faith.

who brand Slavery as a moral evil: and a crime against God, religion, humanity, and society: whereas; it is found to have received the sanction of God, of the Church and of Society at all times, and in all governments. On the other side, I wish to show the conditions under which servitude is legitimate, lawful, approved by all laws, and consistent with practical religion and true holiness of life in masters who fulfill these conditions.[160]

The bishop began by arguing that natural law does not establish slavery but, rather, recognizes that certain human beings are, in their mental and physical makeup, meant to be slaves of others. In speaking of the lot of the slaves as Southern society understood it in the nineteenth century, Verot asserted:

It is truly remarkable how gay, cheerful and sprightly are the slaves of the South. I do not hesitate to say, that they seem to be better contented than their masters; assuredly more so than the sullen and gloomy population found in the work shops and factories of large cities.[161]

He then went on to argue that divine law does not condemn slavery because God cannot commend or authorize anything immoral. In the Old Testament, slavery was clearly not prohibited and was at least implicitly approved, inasmuch as Scripture contains commentary on the rights of masters and the duties of slaves. Abraham himself was a slaveholder (see Gen. 14:14) and, some two chapters later, one reads of how his wife, Sarah, was obliged to inflict discipline on her servant. The handmaid, Hagar, ran away, only to be confronted by an angel, who told her to return and be subject to her mistress. "How strange must all

[160] Peters, *The Catholic Bishops*, 124.
[161] Ibid., 126.

this be," Verot writes, "for Abolitionists who retain their belief in the Bible!"[162]

After citing examples from Exodus and Leviticus, Verot turned to the New Testament to assert that he could find no reference prohibiting slavery. He referred especially to the story in Matthew's Gospel of the centurion who, in asking for a cure for his servant, specifically mentions that he has men under him who follow his directives—and the Lord responds that He had not found so great a faith in all of Israel (Matt. 8:8–10). The Pauline letters as well as the First Epistle of Peter also touch on slavery without condemning it, and Verot even mentioned the ancient Council of Langres, which, he said, "condemns heretics who maintained the principles of modern Abolitionists."[163]

Verot then invoked ecclesiastical history, especially the story of Pope Saint Gregory the Great, who sent the first missionaries to England to convert the island from paganism, buying English and Barbary slaves to aid in the work of evangelization. And in the United States, after the federal Constitution was adopted and implemented in 1789, the relations between master and slave were clearly laid out and understood; the situation, Verot felt, had been stable. There was no doubt in his mind that the American system had gone awry because of the interventions of Protestants who were hostile to the Catholic Faith—that is, who saw it and its emphasis on order and hierarchy as an intrusion on the American way of life. This, by extension, was tied in with abolitionism:

> As for the Protestant clergy, with, of course, honorable exceptions, they have brought about this deplorable state of things, in which the South is arrayed against the North, and in which war, bloodshed, and all the atrocities of civil discord

[162] Ibid., 129.
[163] Ibid., 135.

119

may yet have their sad exhibition. Protestant intolerance and bigotry have demolished this beautiful edifice, which wisdom, moderation and prudence had reared to political liberty.[164]

He then went on, as did each of the Catholic bishops who addressed the issue in this era, to distinguish between the institution of slavery and the slave trade, which is "absolutely immoral and unjust and is against all laws natural, divine, ecclesiastical and civil."[165] Pope Gregory XVI is his chief source for this condemnation, as he was for so many of the American Catholic writers on this subject.

Verot realized that for slavery to continue as a viable institution in the South, it must be made to "conform to the laws of God; a Southern CONFEDERACY will never survive unless it rests upon morality and order."[166] One direct violation of this would be the breakup of slave families, especially, Verot stressed, because it would be almost impossible for a husband and wife to live in continence apart from one another. The fortitude required would be almost miraculous, and it "cannot be expected from the generality of men, much less from a race more inclined to pleasures than any other."[167]

One of the principle reasons separation of families was so deplorable was that it would stifle the religious instruction that Verot felt ameliorated the slaves' condition more than freedom ever could:

As for the generality of masters in the South, they are humane and kind, and more inclined to be too mild than too severe to their servants. This kind treatment is the necessary effect of religious feeling and practical religion among masters. And hence it ought to be the great study

[164] Ibid., 141.
[165] Ibid., 142.
[166] Ibid., 147.
[167] Ibid., 148.

of ministers of religion to spread the spirit of Christianity among the people; it will do incomparably more for the relief and the happiness of the slave than all the fanatical efforts of Abolitionists.[168]

The final portion of Verot's message dealt with the duties of masters to rear their slaves in the practice and knowledge of the Catholic Faith. If this challenge of education, confronted by all the Catholic bishops in slave territories, were met effectively, Verot felt it would be "a just vindication of Southern views sanctioned by the great Arbiter of nations."[169]

While there was certainly difference of opinion among Catholics on the peculiar institution, in both the North and the South, generally speaking, "both scriptural and church tradition were interpreted as recognizing that its existence with certain, qualifying conditions was compatible with the practice of religion."[170] Initially, it seemed that the Church in America desired to be, in a sense, above the fray:

> The spirit of the Catholic Church is eminently conservative, and while her ministers rightfully feel a deep and abiding interest in all that concerns the welfare of the country, they do not think it their province to enter the political arena. They leave to the ministers of the human sects to discuss from their pulpits and in their ecclesiastical assemblies the very exciting questions which lie at the base of our present and prospective difficulties. Thus, while many of the sects have divided into hostile parties on an exciting political issue, the Catholic Church has carefully preserved her unity

[168] Ibid., 149.
[169] Ibid., 154.
[170] Rice, *American Catholic Opinion*, 90.

of spirit in the bond of peace, literally knowing no North, no South, no East and no West.[171]

This proved to be impossible: Prelates and Catholic newspapers did indeed take on the issues of the day, with abolitionism at the top of the list. Archbishop Hughes of New York referred to abolitionist spokesmen such as Theodore Parker, William Ellery Channing, and other ministers as "infidels and fanatics," noting that Channing "was a Socinian, if not an infidel. Parker did not hesitate to preach and write against the divinity of Our Lord — he maintained that there would be other and better Christs than the one who died on Calvary."[172] Richard Whelan, the Catholic bishop of Wheeling, West Virginia, described "abolitionists, infidels and Red Republicans" as the "most deadly enemies of the church."[173] Further North, in Boston, churchmen hardly had better sentiments:

[171] Third Pastoral of the Province of Cincinnati, *Guardian*, May 18, 1861, cited in ibid., 94. The *Guardian* was the diocesan paper of the Diocese of Louisville, Kentucky.

[172] Hughes to Augustine Cochin, January 21, 1862, cited in Rice, *American Catholic Opinion*, 98. Socinians were adherents of a sixteenth- and seventeenth-century theological movement professing belief in God and adherence to the Christian Scriptures but denying the divinity of Christ and, hence, the Trinity.

[173] Whelan to Archbishop Hughes, undated, cited in Rice, *American Catholic Opinion*, 98. "Red Republicans" was a title given to those members of the Republican Party in the North who felt Southern Whites could not be punished severely enough for the system of slavery. These figures would become even more vocal during the postwar period of Reconstruction, regarding the demands made on the former Confederate States before their reentry into the Union. Richard V. Whelan (1809–1874) was born in Baltimore, studied at Mount Saint Mary's, Emmitsburg, Maryland, completed his theological studies at the Seminary of Saint Sulpice, Paris, and was ordained in Versailles in 1831. He served on the faculty of Mount

They [abolitionists] exhibit a striking zeal and earnestness in the propagation of their peculiar notions, and when the sneer or jibe is flung at them, they take up the Sacred Book, and each opposing lunatic conceives he finds something there to arm him in his cause. With audacious irreverence they tell you that such were the doctrines of Christ, and thus they perpetrate their follies under the assumption that they are promulgating His divine code.[174]

The Louisville *Guardian* went even further, exhorting Southern Protestants to condemn their abolitionist coreligionists in the North:

It is time for the enlightened Protestants of the South to open their eyes to the mischievous tendencies of this hypocritical system, which is always invoking the Bible and whose champions are yet the very first to trample on its most sacred principles. Had even one Catholic priest been guilty of one-tenth of the mischievous impiety which is the general rule with these Northern Protestant preachers, we would never hear the end of it. Why should one standard be established whereby to judge Catholics and another to judge Protestants?[175]

Saint Mary's and as pastor of a church in Harper's Ferry. He became the second bishop of Richmond, Virginia, in 1840 and, a decade later, became bishop of Wheeling. He enormously accelerated building in the diocese, fought the strong Know-Nothing influence in West Virginia, and attended the First Vatican Council, where he opposed the doctrine of papal infallibility, thinking it untimely.

[174] *Boston Pilot*, October 22, 1842; June 5, 1858, cited in Rice, *American Catholic Opinion*, 99.

[175] *Guardian*, November 12, 1859, cited in Rice, *American Catholic Opinion*, 100–101.

Faith and Fury

While Northern Catholic thinkers and writers were certainly less monolithic in support of slavery than their Southern counterparts, it seems, especially as the war progressed, that sympathy for the Southern mentality grew stronger among Northern Catholics. Archbishop Hughes, though, changed little with the passage of years. He consistently maintained that

> the teachings of the Church if strictly adhered to would sanctify ... both the master and the servant. The master by requiring him to be the head and guardian and protector of his slaves as well as of his immediate family. The servant by requiring that he should be obedient, faithful, moral and loyal to his master. And thus both would be in the line of obedience to the Supreme Master who created all. [176]

While Hughes proclaimed himself "no friend of slavery,"[177] he was quick to repudiate the extremes of the abolitionists. Even so, years earlier, as a seminarian at Mount Saint Mary's, he composed some verses that indicate his sympathy for the plight of African slaves:

> Those who show a fairer hand
> Enjoy sweet liberty
> But from the moment of my birth,
> I slave along Columbia's earth,
> Nor freedom smiles on me.
> Long have I pined through years of woe
> Adown life's bleeding track
> And still my tears, my blood must flow,
> Because my hand is black.[178]

[176] Kehoe, *Complete Works of Hughes*, 11, 222.
[177] Hassard, *Life of Most Rev. John Hughes*, 485.
[178] Ibid., 42–44.

As years passed, Hughes took a line closer to Lincoln's pre-emancipation position, that whatever became of the slaves was less important than maintaining the Union. On one occasion, responding to an article by Orestes Brownson in which the writer suggested that the abolition of slavery was the sole purpose of the conflict, the archbishop asserted that Catholics had no intention of fighting a war for anything but the preservation of the Union.[179] He reiterated this theme in a well-known letter he wrote to Simon Cameron, Lincoln's secretary of war:

> The Catholics, as far as I know, whether of native or foreign birth, are willing to fight to the death for the support of the Constitution, the Government, and the laws of the country. But if it should be understood that, with or without knowing it, they are to fight for the abolition of slavery, then indeed they will turn away in disgust from the discharge of what otherwise be a patriotic duty.[180]

Finally, one also sees a transformation in Hughes's thinking about the slave trade itself. While he affirmed the teaching of the Church that the slave trade was intrinsically immoral, he felt that Africa was a "country of savages where perpetual warfare and wholesale murder made the slave status in the United States a heaven by comparison." Given this, he could see no serious moral transgression on the part of the "slaver in snatching them from the butcheries prepared for them in their native land," while the purchasers were also blameless "where the traffic was authorized and the masters observant of their responsibilities to care adequately for the 'unfortunate' Africans."[181]

---

[179] *Metropolitan Record*, October 12, 1861, cited in Rice, *American Catholic Opinion*, 120.

[180] Hughes to Simon Cameron, October 1861, cited in Hassard, *Life of Most Rev. John Hughes*, 436–437.

[181] Cited in Rice, *American Catholic Opinion*, 121.

Faith and Fury

The Voice of the Laity

Lay opinion on slavery and abolition varied with regional and political affinities. A case in point is that of Senator David Broderick of California.[182] He allied himself early on with the anti-slavery wing of the Democratic Party, which was rather unusual for Irish politicians of the era. He always denied any connection with the abolitionists, but his concern for the rights of workingmen compelled him to oppose the extension of slavery into the territories. In an early speech in the Senate, he strongly opposed the Lecompton Constitution in Kansas, claiming it would impose slavery on the territory. He joined with Senator Stephen A. Douglas in his fight to defeat the proposed constitution and went on to denounce the Kansas-Nebraska Bill for its repeal of the Missouri Compromise, which he felt was another attempt to force slavery on the people.

A similar story can be told about U.S. Senator James Shields of Illinois.[183] During the discussions over the Compromise of 1850, he

[182] David Broderick (1820–1859) was an attorney and politician, born in Washington, D.C., of Irish immigrant parents. His family lived in New York until moving to California during the Gold Rush. He joined the Democratic Party in New York, was unsuccessful in his first bid for a Congressional seat, and, after his move to San Francisco, went into the business of smelting and assaying gold. He was a member of the California State Senate from 1850 until 1852, and from there he was chosen to be a United States senator from California. He was known for connections with political corruption in San Francisco, and his life ended prematurely in a duel with a political opponent.

[183] James Shields (1806–1879) was a County Tyrone–born Irish American Democratic politician who has the distinction of being the only person in U.S. history to serve in the U.S. Senate from three states. He represented Illinois from 1849 to 1855 in the Thirty-First, Thirty-Second, and Thirty-Third Congresses; Minnesota from 1858 to 1859 in the Thirty-Fifth Congress; and Missouri in 1879 in the Forty-Fifth Congress. Born and initially educated in

The Church and Slavery

announced that he opposed the extension of slavery, denying the claim that "the Constitution carried slavery where it was not positively excluded by law." Since slavery was a violation of a natural right, he argued, it could exist only where people had specifically voted for it. He separated himself from the extremist arguments of the abolitionists, feeling that their rhetoric had made the South rise in rightful indignation—but at the same time, he decried a parallel extremism among white Southerners, whose immoderation damaged the effectiveness of their arguments.[184]

Charles O'Conor was a prominent New York City attorney who holds the distinction of being the first Catholic nominated for president of the United States.[185] In his legal career, he served

Ireland, he practiced law in Illinois, where he nearly fought a duel with Abraham Lincoln over articles Lincoln had written critical of his work as state auditor general. He served with distinction in both the Mexican and Civil Wars and died rather suddenly in 1879, while on a lecture tour in Iowa.

[184] Rice, *American Catholic Opinion*, 116–117.

[185] O'Conor (1804–1884) was the son of Irish-born Thomas O'Conor, who fled Ireland after participating in the Irish Rebellion of 1798. He began to study law at an early age, was admitted to the bar at twenty, and soon became known as a talented trial lawyer. A conservative Democrat in politics, he supported the Union, but was sympathetic to arguments in favor of states' rights. After the war, he became counsel for ex-President Jefferson Davis. In the 1868 presidential election, the Liberal Republicans ran *New York Tribune* editor Horace Greeley against U.S. Grant, the incumbent president who was presiding over a scandal-ridden administration. The Democrats did not hold a convention that year but acquiesced in the nomination of Greeley. Many conservative Democrats, largely Catholics, could not abide some of Greeley's moral positions, and, calling themselves "Straight-Out Democrats," nominated O'Conor and John Quincy Adams II. The ticket received several hundred thousand votes nationwide, though no electoral votes. Very active in Irish affairs, O'Conor is one of several prominent New York

as counsel for masters in many fugitive slave cases. A position he
often repeated in legal briefs was that "Negroes alone and unaided
by guardianship of another race were incapable of sustaining a
civilized political state" and that their makeup made them fit only
for labor in warm climates, work and conditions not at all suited for
the "intellectual white race."[186] O'Conor's pro-slavery and states'
rights views led him to sympathize with the even stronger position
of state sovereignty: He felt that the South should totally control
the institution of slavery, unimpeded in any way by Northern, and
certainly abolitionist, interests. He maintained that

> [slavery] is not unjust; it is just, wise and beneficent.... [In]
> climates where the black race can live and prosper, nature
> herself enjoins correlative duties on the black man and
> on the white, which cannot be performed except by the
> preservation, and if the hissing gentleman please, by the
> perpetuation of negro slavery.[187]

The Catholic Response to Emancipation

In the fall of 1862, President Lincoln announced, after months, if
not years, of soul searching, that "slaves in rebellious states or parts
of states should be then, thenceforward, and forever free."[188] The
president had proposed such a move to his cabinet as early as July
1862. His secretary of state, William H. Seward, advised that he
wait, because it would be, in his view, "a dynamic change in the

---

City Catholics to occupy vaults in the crypt of Saint Patrick's Old
Cathedral at Mott and Pearl Streets on the City's Lower East Side.
[186] Cited in Rice, *American Catholic Opinion*, 117.
[187] Charles O'Conor, *Negro Slavery Not Unjust*, 11, *Freeman's Journal*,
July 28, 1860, cited in Rice, *American Catholic Opinion*, 116–117.
[188] Randall, *The Civil War and Reconstruction*, 480.

The Church and Slavery

war's focus," which had theretofore been fought for the preservation of the Union, and not for the abolition of the South's social and economic identity. Doing so then, Seward felt, would be "little more than a plea for support without a military victory."[189] But a few months later, the president moved forward.

Catholic reaction to emancipation was said by one commentator to have been "divided and ambivalent."[190] There was surely division, but ambivalence is harder to find. Most of the Catholic press remained steadfast in its Democratic allegiance. In New York, James A. McMaster of the *Freeman's Journal* and John Mullaly of the *Metropolitan Record* were avowed peace Democrats, totally sympathetic to the South's position and militantly anti-Lincoln. At the same time, Patrick Donohue, editor of the Boston *Pilot,* and Father Edward Purcell, editor of the Cincinnati *Catholic Telegraph* (and brother of Cincinnati's archbishop, John Baptist Purcell), remained completely pro-Union and devotedly pro-Lincoln and thus supportive of the Emancipation Proclamation.

James A. McMaster, born in 1820 in Duanesburg, New York, was the son of a Presbyterian minister and the descendant of Scottish immigrants who had settled in Vermont. He studied at Union College in Schenectady and later entered General Theological Seminary in New York to study for the Episcopalian ministry. John Henry Newman's writings led him to the fullness of faith, and he briefly entered a Redemptorist Seminary in Belgium. As a married man, he gave two daughters to religious life. He purchased the New York *Freeman's Journal* in 1848, which he used to popularize his views against sending Catholic children to public schools; in favor of slavery; and, in 1861, in favor of secession.

[189] Mark M. Boatner, ed., *The Civil War Dictionary* (New York: David McKay, 1959), 265.
[190] Rable, *God's Almost Chosen Peoples,* 226.

He was outspoken in support of the papacy and, in later years, the doctrine of papal infallibility, while being one of the fiercest critics of the Know-Nothings and other anti-Catholics. He hated abolitionists, had a deep-seated suspicion of Jesuits, and, finally, because of his stridency, incurred the wrath of Archbishop Hughes, who, in 1856, declared that the *Freeman's Journal* was no longer to be considered the official organ of the Archdiocese of New York. McMaster was jailed for six weeks for his activism when President Lincoln suspended the writ of habeas corpus, but, when released, he continued to write against the war effort, believing the South had the absolute right to secede. He died in 1886, in Brooklyn, always a devoted son of the Faith he had embraced years earlier.[191]

John Mullaly was born in Belfast, Northern Ireland, in 1835. After immigrating to New York, he worked for the *New York Tribune* and the *New York Evening Post*. Eventually he became editor of a Catholic publication, the *Metropolitan Record*, which was a source of controversy during the war years. The height of his notoriety came shortly before the New York City Draft Riots of 1863, when he accused the Lincoln administration of perverting the war from an attempt to restore the Union to a "vile" emancipation crusade. After the war, he entered city politics, maintaining strong connections with the corrupt Tweed Ring, as well as Tammany Hall. He died in 1915.[192]

---

[191] When President Lincoln suspended the writ for security purposes during the war, he essentially removed the legal recourse by which a person could reverse an unlawful detention or imprisonment. This was used, as in the case of McMaster, to detain political dissenters who were thought to be undermining the war effort, but it often backfired.

[192] For more information on Mullaly, see Albon P. Man Jr., "The Church and the New York Draft Riots of 1863," *Records of the American Catholic Historical Society of Philadelphia* 62, no. 1 (March 1951): 31–50.

One student of editors such as McMaster and Mullaly contended that their background was determinative of their views on race and politics:

> Most of the editors were of Irish ancestry and their subscribers belonged mainly to the immigrant body. The antipathy to free Negroes prevalent among the workingmen of the lower wage level in the North is a well recognized historical fact. It had become apparent in the course of the abolitionist crusade and it showed itself again when the probability of emancipation raised the specter of mass migration of black workers. Politically minded editors like McMaster of the *Freeman's Journal* or Mullaly of the *Metropolitan Record* were quick to play up these feelings in their fight against President Lincoln and the Republican Party.[193]

The Boston *Pilot*, while strongly Unionist, sounded a concerned note at the idea of thousands of free Blacks emigrating North and replacing the mostly Irish workforce. The paper had been largely anti-slavery before the war, and also strongly anti-abolitionist. In the face of emancipation, it raised the question "[In] the country of the whites where the labor of the whites has done everything, but [that of Blacks], nothing, and where the whites find it difficult to earn a subsistence, what right has the Negro either to preference, or to equality, or to admission?"[194]

The archbishop of Cincinnati, John Baptist Purcell, who was politically conservative prior to 1861, quickly became a staunch supporter of the Union cause and of the Lincoln administration as war broke out. He publicly voiced his support for the Emancipation Proclamation and was denounced by New York's McMaster

---

[193] Rice, *American Catholic Opinion*, 124.
[194] *Pilot*, August 16, 1862, cited in ibid., 126.

as a "political abolitionist." He retorted that those who read the commentary of such editors were "duped and deceived by their malignity."[195]

If an editorial by the archbishop's brother is any indication, however, the Cincinnati prelate was not about to admit the equality of the races:

The natural superiority of the white race ought to be carefully preserved [but this was] impossible so long as slavery exists because the poor white man is just as much, or to a great extent, in the power of the rich planter as the slave. Therefore, let the system be abolished, and then the problem of the freedman "grappled with" in such a way as to protect the legitimate rights of each.[196]

Catholic opinion in the South was, unsurprisingly, a bit more straightforward. One commentator summarized it thus:

Where Northerners in their discussions were inclined as a rule to describe the policy of the Church as looking to eventual abolition, among southern Catholics the chief emphasis was given to the acceptance of the system by scriptural and church authority—with emancipation as a very remote possibility.[197]

This had been the case in the South for decades, of course. In the late eighteenth century, John Carroll of Baltimore had written to a priest convert, Father John Thayer, who had been serving as pastor of a parish in Alexandria, Virginia. Father Thayer felt

[195] *Freeman's Journal*, February 6, 1864, cited in Rice, *American Catholic Opinion*, 127.
[196] *Catholic Telegraph*, July 15, September 23, 1863, cited in Rice, *American Catholic Opinion*, 129.
[197] Ibid., 139.

compelled to leave his post because he could not reconcile slavery with his conscience. Carroll's response indicated that one must accept that which he cannot change in existing norms, no matter how personally difficult (Father Thayer still resigned):

> While you confine yourself within the bounds of solid doctrine, you may act freely, and unrestrained by any ecclesiastical interference, in remedying the abuses of slavery; and when you have done your duty, if all the good effect possible and desirable does not ensue from your endeavors you must bear that, as every pastor must bear the many disorders, which will subsist in spite of his most zealous exertions.[198]

This was also the position taken by Charleston's Bishop John England in response to many queries put to him by the cardinal prefect of the Congregation for the Propagation of the Faith in Rome. England, apparently disclosing some of his deepest inner feelings, told Rome that he was determined to carry on with all his duties in spite of his "disgust with the conditions of the slaves, brought into my diocese under a system which perhaps is the greatest moral evil that can desolate any part of the civilized world."[199] Whether the tension between this statement and his public profile reflects a certain complexity in his thinking, or merely differences in his audiences, cannot be said for sure.

Most of the Southern Catholic press admitted that there were abuses in the system but that they did not occur in the majority of master-slave relationships. Even where these abuses did happen, according to the prevailing opinion among Southern Catholic writers,

[198]"Letters from the Archepiscopal Archives at Baltimore," *Records of the American Catholic Historical Society of Philadelphia* 20, 58–59, cited in Rice, *American Catholic Opinion*, 132.

[199]Peter Guilday, *The Life and Times of John England* (New York: 1897), 1, 531.

they did not justify the violent and unconstitutional methods of the Northern abolitionists. Under the Constitution, the responsibility for managing domestic concerns fell to the states, they asserted, and the federal government had an obligation to safeguard this right.

Deeper in the South, editorial positions became more radical. The *Catholic Standard* of New Orleans and the *Miscellany* in Charleston were adamant that the Southern states were the genuine interpreters of the original federal compact. The latter paper took the position that "it needs but little knowledge of our history to discover, whether it was the men, who revere state sovereignty, or their enemies, that have been pursuing for years an insidious course of aggression upon that constitution, to which these commonwealths have bound themselves as contracting parties."[200] The editors of Charleston's diocesan paper announced that the phrase "United States" would be dropped from the paper's masthead.

In the premier see of Baltimore, notably in the border state of Maryland, many strong differences of opinion could be found. For much of the war, Francis P. Kenrick served as archbishop; only in the final year did the see transfer to Martin J. Spalding. Kenrick, for his part, had Union sympathies, but the editor of his diocesan newspaper, the Baltimore *Catholic Mirror*, was of a decidedly different school of thought. Editorializing on the Emancipation Proclamation, Courtney Jenkins left no doubt about his views:

It compresses all the functions of government into the narrow space of an individual will. Considered in its motive, it contemplates the triumph of a fanatical and reckless faction. Regarded in its anticipated results, it is an invitation to servile insurrection. Its assumptions of power are surpassed in enormity only by the horrors and atrocities it covertly

---

[200] *United States Catholic Miscellany*, December 8, 1860, cited in Rice, *American Catholic Opinion*, 145.

counsels. While invoking the "considerate judgment of mankind and the gracious favor of Almighty God," in its principles it defies the civilization of the age and suggests crimes which are hideous mockeries of God's goodness and providence. Proclaimed as an act necessary to suppress rebellion against the authority and government of the United States, it raises issues and professes objects utterly subversive of legitimate authority, and at variance with the permanence of free institutions.[201]

The details of the American Church's engagement with slavery do not do Her much credit. The institution divided Catholics along regional and political lines, but no prominent member of the Church picked up the banner of abolition — in part, at least, because of anti-Catholic animus within the movement itself. But this was also because Catholic teaching, at least as it had been promulgated in the United States, was, charitably put, conservative — more concerned about disrupting the fabric of society than about the liberty of the millions of bondsmen in the South. Meanwhile, the Faith was spread and passed on among the slaves in a very limited way; so much more could have been done to evangelize both slaves and former slaves in the rudiments of Catholic Faith.

One credit that can be given to the American Church and Her leaders is simply this: that, unlike the country itself, Her unity never faltered, even as regional and political divisions threatened to rend Her.

[201] *Catholic Mirror*, January 10, 1863, cited in Rice, *American Catholic Opinion*, 150.

Chapter 4

∞

The War Years: 1861–1865

Background to War

Sectional tensions had continued to grow throughout the 1850s. At the moment of peak pressure came the election of Abraham Lincoln. Between Lincoln's election and inauguration, seven states of the lower South seceded from the Union and began the creation of the Confederate States of America. Lincoln's strong executive action in defending the federal fort at Fort Sumter, followed by his call for seventy-five thousand militia to be furnished by the states, led an additional four states to join the Confederacy. The South saw these actions as attempts at federal coercion, further validating the decision to secede. By contrast, Buchanan's passivity had given some in the South the hope that an open conflagration might be avoided. But it was not to be so, as William H. Seward accurately predicted two years earlier in a famous speech in Rochester, when he spoke of an "irrepressible conflict" between enduring and opposing forces, which meant "the United States must and will sooner or later become either entirely a slave holding nation or entirely a free labor nation."[202]

---

[202] George E. Baker, ed., *The Works of William H. Seward* (New York: 1853–84), IV, 292, cited in Stamp, *The Causes of the Civil War*, 140.

Faith and Fury

The Union was composed of twenty-three states with twenty-two million people, while the Confederacy had eleven states and nine million people, of whom three and a half million were enslaved. The Union held the upper hand in industry, commerce, and financial power, while the South could boast a certain spiritedness and an aristocratic tradition that produced fine military leadership, and a significant number of interior supply lines. And then there were the border states: Delaware, Maryland, Kentucky, and Missouri, to which would later be added West Virginia. The southern portions of Ohio, Indiana, and Illinois also had significant Confederate sympathies, though most historians argue most of the people in these areas was pro-Union politically and militarily, even while maintaining a cultural sympathy for the South.

Legally the war began with the presidential order of April 15, 1861, summoning the militia to suppress rebellion in the seven states of the lower South. (The president would be assassinated exactly four years later.) No foreign nation intervened on behalf of either side during the war years, though Catholic prelates from New York and Charleston were both to distinguish themselves in diplomatic missions on behalf of their respective sections of the country.

By the time Lincoln's first Congress met in July 1861, he had not only issued a declaration to put down insurrection, but also ordered a blockade of Southern ports, expanded the regular army, directed emergency expenditures, and, in general, assumed emergency executive powers — including suspending the writ of habeas corpus. The president strongly argued that the times demanded an extraordinary exercise of executive power not subject to discussion or negotiation with Congress:

> Lincoln's method of meeting the emergency and suppressing
> disloyal tendencies was not to proceed within the pattern of

regular statutes, but to grasp arbitrary powers by executive orders or proclamations, as in the Emancipation Proclamation (in which the President exercised a power which he insisted Congress did not have even in time of war), and his extensive program of arbitrary arrests wherein thousands of citizens were thrust into prison on suspicion of disloyal or dangerous activity. These arrests were quite irregular. Prisoners were given no trial (usually not even military trial); they were deprived of civil guarantees and were subjected to no regular accusations under the law. Such measures led to severe and widespread opposition to the Lincoln administration.[203]

A Border-State Bishop Diagnoses the War

Catholic bishops were conspicuous even among other religious leaders in their response to the national situation. One of the best-remembered discussions was a paper by Bishop Martin J. Spalding, then of Louisville, Kentucky, titled *Dissertation on the American Civil War*. As the descendant of an English Catholic family who had settled in Southern Maryland in the seventeenth century and joined the significant Catholic migration to Kentucky a few generations later, his views distinctive of a border-state background should come as no surprise.

The difficult matter of opposing views of the federal-state relationship was being solved, Bishop Spalding wrote in 1862, in the worst of ways. After considering the general causes of the war, which he identified as not just African slavery, but the tariff that set regional interests against one another, he expressed deep pessimism about the future prospects for American bondsmen:

[203] Wayne Andrews, ed., *Concise Dictionary of American History* (New York: Charles Scribner's Sons, 1962), 190.

Faith and Fury

Our experience and observation shows us that those who
are in such a way liberated ordinarily become miserable
vagabonds, drunkards and thieves; it would seem a curious
thing, but nevertheless true, that such emancipated ones
are lost in body and soul.[204]

Bishop Spalding then underscored the Constitutional protection
of the institution of slavery and minced no words in condemning
those who wished to overthrow it. Rarely had a Catholic prelate
taken on the abolitionists in such strong language:

Some of these blind fanatics openly proposed their program of modern progress as embracing two principal points!
namely "the violent destruction of those two relics of a
barbarous age — slavery and Catholicism!!" Their shout
was "Down with slavery and popery!!"[205]

Spalding noted that of the thirty-three states composing the
Union, eighteen were free and fifteen had slave populations. Of
the fifteen, eleven were in rebellion, and the other four were border
states that, if they had been allowed to express their governmen-
tal preference, would almost certainly have sided with the South
but were prevented from doing so by occupying Northern troops.
The North was the invading force, said the bishop, whereas the
South's concern was merely defensive. Despite their inferiority
in population, commerce, munitions, and the like, "until now, as
everyone knows, they have succeeded marvelously in defending
themselves from invasion, and have won many signal victories
over their adversaries."[206] The "miserable war," which had begun
to restore the Union, had evolved into a war of "confiscation of

[204] Ibid., 189–190.
[205] Ibid., 192.
[206] Ibid., 193.

140

property, of violent emancipation of the Negroes, of threatened and encouraged slave insurrection, of destruction and desolation of the vast and fair territory of the South, and finally of extermination of all the whites, and perhaps at the same time of all the Negroes themselves, if the revolt cannot by any other means be suppressed."[207]

Spalding's final point, and surely his most significant from the point of view of the household of faith, was about the relation between the war and the Catholic Church, and the duty of bishops and priests. He noted the importance of separation of church and state to our constitutional heritage and emphasized that, at the outset of the conflict, the Church tried to avoid seeming in any way to take sides or to express even slight preferences. At the war's beginning, he noted, the bishops were very careful to emphasize that the Church had taken no position on the issues over which both sides had come to blows. Even so, Spalding admitted that a few bishops—four or five by his reckoning—had taken a more sectarian stand, but these actions were necessary so as not to appear to be working against the government of the land in which they resided.[208]

The war must end sooner or later with one of two results: either there will be here, as before, only one government, or there will be two independent ones; of which results I believe the second to be more probable, at least not impossible. Whichever it may be, there will necessarily be great animosity and strong hate between the men in one section and the other. Now the Catholic Church extending through all the

[207] Ibid., 195.
[208] He refers here to specific pastoral letters, diplomatic missions, and the efforts of New York's Archbishop Hughes during the 1863 Draft Riots in the city.

states of the North and the South will find itself obliged to deal with the adherents of both sides, or governments.... When one reflects, how fierce and terrible are the passions excited by a civil war, in which more than two hundred thousand men will be left killed or dead, and three to four times more wounded or crippled, with thousands of other citizens who will have lost all their goods, one can better imagine what the excitement of the passions will be once the war is ended. The Catholic Church, as a most loving mother of all, must not be an enemy of anyone, nor even seem to be so.[209]

Dialogue: South and North; Lynch and Hughes

It should come as little surprise that the bishop in whose city the first shots of war were fired would take an even stronger pro-Confederate tack than Spalding in Louisville. Bishop Patrick N. Lynch, many years a priest of Charleston before becoming its third ordinary, confided his thoughts to Archbishop Hughes of New York in 1861, some four months after the bombardment of Fort Sumter. He felt that the South had been unfairly blamed for the war's outbreak; in fact, he argued, it was the South that predicted so many times that the triumph of abolitionism would eventually break up the Union. The people, he argued, did not take seriously the sincerity of secession; the Confederate government was formed as a direct result of the "dogged obstinacy of Black Republicans at Washington."[210]

The bishop could not help but lament for the country as it had been:

[209] Peters, The Catholic Bishops, 198–199.
[210] Bishop Patrick N. Lynch to Archbishop John J. Hughes, August 4, 1861, cited in Ellis, Documents, 357–358.

Here was a country, vast, populous, prosperous and blessed in all material interest, if any country was. The South producing cotton, tobacco, sugar, rice and naval stores for the supply, as far as needed, of the North and Northwest, to the value of, perhaps, $50,000,000 a year, and exporting to foreign countries over $220,000,000; the Northwest producing chiefly grain, and supplying the North and the South, and when the European crops failed, having, as last winter, a large European market; the North manufacturing and supplying the South and the Northwest, and struggling to compete with foreign goods abroad, and doing the trading and commerce of the South and the Northwest.... Even a child could see the vast benefits to all from this mutual co-operation. No wonder that in all material interests the country was prospering to an extent that intoxicated us and astonished the world.[211]

But how could this blessed situation have so deteriorated? Lynch's answer was not much different from many of his fellow bishops: "Taking up anti-slavery, making it a religious dogma, and carrying it into politics, [the abolitionists] have broken up the Union."[212] His added comment is especially telling: "We Catholics might everywhere smile at this additional attempt to 'reform' the teachings of our Savior."[213] Lynch surely had in mind the strong anti-Catholic leanings of those in the abolitionist crusade.

Like Spalding, Lynch argued that the rhetoric and result of the 1860 election gave the South no choice but secession. This did not have to mean that all hope was lost in the South: Many felt that some help might still come from Washington. But Lincoln's

[211] Ibid.
[212] Ibid.
[213] Ibid., 359–360.

intransigency (in Lynch's view) ended that hope. "They desired to withdraw in peace. This war had been forced upon them."[214]

> Truly the North has to pay dearly for its whistle of Black Republicanism. The Northwest depended partially on the South for a market for its productions, and so far will suffer from the loss of it. It must also be incidentally affected by commercial embarrassments at the North. They will assuredly have enough to eat and wear, but the 'fancy' prices of real estate and stocks, by which they computed their rapidly increasing wealth, must fall in a way to astonish Wall Street.[215]

Lynch saw the blockade of Southern ports as the chief barrier to peace, which he knew could cripple a Southern economy based on cotton exports. At the time of his writing to Hughes, though, Lynch could attest the blockade had not yet done harm and would not for at least the next six months: It was forcing the South to be active and to do for themselves what they formerly had relied on others, by payment, to do for them. In the end, European cotton production proved sufficient, so that no powers on the continent found it necessary to intervene on the South's behalf.

The last thing Charleston's bishop wanted was a prolonged sectional conflict:

> The separation of the Southern states is *un fait accompli*. The Federal Government has no power to reverse it. Sooner or later it must be recognized. Why preface the recognition by a war equally needless and bloody? Men at the North may regret the rupture; as men at the South may do. The Black Republicans overcame the first at the polls, and would not

[214]Ibid., 360.
[215]Ibid., 362.

listen to the second in Congress, when the evil might have been repaired. They are responsible. If there is to be fighting, let those who voted the Black Republican ticket shoulder their musket and bear the responsibility. Let them not send Irishmen to fight in their stead, and then stand looking on at the conflict, when, in their heart of hearts, they care little which of the combatants destroy the other.[216]

Lynch closed his letter to the Archbishop of New York by saying that "nothing seems now to span the chasm but that bridge of Catholic union and charity of which your Grace spoke so eloquently last Saint Patrick's Day."[217]

Just a few weeks later, Hughes responded to Lynch. He thought the Charleston prelate's assessment "one of the most temperate views of the present unhappy contest that has ever come under my notice from any son of South Carolina."[218] Both of them, Hughes said, had been equally committed to the preservation of peace prior to the outbreak of hostilities. In fact, the nature of their ministry meant they must be friends of peace.

Hughes told Lynch that his explanations of the causes of the war were entirely Southern, but "they are so mildly, and even plausibly stated, that I leave them uncontroverted."[219] Hughes did have his own theories on the origin of the "melancholy strife," though, which he presented to Lynch. He began with the enshrinement of free speech in the American system, one of the basic notions of Anglo-Saxon liberty. The Anglo-Saxon, whether of North or

[216] Ibid., 364.
[217] Ibid. Hughes had delivered an address to the Hibernian Society in Charleston in 1860. See Kehoe, *Complete Works of Hughes*, 11, 756–759.
[218] Kehoe, *Complete Works of Hughes*, 11, 513.
[219] Ibid., 514.

South, Hughes said, "would see the whole world set in a blaze rather than put limits to the freedom of the press or the unbridled license of the tongue, except when the laws interpose for the protection of public authority or individual rights of character and property."[220] While this notion was an important part of the national heritage, the archbishop believed all sides had abused it and, amid all the bombast, emotion, exaggeration, and so on, anger mounted and the balance of the emotions was lost. Reason was all but abandoned and, thus, war broke out.

The slavery question, naturally, was at the root of the argument over theories of government. Though slavery had existed throughout the land at the time of the American Revolution, the North was the first to abandon it, and the bishop felt they should all be free to disagree. But the North turned its moralistic gaze entirely southward, and the South took the regrettable and impossible step of secession:

> Yet, the biggest sin in our day known to the North is not what occurs in its own immediate neighborhood or State, but the monster iniquity of the South, which, between you and me, and as the world goes, might have been permitted to manage its own affairs in its own way, so that its acts should be found either in harmony with, or not in violation of, the Constitution of the United States. I am an advocate for the sovereignty of every State in the Union within the limits recognized and approved of by its own representative authority, when the Constitution was agreed upon. As a consequence, I hold that South Carolina has no State right to interfere with the internal affairs of Massachusetts. And, as a further consequence, that Massachusetts has no right

[220] Ibid.

to interfere with South Carolina, or its domestic and civil affairs, as one of the sovereign States of this now threatened Union. But the Constitution having been formed by the common consent of all the sovereign parties engaged in the framework and approval thereof, I maintain that no state has the right to secede, except in the manner provided for in the document itself.[221]

Hughes found it very difficult to see how the South could reasonably justify its act of secession. The federal government, he felt, had given the South no more reason to secede in 1861 than ten or fifteen years earlier, particularly when one examined the federal legislation passed in that time, which, if anything, supported Southern interests. He again pointed to the general agreement of all the states on the Constitution, which had lasted nearly eighty years and served well as the governing document of the entire nation. He noted that no Northern president had ever been reelected, while several two-term presidents from the South—Washington, Jefferson, Madison, Monroe, and Jackson—had governed under the U.S. Constitution for over half a century.

You say that President Lincoln was elected by Black Republicans in the North. I am inclined to think he was indirectly or negatively elected by Democrats, North and South. The Black Republicans presented one candidate; and, in order to defeat his election, the Democrats, North and South presented *three*. If the latter had only selected one candidate, it is probable that the Black Republicans, as you call them, would have been found as *minus habentes*. But when the Democrats distributed their votes, apparently with a view

---

[221] Ibid., 515. Hughes here gives a clear presentation of the organic theory of government.

of rendering them inefficient, then, of course, the one man of choice was elected over the three candidates and competitors that had been placed in rivalship with each other, and, in the aggregate, all against him alone. That he was constitutionally elected under these circumstances is not denied either in the South or in the North.[222]

Hughes told Lynch that he picked up in his letter a Southern attitude that the North had the purpose of dividing and subjugating the South. He felt this was a great mistake and that the North's only ultimate objective was to bring back the seceded states to their position "*ante bellum.*" Turning specifically to the faith they shared, Hughes wrote:

> You think it hard that foreigners and Catholics should be deluded into the service of the recognized federal Government, in order to be immolated in the front of battles, and made food for Southern powder. If this end were a deliberate policy in the North, I should scout and despise it. I admit and maintain, that foreigners now naturalized, whether Catholics or not, ought to bear their relative burden in defense of the only country on these shores where they have recognized, and which has recognized them as citizens of the United States.[223]

Instead of partisan hostility, Hughes counseled, wise patriots on both sides should outdo themselves in attempting to restore the Union as one nation. While this was inimical to the Southern mind, especially in 1861, Hughes saw the protection and happiness of one united people, their rights and liberties secured, as the only objective worth fighting for. (Of course, Black slaves were not included in this moral calculus.) Hughes even suggested to Lynch

[222]Ibid., 516–517.
[223]Ibid., 518.

the possibility of individual state conventions of the seceded states, to which each governor would send a representative, to examine the situation and clearly list grievances, with the hope these could be collectively gathered, reported to the governors, and resolved peacefully. Once again, like his Southern counterpart, he could not conclude his letter without an appeal to the mutual faith that bound them:

> It only remains for me to add, that the Catholic faith and Catholic charity which unites us in the spiritual order, shall remain unbroken by the booming of cannon along the lines that unfortunately separate a great and once prosperous community into two hostile portions, each arrayed in military strife against the other.[224]

Divergent Catholic Views in the North

There is little doubt that deeper political divisions were to be found in the North than in the South. While many editors, as we have seen, took a more pro-Union position, the convert editor James A. McMaster, who lived and worked in an era of controversial newspaper men such as Horace Greeley of the *New York Tribune*, Henry J. Raymond of the *New York Times*, and Charles A. Dana of the *New York Sun*, did the very opposite. The *Freeman's Journal* had been founded in 1840, and McMaster became its editor eight years later. Early on, he reserved editorial comment to church issues, but gradually he became involved in the slavery controversy—so much so that Archbishop Hughes, who disagreed with him, withdrew his episcopal approval and began his own official diocesan paper, the *Metropolitan Record*. As McMaster's views and

[224]Ibid., 520.

Faith and Fury

tone became increasingly strident, he came under the suspicion of the Lincoln administration. One historian, speaking of this period of journalistic history, noted that "never was there a war in which arm-chair generalship from newspaper offices was more vociferous, in which more editors became military strategists overnight."[225]

The same summer of 1861 in which Archbishop Hughes wrote his reply to his episcopal colleague in Charleston, McMaster penned an editorial sharply critical of Lincoln's decision to call out the state militias. McMaster felt that despite the president's appeal to emergency authority, it was too raw an exercise of executive power. The editor further questioned why the president had, without congressional approval, expanded the regular army and navy of the United States. In the appointment of generals, such as George B. McClellan, the president had "no more authority ... than Mr. Dogberry Kennedy of the New York Police."[226] McMaster argued that Lincoln had "sought to absorb and confound in his own action the legislative and executive functions, which the Constitution of the United States, with such pre-eminent care, has distinguished and placed in separate hands."[227]

Lincoln's present course of action, according to McMaster, was "unconstitutional, outrageous, and *an open rebellion* against the United States Government as established and recognized."[228] He was sharply critical of the new Republicans, and he especially singled out the "Red-Republican ravings of the *Tribune*," among others, for stirring up sentiment that was leading to a "centralized despotism."[229]

[225] Frank Luther Mott, *American Journalism* (New York: 1941), 339, cited in Ellis, *Documents*, 351.
[226] Ibid., 352.
[227] Ibid., 353.
[228] Ibid.
[229] Ibid., 354.

Let those heed it who, one year ago, scoffed when we said that the election of Lincoln would cause civil war! We say, now, that if there be not conservativism enough in the country to stop and to rebuke the course of Lincoln and his Cabinet, we will have a bloody revolution and anarchy, resulting in a military despotism, with a different man from Lincoln at its head. We speak what we see and know. Our conscience forces us to speak, whether it please or offend.[230]

The administration in Washington was not pleased: McMaster was sentenced to six weeks in Fort Lafayette in the Narrows of New York Harbor.

Becoming American

Despite these divisions, the Catholic experience of the Civil War was in many regards another in a series of rites of passage for Catholics in this country, an important moment in the process of Catholic assimilation into American life. Since the colonial days, the Church had been suspect in the minds of many Americans. Anti-Catholic bigotry had been fueled by oratory, literature, and especially the distrust inherent in the Calvinist tradition that had entrenched itself in the American civil religion. But even as Catholics achieved a more mainstream status, other barriers were soon put up.

Catholic participation in the war effort was substantial on both sides:

On both sides, thousands of Catholics took up arms. The "Montgomery Guards" of the First Virginia Infantry donned green and gold uniforms and marched to the basement of Richmond's St. Peter's Cathedral, where Bishop John McGill

[230]Ibid., 356.

blessed the pikes they carried. At Bull Run they would confront New York's Irish Catholic Sixty-ninth Regiment. At a
Mass in the Mobile Cathedral, Bishop Quinlan blessed the
flag of the "Emerald Guards," Company 1 of the Eighth Alabama. Of 109 men on the roster, 104 were Irish born. When
Texans threatened the New Mexico Territory, the governor
commissioned Colonel Kit Carson and Ceran St. Vrain,
both parishioners of Taos, to raise troops. French Catholics
enlisted in Louisiana regiments. Lieutenant General William
J. Hardee, C.S.A., defended the state, while another Catholic, General Philip H. Sheridan, U.S.A., made his name in
the Shenandoah. Bishops took comfort from General Pierre
G. T. Beauregard's attendance at religious services and hoped
it might be a sign of better practice to come. The Confederate
hero was a Catholic, but also a Free Mason. A prominent
Charles County, Maryland, Catholic family contributed rear
Admiral Raphael Semmes to the Confederate navy. He cap-
tained the C.S.S. *Alabama* during the two year cruise which
cost the Union seventy ships taken as prizes and $6 million
in shipping losses. The highest-ranking Catholic in either
government, after the aged Chief Justice Taney, was Confederate Secretary of the Navy Stephen R. Mallory. Over seventy
Catholic chaplains, commissioned and volunteer, served the
two armies: Jesuits from the French missions in New York
and the south and the Maryland province, Holy Cross priests
from Notre Dame, Redemptorists and secular priests from
a score of dioceses.... Between five and six hundred sisters
from twenty religious communities were nurses in military
hospitals. Outstanding were the Emmitsburg daughters of
Charity with two hundred and thirty-two nursing sisters.[231]

[231] Hennesey, *American Catholics*, 154–155.

Whatever the stature of Catholics and Catholicism in the American mind, it was clear that members of the Church of Rome were doing their part on both sides of this country's defining civil strife.

Debating Slavery

Meanwhile, both Protestants and Catholics engaged in deep theological discussions of the morality of slavery. The Bible is replete with passages that seem to argue for the legitimacy of slavery. But a new generation of what would have been considered liberal or progressive Protestants, such as Harriet Beecher Stowe and her brother, Reverend Henry Ward Beecher, was trying hard to assert what they believed to be Scripture's real emphasis: the love all Christians should have for one another. Perhaps the era's most blistering biblical attack on slavery came from George Cheever, a Congregationalist minister from upstate New York, in his work *The Guilt of Slavery and the Crime of Slaveholding, Demonstrated from the Hebrew and Greek Scriptures.* Cheever, it is said,

> labored diligently, if not too convincingly, to show that Old Testament "bondmen" and New Testament "servants" were not slaves at all. He certainly scored points in using biblical prohibitions against "manstealing" when he excoriated the internal trade in slaves, and, by implication, all slaveholding. Yet over and again he appealed to the inconsistency between slavery and "the benevolence commanded in the Scriptures."[232]

A much richer theological commentary on the morality of slavery came from European Catholics, progressive and conservative.

---

[232] Mark A. Noll, *The Civil War as a Theological Crisis* (Chapel Hill: University of North Carolina Press, 2006), 44.

Faith and Fury

Progressive Catholic writers, found in such areas as Quebec, France, Switzerland, and Ireland, were quick to dismiss biblical remarks apparently favoring slavery and simply called for immediate emancipation. They argued that slavery was not only unchristian but totally at odds with the precepts of republican institutions. Writers such as Bishop Félix Dupanloup, onetime ordinary of Orleans, France, and Augustin Cochin, a French politician who enjoyed a central place among liberal Catholics of his time, begged Catholics to look to scriptural examples of love and brotherhood.

> Cochin challenged defenders of modern slavery to stop taking "arguments" from the Bible: "Let them rather take examples." His conclusion resounded: "On the day that the law of the Jews shall become the law of one of the self styled Christian Southern States of the American Union, immense progress will be accomplished, and the unhappy slaves may await and catch a glimpse of full liberty."[233]

But more conservative Catholics played an equally important role in European Catholic journalism, especially with their emphasis on the spiritual authority of the Church and the temporal authority of the popes, who then still ruled the Papal States. Taking Gregory XVI and Pius IX as their lead, such writers and thinkers were skeptical about the "supposed virtues of modern society — including democracy, unrestricted capitalism, free speech, liberty of conscience, public schools, denominational pluralism, and the separation of church and state."[234] At the same time, they also entertained serious doubts about what they perceived to be modern tendencies to undermine "paternal authority, corporate

[233] Augustin Cochin, *The Results of Slavery*, trans. Mary Booth (Boston: Walker, Wise, 1863), cited in Noll, *The Civil War as a Theological Crisis*, 136.
[234] Noll, *The Civil War as a Theological Crisis*, 138.

economic solidarity, disciplined public utterance, consciences bent to the truth, religious education, Catholic supremacy, and a well regulated cooperation of church and state." [235]

In Quebec, an expatriate American, Jules-Paul Tardivel, described American republicanism as an "essentially anti-Christian extension" of the godlessness of the French Revolution. In Germany, a political and historical newspaper founded by Joseph Gorres, aided by his well-known colleague Ignace Dollinger, aimed at promoting Catholic devotional life and traditional Catholic theology to influence the political and social development of the modern German state. Their greatest enemies were "political and social liberalism, state-dominated churches, and progressive Protestantism." [236]

But what one author has described as the "gold standard" for Catholic commentary on the American Civil War was the Roman Jesuit publication *La Civiltà Cattolica*. Founded in 1850 by a group of Italian Jesuits at the request of Pope Pius IX, the publication had continued to grow in prestige since then. Pius had become disillusioned with modern notions of liberalism, democracy, and progress, and he desired a journal in which renowned Catholic scholars would publish Catholic responses to modern-day errors. Their editorial positions tried to walk a fine line between rapprochement with liberal society and capitulation to ultramontane—that is, entirely papally directed—solutions to problems of modernity.

> *La Civilta cattolica*'s general position [on American slavery] resembled in some respects the stance of American modern emancipationists.... Where it went further was in adding long historical accounts of papal actions against the excesses of ancient, medieval, and modern slavery. The

[235] Ibid.
[236] Ibid., 140.

basic argument maintained that, unlike radical liberals, the Catholic Church could never categorically condemn slavery, but that it had nonetheless worked consistently through its entire history to mitigate the wrongs of slavery, to move toward gradual and peaceful emancipation, and to act for the benefit of slaves and masters in harmony together.[237]

The journal's contributors observed that slavery was not, of itself, contrary to the laws of nature—but that the institution should never be allowed ride over the person's basic human rights to life, sustenance, and so on. They found support for this view in Scripture: The apostles Peter and Paul had both advised slaves how to act with regard to their masters, but also masters how they must treat their slaves.[238] Properly understood, the kind of relationship of authority between master and slave was acceptable—but it was easily abused and had been quite seriously abused in the American system.

Indeed, the Roman Jesuits contrasted the Church's proper approach to mitigating the evils that slavery tended to create with what the paper called the more utilitarian approach found in America, exemplified by Abraham Lincoln. Considering Lincoln's promise to preserve the Union first, with partial or no emancipation if necessary, the journal observed that "only when it became useful as a war stratagem did Lincoln move against slavery." What had done more to mitigate slavery over the centuries, the journal asked: the "steady practices of the Church" or the approach in America, where "the philosophy of revolution was so strong?"[239] It was better, La Civiltà Cattolica meant to say, for slavery to be phased out through the kind of moral suasion by which all come

[237] Ibid., 146.
[238] Eph. 6:7; Col. 3:22; 1 Pet. 2:18.
[239] Noll, The Civil War as a Theological Crisis, 149.

to recognize the humanity of all, rather than merely as a means to some other—and, in this case, violent—political end.

The journal saw this kind of utilitarianism as a foundational problem in the American system, and specifically as the heritage of the Reformation. Protestant sects, agreeing on viewing the individual as "standing in a direct relationship with Jesus Christ," had excluded Catholic doctrine "concerning the nature and authority of the church as a divine institution established by God for the salvation of men." The idea of mediating authorities between God and man was gone, with implications for the American view of political authority. This had begun, the argument went, with the seventeenth-century English Puritans who had sought to establish their religious beliefs, leading, in turn, to the enshrined concept of separation of church and state. This idea was at the heart of the Protestant revolt of the sixteenth century, a type of "religious individualism."

By the winter of 1861, *La Civiltà Cattolica* was arguing that European liberals who looked on the American experiment with such awe should take a second look, in view of the breakup of the Union. The journal made the somewhat cheeky observation that the breakup of the United States was in keeping with its "history as an experiment in Protestant public order."[240]

While there was much to praise in American religion, the Jesuits nonetheless saw a "great mistake," a "missing principle ... dissolving a great union." That missing element was "religious unity." Reconciliation, so the Jesuits thought, would elude the Americans "because they are divided on a moral question, and moral questions are fundamentally grounded in religious dogma."[241]

[240] Ibid., 147–153.
[241] Ibid., 154.

Faith and Fury

Some of this was exemplified in the life of Lincoln, a man who never formally joined a church and who, through most of his life, seemed to reject the Calvinism inherited from his parents. A study some years ago of his Gettysburg Address saw in it a possible "rebirth" of Christianity in the chief executive. In the speech, the president made no specific reference to Christianity, nor would he have been previously familiar with the idea of sanctifying a piece of ground for the burial of the dead. In fact, if he had truly realized the religious significance of what was being done at the Gettysburg cemetery that day, he might have felt uncomfortable participating. It seemed that only after carefully observing the at-mosphere at the cemetery that day—the prayers, the hymns, the bowed heads—did he inserted into his address the phrase "under God have a new birth of freedom."

And yet, whatever expectations he may have taken to Get-tysburg, however reluctant he was to make a public profes-sion of Christianity, much of what Lincoln said carried the rhythms of the Bible. This was the music of the ancient Hebrew and Greek turned into King James's English. This was the language he was raised on. "Four score and seven years ago." Psalm 90: "The days of our years are three score and ten," one of the best known sentences of the Book. "Brought forth" is not only the biblical way to announce a birth, including that of Mary's "first born Son," but the phrase that describes the Israelites being "brought forth" from slavery in Egypt."[242]

In combination with the words of his second inaugural on March 3, 1865 — "with firmness in the right, as God gives us to

---

[242] Gabor Boritt, The Gettysburg Gospel: The Lincoln Speech Nobody Knows (New York: Simon and Schuster, 2006), 120.

see the right"—this could be used to advance the notion that the Protestant Christianity of his youth was starting to reclaim him. On the other hand, as has been pointed out, Lincoln spoke also to the secularists in the audience in Gettysburg that day, "for in some part he remained one of them ... [he] could not accept the Christian Doctrine of sin and redemption, kept mostly silent about Jesus, and showed no inclination to build a personal relationship with God."[243] While some Christians might have been disappointed that he was not overly zealous, and some secularists might have been chagrined that religiosity had overcome him, it appeared the "majorities embraced him as one of their own":

> The rationalism of the Enlightenment combined with Protestant conscience. Lincoln's nine sentences had been welcomed by opening applause, interrupted by applause five times, and followed by applause. His perhaps two-and-a-half minute speech grew into something like three minutes. The people loved him. Lincoln had both voiced the beliefs of mainstream America and urged America on toward a "new Birth."[244]

La Civiltà Cattolica had summarized America very well.

The European Theater

Throughout the war years, diplomacy, especially with principal European nations, was a high priority of government officials on both sides. There were often fears of intervention, especially by England, France, and even Spain. The Vatican's position was also not to be taken lightly, because the weight of its moral authority could have lasting ramifications.

[243] Ibid., 121.
[244] Ibid.

Faith and Fury

England set the pace for the rest of Europe: For example, French Emperor Napoleon III would make no move unless England acted first. The North was concerned about both nations: England could have been a source of naval vessels for the Confederacy, and France might also have recognized the new country and given substantial aid.

For the Union, Secretary of State William H. Seward generally handled foreign affairs as he saw fit and kept his president informed as needed. Most historians have felt that he did a fine job, ably assisted by the U.S. ambassador to England, Charles Francis Adams. In France, U.S. minister William Dayton played a lesser role, while the consul in Paris, John Bigelow, carried on most of the important work. Also figuring significantly was Senator Charles Sumner of Massachusetts, chairman of the Senate Foreign Relations Committee. With eleven states out of the union, every weapon, including diplomacy, would have to be used to restore unity.

Lincoln's government felt it had to avoid all forms of European intervention, even mediation, because if they rejected it, help might be offered to the Confederacy. And if England officially recognized the independence of the Confederacy, Lincoln felt the situation could develop as it did with the intervention of France during the War for American Independence. Even a modest influx of British resources and materiel for the Confederacy, it was feared, could shift the outcome.

Many in the South, on the other hand, felt that either England or France would be so in need of cotton they would have to intervene in some way on the Confederacy's behalf. As it turned out, no drastic shortage occurred in Europe; in fact, the British seemed quite content to have stopped receiving surplus cotton. When shortages did begin to occur late in 1862, the North was not quite so concerned about intervention. King Cotton diplomacy never worked as the South had hoped.

In fact, British attitudes on the war never reached a fever pitch either way; some initial fears of a major uprising in England favoring one side or the other never materialized. It is true that many in the British aristocracy favored the lifestyle they observed in the South, and it is also true that the American form of government was still relatively new, and that many political conservatives in England would have been happy to see the experiment fail. These points gave some credence to the Northern fear of British intervention on behalf of the South, and, by the summer of 1862, there were many in England who feared that neither side was going to win the war.

A motion was introduced in Parliament in June 1862, in light of General George B. McClellan's failure in the Peninsula Campaign, to intervene for the Confederacy, but it never resulted in any action by the ministry of Viscount Palmerston. But after the Second Battle of Bull Run, in August 1862, and General Robert E. Lee's subsequent invasion, thinking changed in Britain, and the Palmerston ministry felt that if either Washington or Baltimore fell to the Confederates, England should indeed intervene. With the decisive Northern victory at Antietam, though, British thinking changed again, now in favor of an ultimate Union victory. By 1863, with the battles of Gettysburg, Vicksburg, and Chattanooga, all chance of intervention had ended, and the priorities of the British had shifted from the American Civil War to the balance of power in Europe.[245]

Hughes's Junket

Early in the war, the North was the first to see the value of the Catholic Church's cooperation in diplomacy. In October 1861,

---

[245]Though England had abolished the institution of slavery some decades earlier, most historians believe that the South's attachment to it would not have precluded British intervention on their behalf.

Archbishop Hughes received a cable from his old friend Secretary Seward, whom the prelate always addressed in letters as "My Dear Governor," to meet with him about a matter that had recently been discussed by Lincoln's cabinet. The proposal was that the archbishop and some other like-minded individuals be sent to Europe, at the government's expense, "to promote healthful opinions about the war, the righteous cause of national unity, and the need for foreign governments either to support the United States as friend and ally or to refrain from giving such support to the rebels."[246] It was understood that the members of the company were not to hold any sort of diplomatic title, had no power to negotiate treaties, and were not, in any way, to speak publicly for the United States government. The plan became all the more urgent when it became known that two confederate agents had run the blockade, sailed to Havana, and were making their way to Europe to advance the Confederate cause.[247]

Hughes was to travel in company with a bishop of the Episcopalian church, Charles McIlvaine, who subsequently was to go on to England. Hughes strongly recommended his old friend Thurlow Weed, editor of the *Albany Evening Journal*, to accompany him. The two had been friends at least since the fight for Catholic schools in New York in the 1840s, and Weed was a man in whose company the archbishop could be completely relaxed. While Seward had initially been reluctant about this part of the arrangement, he did agree, though Weed was to pay his own expenses, a stipulation to which the editor did not object.[248] While the administration was

---

[246] Loughery, *Dagger John*, 5.

[247] James Mason and John Slidell.

[248] Thurlow Weed (1797–1882) was a New York newspaper publisher and Whig and Republican politician. He was the principal political adviser to William H. Seward and was instrumental in the presidential nominations of William Henry Harrison, Zachary Taylor,

taking a gamble in choosing a Catholic prelate for such a mission, this particular bishop

> had been courted by Henry Clay and Winfield Scott. He had dined with Millard Fillmore in the White House and was on friendly terms with James Buchanan. He had addressed Congress at the invitation of John Quincy Adams. He had met two popes in Rome and, on his first trip to Europe in 1839, had been introduced to the Emperor and Empress of Austria.[249]

Even more to the point, "a Catholic Archbishop, if he could get the ear of a Catholic monarch—and the monarch's wife, the empress Eugenie, a woman known to have a lively interest in foreign affairs herself—might, just might, do more than official communiques and ministerial briefs."[250] With this in mind, the trio departed on November 7, 1861, on what would prove to be a most interesting sojourn. Before leaving, however, Hughes felt it important to convey his true feelings to Seward regarding the country's situation. No political friend of the South's theory of government, he totally approved of the blockade of Southern ports, and strongly felt that

> the President is the responsible man of this nation. No President has ever been so severely tested as he. A great conspiracy, of which he knew nothing, was in existence when he was elected. It burst forth immediately after his inauguration. There was no preparation to meet its extravagance, for it was a foolish enterprise, and a snare sprung upon him before he could be aware of it. Things are changed, however, and

---

and John C. Fremont. He was a particularly strong player in New York State Republican politics.
[249] Loughery, *Dagger John*, 7.
[250] Ibid., 10.

the country begins to know, if it did not know before, that Mr. Lincoln is not less than equal to the emergency which had been prepared for the first months of his administration. He had been fortunate in surrounding himself with advisers competent from their understanding of the whole case, from their ability in their several departments, from their unity as a cabinet, and their loyal devotion to the interests of the country, to strengthen and sustain its chief magistrate during the unexpected events that have occurred since his election.[251]

For his part, the secretary of state assured the archbishop, "I submit your letters to the President, who reads all you write to me with deep interest."[252]

No sooner had the mission begun than an international scandal erupted. The U.S. Navy illegally captured the two Confederate diplomats, James Mason and John Slidell, from the British ship on which they were traveling. The U.S.S. *San Jacinto*, commanded by Captain Charles Wilkes, intercepted the British mail packet R.M.S. *Trent* and removed the two diplomats as contraband of war. The envoys were bound for Britain and France to make a case for diplomatic recognition of the Confederacy, and possibly to obtain military or financial support. While the British protested strongly, most Americans applauded the capture — with many in the South hoping it would lead to a permanent rupture in Anglo-American relations. For their part, the British saw the incident as a violation of their rights as a neutral nation, and as an insult to their national honor. They demanded an apology and the release of the prisoners, while they also took steps to strengthen their military forces in Canada and the Atlantic.

[251] Hassard, *Life of Most Rev. John Hughes*, 445–446.
[252] Ibid., 447.

President Lincoln and his advisers did not want to risk war with England over the issue. The administration announced that the diplomats were to be released, and they disavowed the action of Captain Wilkes—though they offered no formal apology. Mason and Slidell resumed their voyage to England, but, in the end, their efforts were unsuccessful.

Writing to Seward from Paris, Hughes saw two possible solutions to this affair: The French emperor could act as an impartial arbiter, or the prisoners should be tried according to the laws of the land—and while there was no doubt they would be condemned to death, the archbishop suggested to Lincoln, "I presume that it would be competent for the President, in the exercise of his constitutional privileges, to commute the sentence of the culprits, and allow them, under that commutation, to go on board any neutral vessel, and forsake the United States forever, except at the peril of their lives, or by virtue of an act of Congress permitting them to return to the country which they have left nothing undone to betray."[253]

The archbishop would wait one month before being received by Emperor Napoleon III and Empress Eugenie on Christmas Eve 1861. He had secured the audience, he admitted to Seward, merely by writing to the emperor "as one man would write to another, in a polite and brief note to the effect: Sir, I wish to have the honor of a conversation with you."[254] To the archbishop's request that the

---

[253] Hughes to Seward, December 5, 1861, cited in Hassard, *Life of Most Rev. John Hughes*, 459.

[254] Hughes to Seward, December 27, 1861, Seward Manuscript Collection, University of Rochester; New York Archdiocesan Archives, Guilday Collection; Hassard, *Life of Most Rev. John Hughes*, 463–464, cited in Charles P. Connor, *The American Catholic Political Position at Mid Century: Archbishop Hughes as a Test Case* (unpublished Ph.D. thesis, Fordham University, New York City, 1979), 376.

emperor act as a mediator in the Trent Affair, Napoleon replied that what was involved was a point of honor between two equally proud nations, each duty-bound, and thus arbitration by a third party would likely be unacceptable to both. Beyond this, Napoleon stated that the United States made an error in the high tariff it had imposed on foreign importations, a criticism resonant with the South' position. Hughes responded that the causes of secession went far deeper than this specific tariff.

Having exhausted that topic, Hughes stressed the value of France and England cultivating a cotton crop in their respective colonies, while assuring the empress of the effectiveness of the North's blockade. These appear to have been the only substantive issues discussed, or at least recorded, in the one-hour-and-ten-minute interview, which was not "unsatisfactory or discouraging,"[255] and ended with the prelate imparting his episcopal blessing to the young prince regent. With the view from London, Weed wrote to Hughes, "There were curious conjectures about the object and nature of your interview with the Emperor," adding that "the apprehensions of war are abating, though we have no knowledge of the intentions of our government."[256]

Hughes had envisioned a lengthy stay in Europe, visiting any number of nations for the administration's benefit, but Seward felt this was unnecessary. Nonetheless, he did spend some four months

[255] Hughes to Thurlow Weed, December 24, 1861, Weed Manuscript Collection, University of Rochester. See also Hughes to Seward, December 27, 1861, Hughes to Mrs. Rodrique, December 27, 1861, in Hassard, *Life of Most Rev. John Hughes*, 468. See also Connor, *American Catholic Political Position*, 377. Mrs. Rodrique was the archbishop's sister.

[256] Thurlow Weed to Hughes, January 6, 1862, Hughes Manuscript Collection, Archdiocese of New York, cited in Connor, *American Catholic Political Position*, 377.

in Rome, where he spoke with the reigning pontiff, Pius IX, and met with the Spanish bishops, who were in the Eternal City for the canonization of the Japanese martyrs, to warn them of possible designs the Confederacy might have on Cuba. Hughes found a good deal of favorable opinion in Rome for the North, as he had in France, and, for that matter, in England during his brief time there. In two missives to Seward, he told the secretary that one could not find a public servant "more capable, more honest, more moderate, more safe and reliable" than President Lincoln and that the press in countries he visited regarded Seward very highly.[257]

The conversations Hughes had with Pius IX while in Rome seemed to pertain more to the spiritual aspect of his episcopal office. In fact, no evidence has ever been uncovered to suggest that the two men personally discussed America's domestic strife. Several factors account for this: unfamiliarity on the pope's part with the particulars of the American war; possible repercussions among European powers if the Church's leader attempted to intervene by word or action; and the nativist outcry that could ensue in the United States should it appear the Church were intervening in the country's affairs.

The only action Pius IX did take was to dispatch a letter to the archbishop some three months after he returned to New York, and a similar one to the archbishop of New Orleans, John Mary Odin, stating that he was impelled by "no political reasons [and] no earthly considerations" when he urged both prelates to use their offices to advance the cause of peace as quickly as possible. The message was typical of papal correspondence in that it was veiled in ambiguity and full of lofty expressions of peaceful sentiments; it

---

[257]Hughes to Seward, February 21, 1862, Seward Manuscript Collection; Hassard, *Life of Most Rev. John Hughes*, 473–474, cited in Connor, *American Catholic Political Position*, 381.

was simultaneously carefully crafted for the contemporary American situation and a genuine expression of the Holy Father's interest in world peace as the Vicar of Christ.[258] In addition, Hughes confided to Seward that the information he had received from the papal secretary of state and the prefect of the Sacred Congregation *Propaganda Fidei*, Cardinals Antonelli and Barnabo, was that, far from being in any way critical of Hughes's mission for the United States government, the pope showed a "disposition to confer additional honors" on the archbishop of New York.[259]

Hughes left the Eternal City on a more pessimistic note than when he arrived. Perhaps it was because his papal meetings had failed to produce, in his mind, tangible results favorable to the Northern cause; more practically, it likely also stemmed from what he perceived as a change in position in the British press—an increase in anti-Americanism through 1862. Italian and French newspapers tended to take their lead on American matters from British journalism, and the current tone was no longer "favorable to the prospects of insurrection or rebellion against our Washington

[258] For this reason, Pius's words have lent themselves to multiple interpretations. Many have argued that his ambiguity merely disguised his sympathy for the Confederacy. While this may be the case, it is possible and has been argued that too much has been read into letters such as this one and those from Cardinals Antonelli and Barnabo to officials of the Confederacy, none of which ever explicitly expressed Vatican support for the South. It must be said, however, that the natural conclusion one would draw from the predominance of communication between Richmond and Rome is that Pius IX sympathized with the Southern cause. Rena Andrews, *Archbishop Hughes and the Civil War* (unpublished Ph.D. thesis, University of Chicago, 1935), 204–209, cited in Connor, *American Catholic Political Position*, 384.

[259] Hughes to Seward, March 1, 1862, Hughes Manuscript Collection; Hassard, *Life of Most Rev. John Hughes*, 474, cited in Connor, *American Catholic Political Position*, 384.

government," but rather one that adopted a "tone of sympathy for the vanquished ... with a sting of malaise against the unity of the American people under the sacred constitution of the whole country."[260] While there were exceptions, Hughes stood by the general observation that "there are no friends on this side of the Atlantic."[261] Before his European sojourn ended, Hughes returned to his native land of Ireland, once again to attempt to speak to any and all about the uprightness of the Northern cause.[262]

Once back in New York, the archbishop lost no opportunity to champion the Union, urging in a sermon in Saint Patrick's Cathedral that all citizens put forth their strength and finish the war in one gallant effort. He strongly supported Lincoln's call for six hundred thousand men, saying, "If I had a voice in the councils of the country, I would say let volunteering continue.... It is not cruel, this. This is mercy, this is humanity.... [Anything that will] put an end to this drenching with blood the whole surface of the country, that will be humanity."[263]

The Lynch Mission

Naturally, Southern Catholics were not at all happy with either the Hughes mission or his strong rhetoric following his trip. He was strongly criticized by Baltimore's *Catholic Mirror*, though he

[260] Hughes to Seward, May 23, 1862, Seward Manuscript Collection, cited in Connor, *American Catholic Political Position*, 385.

[261] Hughes to Seward, May 10, 1862, Seward Manuscript Collection, cited in Connor, *American Catholic Political Position*, 385.

[262] Recent historical studies have alleged that Irish public opinion consistently supported the South, for such diverse reasons as Britain's commercial prosperity, her prestige as a world power, the principle of self-determination on the slavery question, and the nationalistic character of the Southern rebellion.

[263] Hassard, *Life of Most Rev. John Hughes*, 487.

defended himself in the pages of the *Metropolitan Record* in New York, resulting in an "acrimonious controversy which continued several months."[264]

In the Confederate Museum in Charleston, South Carolina, one may see a replica of the Crown of Thorns, which was sent to Confederate President Jefferson Davis by Pope Pius IX. Davis, a native of Mississippi, had been educated by the Dominican Fathers at their first foundation, Saint Rose's, in Springfield, Kentucky. As a young man, Davis had entertained thoughts of becoming a Catholic but was advised to wait. It is not surprising, then, that Davis would seek Vatican recognition of the legitimacy of the Confederate government. He sent Bishop Lynch of Charleston as a special emissary to Rome with this in mind.

Almost since its inception, the United States government had consular representation in the Papal States, and in the mid-nineteenth century, Congress approved a proposal by President James K. Polk to have a chargé d'affaires at the Papal Court. These representatives had always been received most graciously, and, in time, the Vatican appointed a consul in New York, and then twenty-one vice-consuls in American cities, including Charleston.

The Vatican's official newspaper, *L'Osservatore Romano*, and the Jesuit-edited *La Civiltà Cattolica* had both expressed skepticism about the Lincoln administration's aims and motives. Writers in both publications favored the continuation of the American union but expressed doubts about the administration's genuine concern for the slaves, and the violence that could erupt if emancipation became a reality. While the latter publication did not carry the official weight of the former, the text of every issue was still read and approved by the Vatican Secretariat of State, and the pope himself met with the editorial board every other week to review plans for the

---

[264] Ibid., 489.

forthcoming issue. Given all this, historians have generally argued that Vatican and papal sympathies leaned toward the Confederacy.

The Confederate government took notice of the Holy Father's letter to Archbishops Hughes and Odin and saw in it a possible opening to the Holy See. The Confederacy was especially interested in whatever influence Rome might have in discouraging young Catholic men, especially from Ireland and the southern German states, from immigrating to the United States and joining the Union Army. To this end, the South began dispatching agents to Ireland by 1863. Especially well known was the Irish-born Confederate chaplain Father John Bannon, who accepted a commission to be a secret Confederate agent. He was well connected in his native land and had easy access to the Irish hierarchy and clergy. It is not altogether clear to what extent his efforts were successful.

Father Bannon did play a role in communication between the Confederate president and Rome. Jefferson Davis prepared a letter to be delivered to Pius IX and gave it to Father Bannon to take through the blockade. Bannon, in turn, delivered the letter to Henry Hotze, a Confederate propaganda agent in London. Hotze then delivered it to Ambrose Dudley Mann, the Confederate Commissioner based in Brussels, Belgium. After expressing kind sentiments of esteem, Davis got to the point:

> That we desire no evil to our enemies, nor do we covet any of their possessions, but we are only struggling to the end that they shall cease to devastate our land and inflict useless and cruel slaughter upon our people, and that we be permitted to live at peace with all mankind, under our own laws and institutions, which protect every man in the enjoyment not only of his temporal rights, but of the freedom of worshiping God according to his own faith.[265]

[265] Cited in Heisser and White, *Patrick N. Lynch*, 98.

Faith and Fury

Dudley Mann was the first high-ranking Confederate to be received in audience by Pius IX. The Holy Father noted that the Lincoln administration had created the impression that the Union was fighting for the abolition of slavery and observed that it might be more prudent to pursue gradual emancipation, rather than face the unpredictable consequences of an immediate mass liberation. Mann replied that such considerations were the concern of individual states rather than the central government.

Later, Pius addressed a letter to President Davis, similar to that which he had sent to the two American archbishops, pleading in the loftiest terms for peace. It was that letter that accounted for the Confederate government's decision to send a high-ranking Catholic to Rome to plead their cause. After initial discussions about whether that person should be a layman or a cleric, the government decided on Bishop Lynch.

The bishop's commission was signed by President Davis and his secretary of state, Judah P. Benjamin,[266] on March 4, 1864—two months after the death of Archbishop Hughes. He was given full power "to agree, treat, consult and negotiate concerning all matters and subjects interesting to both governments, and to conclude and sign Treaties, Convention or Conventions."[267] This was a far more sweeping mandate than Hughes had received two years earlier, though given the newness of the Confederacy, one wonders what diplomatic weight it carried abroad.

Bishop Lynch traveled with two young men, Conrad Wise Chapman, son of the Virginia artist John Gadsby Chapman, and Daniel J. Quigley, a Charleston seminarian studying at Mount Saint Mary's and soon to complete his studies at Rome's North American College. The bishop took lodging on the fashionable Via Condotti

---

[266] Benjamin, a Jew, was married to a Roman Catholic.
[267] Heisser and White, *Patrick N. Lynch*, 103.

and called on Cardinal Barnabo, the *Propaganda Fidei* prefect, who, very interestingly, told him that at the time Pius IX had written his plea for peace to the two archbishops, he had had no idea how seriously the two sections of America were divided. He also told Lynch that when the pope's subsequent letter to President Davis had been published, the U.S. minister in the Papal States, Rufus King, had inquired why Davis had been addressed in such exalted terms. Barnabo had replied to King that the Vatican believed "the Confederate Government had an existence, and exercised the functions of a Government."[268]

On the Fourth of July 1864, Lynch and his party were received by the Holy Father in his "quality as a Bishop," not as a Confederate emissary, just as any bishop making his five-year *ad limina* visit to the Holy See would be received. Once again, as in the case of Archbishop Hughes, Pius spoke in veiled terms. He inquired about the state of Charleston in the wake of the bombardment of Fort Sumter, deplored the destruction of human life since the outset of the war, strongly asserted that his office would not permit him to serve as an arbiter in any way, praised the work of the religious orders of Sisters on the battlefield, and argued once more against sudden emancipation, favoring instead a period of preparation for the freedom of the slaves at a "future opportune time."[269]

A curious episode occurred later in July, when the British minister to the Holy See, Lord Odo Russell, was received by the pope. Russell reported that Pius had confided to him his sympathies for the South and personally wished them great success. He also noted that there appeared to have been more conversions to Catholicism from the South than from the North, though this

[268] Ibid., 109.
[269] Ibid., 111.

may have been because more reports and letters arrived from Southern bishops.[270]

As to the success of the Lynch mission:

> The end result ... can be judged as nothing more than inconclusive. He never presented himself in any official capacity to Pope Pius IX. He had friendly meetings with various Vatican officials, and he impressed them with his intelligence and sincerity, yet no official responses to his conversations were ever pronounced. He became subject to suspicion and condemnation from officials of the soon-to-be triumphant government of the United States and thus was forced to remain in Rome as a wanted belligerent-fugitive until a presidential pardon ended his exile. In this mission he risked much and lost much. The Confederate States gained little and soon were forced to surrender.[271]

Church and State in the South

Back in America, the Church was not always able to remain as above the fray, as Her leaders would have liked. Divided allegiances in the city of Baltimore proved to be especially sticky. That city's Archbishop, Francis P. Kenrick (himself a Union sympathizer), asked that a prayer written decades earlier by Archbishop John Carroll for government officials—including the president of the United States—be read at Mass. A number of pro-secession priests of the cathedral parish refused to say it, and so the archbishop went out himself after Mass to do so, but much of the congregation walked out, while others "rustled papers and silks."[272]

[270] Ibid.
[271] Ibid., 112.
[272] Hennesey, *American Catholics*, 154.

A far more complicated story involved the Bishop of Natchez, Mississippi, William Henry Elder. Bishop Elder, the descendant of English Catholics who had settled in Southern Maryland centuries before, was born and raised in Baltimore. Whatever his private political sympathies, as a shepherd he felt it was his duty not to take sides but simply to inform Catholics of their duty to pledge allegiance to the government under which they were living, "without reference to the rights or the wisdom of making the separation — or the grounds for it."[273] He instructed his clergy to tell the people not to recommend secession, but also that nothing in their religion forbade them from accepting it.

There had been a custom in the Natchez cathedral of offering prayers for the civil authorities of the United States, and, after the creation of the Confederacy, for the officials of the new government. In mid-1863, Elder informed President Lincoln that he had laid aside these prayers, though, because of the controversy they were causing and had substituted other traditional prayers, such as the Litany of the Saints.

But in the early part of 1864, while the region was under Union occupation, the federal commander in Natchez demanded that Bishop Elder recite a specific prayer for all federal authorities; failure to do so would be "proof of disloyalty which would be subject to punishment."[274] Elder protested directly to the president that his episcopal authority was being interfered with and sent the missive also to the president of Georgetown University in Washington, who forwarded it to a Catholic member of Congress, who, in turn, delivered it to Secretary of War Edwin Stanton. The same day, the commander in Natchez received a letter from an assistant adjutant general informing him he was not to "proscribe any form of prayer

[273] Peters, *The Catholic Bishops*, 158.
[274] Ibid., 174.

or of service or in any other way interfere in matters of church administration except in cases of disloyalty when you will report the facts to this Department and take its orders."[275]

In June 1864, a new commander took over, with a new special order that a pastor who neglected to offer prayers for the president of the United States would be prohibited from exercising any public functions in Natchez and would "render himself liable at the discretion of the commandant, to banishment beyond the lines of the federal forces."[276] Bishop Elder was absent from his diocese when this order was published but, upon return, respectfully declined to comply. The issue was tabled until a third commander, even after conversations with Elder, felt that orders were orders and planned to remove the bishop. In July, Elder asked Secretary Stanton to intervene and settle the matter, though after three days no word had come down, and the current commander's order, that the Catholic bishop was "still in rebellion against the United States, and ill disposed toward the government thereof,"[277] remained in force.

The commander ordered the closure of St. Mary's Cathedral in Natchez and all other churches under Elder's jurisdiction in which the prayers for federal authorities were not being read. Elder, meanwhile, was ordered to report to "the officer commanding the U.S. forces at Vidalia [Louisiana] and remain within his military lines under penalty of the immediate execution of the before named orders."[278]

At no time was the bishop held in close confinement. For a few days, he remained in the town hotel; then he moved to a private family home. As soon as he arrived, he attempted again to

[275] Ibid.
[276] Ibid., 175.
[277] Ibid.
[278] Ibid., 176.

correspond with Stanton. While Elder didn't hear from the secretary, he did receive a letter from a friend in Washington informing him that the commanding officer of the Department of the Mississippi had been told that the rights of Catholics were not to be interfered with and that this was to be passed on to subordinates in the form of an order. And so, early in August, the bishop was released and allowed to return home. The press was filled with various accounts of this story, many of them wildly exaggerated. To quell speculation, Elder requested that his vicar-general issue a statement of the true facts of the case. As to the historical judgment of Elder:

> Throughout the crisis of secession and war, when he was not subjected to enemy control, Bishop Elder recognized that the government of Mississippi and of the CONFEDER-ATE STATES were the *de facto* governments and the ones to which he and his fellow citizens owed their allegiance and support. With the problems occasioned by the blockade and the consequent shortages, he manfully wrestled although forced to utilize improvisations. For the men in military service he maintained an unflagging concern and nobly tried to supply them with chaplains. When Natchez was occupied by the Federal army Bishop Elder without hesitation professed obedience to the Union, but he stoutly and successfully resisted all attempts by commanders to interfere with his ecclesiastical administration. A true son of the Church, William Henry Elder served it to the utmost of his ability. At *the same time* he displayed a high sense of patriotism and civic responsibility during the crisis that overtook his divided country.[279]

[279] Ibid., 178.

Faith and Fury

Catholic Gettysburg

Civil War historians largely agree that the turning point of the conflict was the Battle of Gettysburg on the first three days of July 1863. The town of Gettysburg was settled as early as 1780 and had a decidedly Protestant cast. Anti-Catholicism had been rampant for decades; nativists and Know-Nothings had made advances there as elsewhere, and there was significant hostility toward foreigners and Catholics, even as the thriving parish of Saint Francis Xavier sprang up.

Lutherans were especially prominent in Gettysburg, owing to the presence of a significant seminary, and were quite vocal in their disagreement with the Catholic practice of infant Baptism. Referring to it as a "Romish superstition," they believed that all children who died young went directly to Heaven and could not be penalized simply because of the neglect of their parents.[280] The principal anti-Catholic mouthpiece in Gettysburg was *The Star and Banner*, a newspaper published by a prominent abolitionist attorney, David Buehler. He described foreigners (and, by extension, Catholics) as a "mass of undesirable social material in the shape of restless agrarian agitators, criminals and paupers."[281] They brought "crime and poverty ... from the hotbeds of European vice and destitution" into small rural communities such as Gettysburg.[282]

Buehler saved his most serious contempt for Catholic Irish, often quoting America's founding Fathers on the dangers of diluting true Americanism with too broad a toleration for those whose background and upbringing were not suited to the country's values (at least as understood by certain newspaper editors). He alerted

---

[280] Steve Longenecker, *Gettysburg Religion* (New York: Fordham University Press, 2014), 92.
[281] Ibid., 93.
[282] Ibid.

his readers that a Jesuit conspiracy had made its way to the county. claiming that a special agent of the U.S. Postal System, an Irish Catholic, had entered the county incognito to have the local post-master removed. Though the postmaster remained in his position, and all attempts to have the postal system "prostitute to Jesuit purposes" apparently failed, Buehler still felt the local citizenry had not sufficiently risen to protest such an invasion of the community.

One would think that Catholics might have found life in Get-tysburg quite unbearable, but this does not appear to have been the case:

> Viewed broadly, antebellum Catholics, though remote from Gettysburg's Protestant mainstream in doctrine and polity, enjoyed general acceptance. Although some in the Border North public square detested Catholics and while never asking them to leave, denounced them for an unholy com-bination of political and religious sins, Pennsylvania's famed tolerance endured as a future saint laid the cornerstone and priests turned their backs on the congregation to pray in a language almost nobody else understood.... More than any other group, Catholics tested tolerance but without breaking it.[283]

Just a few miles south of Gettysburg lies the hamlet of Emmits-burg, Maryland, which had been home to Mount Saint Mary's Col-lege and Seminary since 1808.[284] An early history of the seminary

---

[283] Ibid., 97. The saint referred to was John N. Neumann, bishop of Philadelphia from 1852 to 1860.

[284] The seminary was begun in 1808 by Father John Dubois, S.S., an émigré from the French Revolution. The college, initially founded to be a source of revenue for the young seminary, followed two years later in 1810. A pleasant legend, perhaps more accurate than not, holds that General George Gordon Meade, commander of

relates that officially it was considered neutral ground. In fact, though, the sympathies of faculty and seminarians leaned strongly toward the South. The reasons for this largely paralleled those of other Southern-sympathizing Catholics, with an additional geographic factor:

> Added to these reasons was the large number of students from the Southern States, whose companionship and arguments greatly influenced the whole body. The greatest number of these was from New Orleans and other parts of Louisiana, and nearly every seaport from Vera Cruz in Mexico, along the gulf and the shores of the Atlantic Ocean to Baltimore had its representative.[285]

the Union forces at the Battle of Gettysburg, visited his sister, a member of Mother Seton's Daughters of Charity, to inform her and the community of the impending and dangerous crisis. The Sisters undertook a serious campaign of prayer, pleading with Heaven that Emmitsburg might be spared the ravages of battle. The final locale of the battle moved up the road, some ten or eleven miles, into Pennsylvania. For decades, a statue of Our Lady of Victory has stood on the grounds of the convent and motherhouse of the Emmitsburg Daughters of Charity in thanksgiving for the diversion of hostilities from Emmitsburg.

[285] Edward F. X. McSweeny, *The Story of the Mountain: Mount Saint Mary's College and Seminary, Emmitsburg, Maryland* (Emmitsburg: Weekly Chronicle, 1911), 11, 14–15. Father McSweeny, an early president of the Mount, lists the faculty this way: "The adherents of the South were: The President, Dr. McCaffrey; Henry McMurdie, Professor of Logic and Director of the Seminary; George H. Miles, Professor of English Literature; Col. Daniel Beltzhoover, a graduate of West Point and a class-mate of General Grant, Professor of Mathematics and Commandant of the Mountain Cadets; and James Hickey, professor of Writing and Drawing. The Union men were: Rev. John McCloskey, Vice President and Treasurer; Rev. Leonard Obermeyer and Rev. John B. Byrne, during the short time he stayed at the College during the war. Henry Dielman, Professor of Music,

A priest alumnus of the Mount stated of his rector of four decades earlier, a certain Dr. McCaffrey, that he displayed

> a very bitter feeling towards the North. Dr. McCaffrey in his remarks was exceedingly bitter. You know, all were hot, those from the North as well as those from the South. I do not remember Dr. McCaffrey showing any special feeling towards the college boys. I thought the college authorities were very generous to the boys from the South. I am sure we of the North asked no special favors. I remember him very kindly. If he made harsh remarks to others I do not know; he was very kind to me.... We had a very exciting time at the Commencement of 1863. Lee with his army was north of us. We had few visitors.[286]

While Gettysburg was a notably anti-Catholic town, the Union victory that spared it was due in no small measure to the "Fighting 69th," the famous Irish Catholic Brigade. These soldiers, as well as others, would then be called on before the end of the month to put down a disturbance in New York City, also involving Irish Catholics.

The Draft Riots

In August 1862, President Lincoln called on the states for three hundred thousand more soldiers to serve for nine months, ordering governors to draft from the militia if the quota could not be

---

and leader of the band and choir, and Jean Maurice, Professor of French, were neutrals. In the Seminary John D. Crimens was the most pronounced Republican or Abolitionist."

[286] Ibid., 13. The alumnus was Monsignor John F. Kearney of the class of 1862. He was a student prefect at the Seminary and was in attendance at the commencement of 1863.

filled by volunteers. As a result, riots broke out in Wisconsin and Indiana and threatened Pennsylvania. Then, in March 1863, just two months after the Emancipation Proclamation, Congress passed a draft in the form of the Enrollment Act, which precipitated the New York City Draft Riots of July 13–16, 1863. The draft stipulated that men could pay others to do their fighting for them or simply pay the government three hundred dollars in lieu of military service.

On Saturday, July 11, 1863, the provost marshal drew the first names for the draft, and they were published in the city's newspapers the following day. That afternoon, mobs started to gather, and the next day, when the draft resumed, the rioting began. "New York immigrants felt like scapegoats. Not only were they cannon fodder; they expected Blacks to flood into New York City where nobody doubted they would undercut the already atrocious market for unskilled workers."[287] Indeed, the mood in the city about the war had been negative for some time; the fact that a good deal of Southern cotton used to pass through the city accounted for a large number of Southern sympathizers. What followed was three days of arson, looting, lynching of several Black men, and, in the end, the loss of nearly one thousand lives. Federal troops from Gettysburg had to be diverted from their pursuit of Robert E. Lee to quell the riots. They were "in no mood to tolerate what they took to be an assault on the honor of their military service."[288]

Archbishop John Hughes was six months away from death, and in very poor health. Nonetheless, it was widely believed that his authority could quell the rioters, since most of them were members of

[287] Marlin, George J. and Brad Miner, *Sons of Saint Patrick: A History of the Archbishops of New York* (San Francisco: Ignatius Press, 2017), 75.
[288] Ibid.

182

his flock. A specific request came from Horatio Seymour, governor of New York, stating that while he did not wish to ask "anything inconsistent with your sacred duties," he hoped that Hughes could "with propriety aid the civil authorities at this crisis."[289]

The archbishop circulated a public notice throughout the city indicating that his health would not permit him to meet people individually, but that he would be able to come to the balcony of his residence and deliver an address to anyone who gathered.[290] It was estimated that three to four thousand came, "but they were apparently decent, well disposed working-men, not at all resembling the savage mob which had been burning, and pillaging, and killing for the previous three or four days."[291] Most contemporary observers who reported on the speech would agree with Hughes's earliest biographer that, though there were some sparks of his old brilliance and pointedness, it was, for the most part, "long and rambling, [and] indicated but too plainly that the disease which had destroyed his physical strength, had also weakened his mind, and that the Archbishop's speaking days were over."[292]

George Templeton Strong, a famous New York diarist not known for his love of Catholics or the Church, observed that it would have been far more merciful if the archbishop had died before having to give the address so as not to have to deliver "of himself in public such a piece of imbecility." He went on to observe that England had been right about the Irish all along: They were a "brutal, base, cruel people, not ready for civilized life in the United States."

[289] Hassard, *Life of Most Rev. John Hughes*, 499.
[290] The archbishop's residence was at the corner of Thirty-Sixth Street and Madison Avenue, the site of the present-day Pierpont Morgan Library.
[291] Hassard, *Life of Most Rev. John Hughes*, 500.
[292] Ibid.

Faith and Fury

Priests on the Lines

One of the greatest contributions the Church made during the Civil War came in the form of the chaplains who served the spiritual needs of the men who endured the fighting on both sides. This spiritual service had its beginnings with a letter Abraham Lincoln wrote to Archbishop Hughes, which is telling in several ways:

Archbishop Hughes,

Rt. Rev. Sir: I am sure you will pardon me if, in my ignorance, I do not address you with technical correctness. I find no law authorizing the appointment of chaplains for our hospitals; and yet the services of chaplains are more needed, perhaps, in the hospitals than with the healthy soldiers in the field. With this view, I have given a sort of quasi appointment (a copy of which I enclose) to each of three Protestant ministers, who have accepted, and entered upon the duties. If you perceive no objection, I will thank you to give me the name, or names, of one or more suitable persons of the Catholic Church to whom I may with propriety tender the same service. Many thanks for your kind and judicious letters to Gov. Seward, and which he regularly allows me the pleasure and the profit of perusing. With the highest respect, your obedient servant, A. Lincoln.[293]

Thus began the volunteering of many priests who accomplished untold good. Perhaps the best remembered in the Union Army was a member of the Congregation of Holy Cross from the University of Notre Dame, Father William Corby.

Corby was born in 1833 in Detroit, Michigan, to an Irish father and a Canadian mother. He attended public school until he was

---

[293] Hassard, *Life of Most Rev. John Hughes*, 445. The letter was dated from Washington, D.C., October 21, 1861.

sixteen, then worked in his father's real estate business. Notre Dame was only ten years in existence when he entered as a student; within a few years, he had begun studies for the priesthood and was eventually ordained for the Congregation of Holy Cross. He served as chaplain of the Eighty-Eighth New York Infantry, which was one of the five original regiments in the Irish Brigade. He is perhaps best known for giving general absolution to the Union soldiers preparing to go into battle at Gettysburg in July 1863, a scene depicted in an 1891 painting, *Absolution Under Fire*, by Paul Wood.[294]

After the war, Corby went on to serve first as vice president of Notre Dame, then two terms as president, from 1866 to 1872 and from 1877 to 1881. He would begin construction on the famed Basilica of the Sacred Heart, and, following the great Notre Dame fire of 1879, he rebuilt Old Main with its golden dome. He also founded Notre Dame's Law School.

Corby also contributed to Civil War history through his memoirs. Perhaps the most remarkable story he recounted was his attempt to save the life of an enlisted man, Thomas R. Dawson. Dawson was a member of the Nineteenth Massachusetts regiment who had been condemned to death on charges of desertion, drunkenness, and rape. The two men who had wandered from camp and broken into a country home with him escaped, but Dawson did not. Corby vouched for Dawson's character, and the officers of his regiment did not want to see him die. They drew up a petition

[294]Of the Brigade's three thousand men, only about five hundred remained, and more than a third of them were either killed or wounded in the battle. Corby's action was dramatized in the 1993 film *Gettysburg*. A statue by Samuel Murray depicting Father Corby with his right hand raised in absolution now stands where he stood more than 150 years ago. It was the first statue of a non-general erected on the Gettysburg battlefield, and it was dedicated in 1910.

to President Lincoln and asked Father Corby to deliver it to the White House and to try to persuade the president to pardon the soldier. The chaplain agreed and, upon identifying himself at the presidential mansion, was promptly escorted in to meet with the president. As Corby recounted the story:

> The good President was inclined to be positive; said it was a "hard case," promised to take the matter into consideration, and, across the back of the petition, which was foiled in the long form usual with military papers, wrote: "See for the 25th of April." This was intended for a note to remind him of the time set for the execution. The president then asked what I had to say in extenuation of the crime. I answered that I could not say anything on that score, since the man had been tried by court-martial and had been found guilty; but I added that good reasons had been set forth in the petition for mercy and pardon. I showed that an actual injustice had been done, according to military standards, in keeping the man so long—some months—under sentence; the suspense he had undergone must be considered as unnecessary cruelty. Still the President was not inclined to grant the pardon, and said that suspense was more or less inevitable, on account of the movements of the army. But, finally, I touched a tender cord. All who knew President Lincoln knew that he was a very tender-hearted man. I said almost in despair of my case: "Well, Mr. President, since I have seen from the start that it was out of the question to plead the innocence of this man, or to say anything in mitigation of his crime, I have confined myself to pleading for his pardon; but, since Your Excellency sees fit not to grant it, I must leave his life in your hands." This was too much! His tender heart recoiled when he realized that a man's life depended upon his mercy.

As I started across the "green room" to take my departure he turned in his chair, and, throwing one of his long legs over the other, said: "Chaplain, see here! I will pardon him if Gen. Meade will, and I will put that on the petition."[295]

Corby was not optimistic about General Meade granting any such pardon. He called on the general, then commander-in-chief of the Army of the Potomac, and produced Lincoln's statement, to which the general replied that while Father Corby's mission was one of charity, "sometimes charity to a few means cruelty to many." If military discipline had been more severe from the beginning, the commander asserted, there would not be so many cases up for pardon. "Besides, the President has the final acts of that court-martial in his possession, and he should have given the final and positive decision. I will *not* act."[296]

Meade suggested that Corby see the president again, but the chaplain replied there was not sufficient time before the execution. He returned to his unit "with a heavy heart," but the officers suggested he try to telegraph the president. The priest went immediately to General Winfield Scott Hancock, a good friend, who was most happy to help. The president, however, never received the message, and Thomas Dawson went to his death after having made a good confession with perfect contriteness. The priest observed that "by his death, encountered with Christian sentiments and united with the merits of Christ, he wiped out the sins of his

---

[295] William Corby, C.S.C., *Memoirs of Chaplain Life: Three Years with the Irish Brigade in the Army of the Potomac* (New York: Fordham University Press, 1992), 223–224. Lincoln's note read: "If Gen. Meade will say in writing he thinks this man ought to be pardoned, it shall be done. A. Lincoln." The note was dated April 19, 1864. Corby, *Memoirs of Chaplain Life*, 225.

[296] Ibid., 226.

past life. Had he been pardoned he might not in the end have died in as excellent dispositions."[297]

Father Corby described with great pride the members of the Congregation of Holy Cross from Notre Dame who served in the Union forces.[298] In addition, he lauded others not of his religious congregation, such as Father Thomas Ouellet, S.J., a Canadian Jesuit assigned to Fordham University who heard that a Catholic regiment was in need of a chaplain and offered his services to Archbishop Hughes.[299] The regiment was the "Fighting 69th," and the Jesuit ended up serving them all four years of the war and through some of its most grueling battles. He was remembered for his care for all the soldiers he encountered, regardless of their beliefs. One especially poignant story occurred at the battle of Malvern Hill in 1862. Ouellet was walking among the dead and dying, asking if any were Catholic and desired absolution. A seriously wounded Confederate soldier—not a Catholic, replied that he would like to die in the faith of any man who had the courage to come and see soldiers under such devastating circumstances—a wish that became a reality.

Another notable chaplain was the Dominican Constantine L. Egan. He was stationed at Saint Dominic's Priory in Southeast

[297] Ibid., 228.

[298] They were Fathers Dillon, Cooney, Kilroy, Carrier, Gillen, Leveque, and Corby. In addition, he notes that John Ireland, a future archbishop of Saint Paul, Minnesota, and Lawrence S. McMahon, a future bishop of Hartford, Connecticut, both served with distinction. Also, he praises a Father Hamilton, a priest of the diocese of Mobile, Alabama, quoting from an issue of the publication Century that he was "the only authorized representative of the Christian religion" in the infamous Andersonville Prison. Father Hamilton, according to Corby, would visit prisoners every Sunday. Ibid., 273–274.

[299] Ibid., 299.

Washington, D.C., and was asked by the War Department in August 1863 to go to General Meade's camp. After a ten-day stay with the soldiers, Father Egan was preparing to return home when the commander of the Ninth Massachusetts Volunteers, as well as several of their officers, requested that he remain with them as their chaplain. The Dominican provincial agreed, and his commission was officially granted by the famed war governor of Massachusetts, John Andrew. Father Egan's chaplaincy was marked by several dire encounters in which he served his flock bravely.[300]

Father Corby also recounted a story about one of his fellow Holy Cross priests, Father Paul Gillen. Gillen had come to the United States from Ireland in 1840 and worked as a correspondent on an Irish weekly paper. After ordination, he offered to serve as a chaplain in the Union Army. Rather than secure an official commission, Gillen purchased an "old fashioned, flat-bottomed rockaway," had the front seat removed, and traveled the war-torn country, seeking out and finding Catholic soldiers in need of his ministry. He became well known, especially throughout Virginia, for his "piety and general zeal." Gillen's difficulties, however, began after a general order was issued forbidding any citizen to come or remain within army limits:

> One day, at a distance, [General] Grant saw the strange-looking land-boat in which Father Gillen was making his way, and ordered him arrested and sent out, rockaway and all. After this, Father Gillen went to the Corcoran Legion, then at Norfolk, Va., and accepted a commission of one of the regiments of that organization. They were only too glad

---

[300] An article by Brother Richard King, O.P., "Dominican Chaplains in the Civil War," is to be found in the Archives of the Eastern Dominican Province of Saint Joseph, and recounts in full the battles in which Father Egan distinguished himself.

to receive the experienced war chaplain. In this command he labored with marked success, and gave general satisfaction until the end of the war. He was beloved and respected by Catholics and non-Catholics.[301]

Finally, Father Corby provides an interesting description of what he describes as a "Military Mass." He asks his reader to imagine the entire camp, the "church tent," and the "great avenue leading to this tent lined on either side with green trees—put down for the occasion—all decorated with fresh branches, flags and other military emblems—a preparation like that made for a triumphal entry into a city." He continues

The congregation is composed exclusively of officers and soldiers, "rank and file," each one armed as for dress parade. The officers carry dress swords suspended from their belts, and wear the full insignia of their office. The cavalry men carry their heavy sabres in the same way, and on their boots the well-known formidable spurs that rattle and click at every motion of the foot.... Here the priests, vested in rich silk vestments embroidered with gold and artistic needle work, begin Holy Mass, in presence of the several thousand men and officers on whose bright, neat uniforms the gold ornaments sparkle in the sunlight, while dress swords, many of them diamond hilted, make a pleasing contrast to burnished sabre and polished steel bayonet.... The music consists of the stirring, martial strains of the infantry and marine bands. During the more solemn parts of the Mass the soldiers "present arms"—an act of the highest respect—while outside, at the time of the Consecration (if we are not in the presence of the enemy), cannons boom in various directions; going

[301] Corby, *Memoirs of Chaplain Life*, 307–310.

forth like thunder in the heavens, to represent, as it were, the voice of God, or at least to speak in the presence of him who rules from above, amid the crash of nations. Thus we see how God is served, even in camp.[302]

Southern Priest Poets

The Confederate Army was not to be outdone in the quality of sacramental ministers found in its midst. One example is the "priest poet of the South," Father Abram J. Ryan. Given the name Abraham at his birth in Hagerstown, Maryland, in 1838 to parents from County Tipperary, he relocated with his family in 1840 to Missouri, where his father opened a general store in St. Louis. As a young man, Ryan entered the College of Saint Mary's of the Barrens in Perryville, run by the Vincentians. He felt he had received a calling to be a Vincentian priest, and his formation eventually brought him to the Seminary of Our Lady of the Angels in Niagara, New York, in 1858. With their beginnings in Maryland, the Ryans had always considered themselves Southerners, and Abraham and his brother, David, who had joined him in the seminary, were becoming increasingly discontent in their Northern surroundings. Following his ordination, Abraham was sent to do parish work in LaSalle, Illinois. His brother did not pursue the priesthood and eventually taught at St. Mary's College in Marion County, Kentucky, until he enlisted in the Confederate Army in 1862.

The young Father Ryan's intense dislike for President Lincoln inspired him to change his name to Abram, though his Vincentian superior forbade him to engage in any political discussions because his Southern feelings were so intense. He eventually concluded that he must be released from his Vincentian vows and be incardinated

[302] Ibid., 99–101.

into a diocese as a secular priest. The bishop of Chicago welcomed him, and he began serving in Peoria, where his reputation as a preacher grew rapidly.

In 1863, Ryan received word of his brother's death on the battle-field near Monticello, Kentucky, though it was not determined if he died from wounds received in battle or from illness. Even after intense searching, David's body was never recovered; to a man with an already melancholic disposition such as Father Ryan, this plunged him into obsession. The war became the center of his life, and his poetry reflected his irrepressible love of a cause that he increasingly saw as doomed.

During the war years, Father Ryan traveled around the South, serving the sick and the dying in places such as New Orleans, Knoxville, and Augusta, where he served in a parish and edited a newspaper, *The Banner of the South*, for Bishop Verot of Savan-nah. (Ryan would fall out with Verot over the question of whether to define papal infallibility, which the priest strongly supported, years later.)

The priest poet settled in Mobile, Alabama, where he drew significant crowds of both Catholics and non-Catholics to his lec-tures and sermons. He became very close to the Children of Mary Sodality at Saint Mary's Church in Mobile and requested he be buried among them in the parish cemetery. His final years were spent in a small home on the beach in Biloxi, Mississippi, where he could concentrate on his writing. His death came suddenly in 1886 in Louisville, Kentucky, while at a Franciscan Monastery making a private retreat.

Father Ryan has received serious scholarly consideration for his acclaimed poems, particularly "The Conquered Banner" and "The Sword of Robert E. Lee." The former "swiftly penetrated popular consciousness across the South ... it also echoed and re-echoed across the Atlantic as the redoubtable Sir Henry Houghton of

England brought forth in short order his sympathetic verse 'A Reply to the Conquered Banner.'"[303]

> Ryan sacralizes the banner that he would have treated like the Body of Christ. He was one of the very first postwar authors to so explicitly link the Confederate Cause to ambient Christian tradition.... "The Conquered Banner" is not a particularly subtle poem, and so it is not very difficult to see the connections that Ryan draws. One argument for putting away the flag is that "there's no one left to lave it In the blood which heroes gave it." "Laving" the flag—that is, soaking it in the blood of the slain—presents a rather strange image. But a bloody Jesus was laved in preparation for the tomb, and there were few southerners who would not understand the deeper meaning of "washed in the blood."[304]

Due to his sacralizing the Confederate cause and his eloquence in the pulpit, Ryan became in his day what one biographer has called a Southern Catholic icon. His funeral was attended by members of the Confederate military, as well as by John C. Breckinridge, former vice president of the United States and Confederate secretary of war. Funeral orations in the city of Mobile crossed sectarian lines, and his death was considered "peculiarly and strikingly a poet's death."[305]

Yet another unique priestly personality in the South was that of Father John Bannister Tabb, who was born in 1845 near Richmond into one of the old, wealthy, Episcopalian families of Virginia. His ancestors claimed friendship with the families of George Washington

---

[303] Donald Robert Beagle and Bryan Albin Giemza, *Poet of the Lost Cause: A Life of Father Ryan* (Knoxville: University of Tennessee Press, 2008), 106–107.

[304] Ibid., 109–110.

[305] Ibid., 247.

and John Randolph. His family patrimony included more than a dozen fertile plantations and numerous slaves. By the time he was fourteen, he began to notice his eyesight was failing—an affliction that would only worsen, plaguing him throughout life.

At the beginning of hostilities in 1861, Tabb enlisted in the Confederate Navy and served as a captain's clerk on the steamer *Robert E. Lee*, which had run the Union blockade at Wilmington, North Carolina, some twenty-one times. On his first voyage to England, he met a passenger well known in Southern circles, Father John Bannon, who apparently made quite an impression on the young Episcopalian:

> Sometime after 1894, Father Bannon may have become aware of the poetry of an American priest, John Bannister Tabb, whom he helped move toward the Catholic faith. Young Tabb had been a sailor on the blockade runner the *Giraffe*, later to be called the *Robert E. Lee*, that took Father Bannon from Wilmington, North Carolina, to the British West Indies in 1863. Tabb had asked the priest many questions about religion and was later to acknowledge his indebtedness to the Confederate chaplain.[306]

Tabb continued to serve in the navy until June 1864, when he was captured off Beaufort, North Carolina, on the *Siren* by a federal ship, the *Keystone State*. The following day, he and four others were court-martialed and remained in prison until February 1865. At war's end, he was offered a teaching position at a school attached to Mount Calvary Church in Baltimore, long a center of Anglo-Catholicism, where the high-church rector believed in the Real Presence of Our Lord in the Blessed Sacrament, offered

---

[306] William Barnaby Faherty, S.J., *Exile in Erin: A Confederate Chaplain's Story* (St. Louis: Missouri Historical Society Press, 2002), 199.

Mass each day, and heard confessions. He instilled deep devotion to the Blessed Virgin Mary, wore his cassock and biretta daily, and deeply influenced young Tabb. The rector was Alfred Curtis, who eventually became a Catholic (at the hands of John Henry Newman, no less), was ordained a priest, and became the Bishop of Wilmington, Delaware.

Tabb moved on to a teaching position at Racine College in Michigan, clearly influenced by Curtis's conversion. In 1874, before Reconstruction had ended, Tabb entered Saint Charles College, Ellicott City, Maryland, to begin his own studies. We get a glimpse of his spiritual progress through the years in a verse of his:

> This is the Catholic priest
> Who in piety never increased
> With the world and the Devil
> He kept on a level
> Tho' from flesh he was wholly released.[307]

Tabb had hoped to have a priestly career centered on education, and, according to one biographer,

> God heard his prayer and granted it in fullness for ... until the day of his death the gifted priest-poet was part of [Saint Charles] College. He gave to it the service of his whole being; and the angels alone could measure the height of moral, spiritual, and literary influence which he exerted not only on those who came under his gentle academic scepter, but on hosts of friends and strangers alike, by his counsels, his cultured conversation, his kindly, helpful letters—each a veritable *multum in parvo*—and by his published poems.... He added fame and distinction to the already famous institution

---

[307] M. S. Pine, *John Bannister Tabb: The Priest-Poet* (Washington, D.C.: Georgetown Visitation Convent, 1915), 35.

founded by Charles Carroll of Carrollton for "the education of pious young men of the Catholic persuasion for the ministry of the Gospel," as its ancient Maryland charter states. His "Poems" and "Lyrics" were read and appreciated by an ever-widening circle of cultured admirers wherever the English language is spoken.[308]

"From the Sacred Presence of the Tabernacle, where, like his saintly model, Bishop Curtis, he spent hours of fervent adoration," Tabb's biographer writes, "he would pass to his sanctuary of the woods, and there wait, assured of poetic inspiration."[309] From such moments sprang verses deeply rooted in faith:

> My God has hid Himself from me
> Behind whatever else I see;
> Myself—the nearest mystery—
> As far beyond my grasp as He.
> And yet in darkest night I know,
> While lives a doubt—discerning glow,
> That larger lights above it throw
> These shadows in the vale below.[310]

In his later years, his works came to the attention of Alice Meynell, wife of Wilfrid Meynell, who was editor of *Merry England*, a publication in which the British Catholic poet Francis Thompson was often published. Some have placed Tabb on an equal footing with Thompson, though "he did not seek in the Elizabethan treasury words, however beautiful, that had a stamp of antiquity; nor did he ever coin new words for his purpose."[311]

---

[308] Ibid., 39.
[309] Ibid., 63.
[310] Ibid., 44.
[311] Ibid., 59.

The War Years: 1861–1865

Father Tabb's death on November 19, 1909, brought a significant literary career to a close. This true son of the American South, after a Requiem Mass in the college chapel of Saint Charles, was buried, at his own request, in Hollywood Cemetery in Richmond, where Jefferson Davis, many Confederate generals, and two American presidents rest.

Father Bannon's War

Father John Bannon served the Confederacy in a unique role. Born in County Roscommon in 1829, he spent his college years in Dublin and his seminary years at Saint Patrick's, Maynooth. He was ordained for the Archdiocese of Dublin by Archbishop Paul Cullen in 1853.[312] Shortly after, he left for the United States, settling in St. Louis, where he soon became pastor of one of the city's most prominent parishes. When war began, he volunteered for the First Missouri Confederate Brigade and ministered at the battles of Corinth and Fort Gibson and at Big Black during the Vicksburg campaign. He was detained when Vicksburg surrendered in July 1863 and, after being released, went to Richmond, where he met President Jefferson Davis and his secretary of state, Judah P. Benjamin. They asked him to go to Ireland to discourage recruitment for the federal forces and to try to obtain international help for the Confederacy.

> Both the Confederate President ... and the Secretary of State ... knew the influence of priests among Catholics. Davis had gone to a Dominican school as a boy in Kentucky, and Benjamin, whose wife was a Catholic of French ancestry, represented Louisiana, a state with a large Catholic population. The two men readily saw the value of having

[312] Paul Cullen would later become Ireland's first cardinal.

a Catholic priest, a native of Ireland.... Father Bannon ...
agreed to transfer from the army to the special service of
the State department on September 1, 1863.[313]

Benjamin suggested to Bannon that he could discuss with his
countrymen the slaughter of so many in the Irish Brigade in the
Battle of Fredericksburg; the fact that Irishmen in the Union Army
would be killing their fellow countrymen who wore the gray; the
anti-Catholic bigotry found in so many parts of the country; the
effect of political parties such as the Native Americans and the
Know-Nothings before the war; and the desecration of several
Catholic churches by New England soldiers.

Bannon initially tried to circulate newspapers like *The Richmond Whig* and the New York *Freeman's Journal*, which contained
detailed explanations and defenses of the Southern position. He
soon realized, though, that most emigrants spent little, if any, time
on newspapers; he therefore decided to publish a pamphlet of his
own to be given to potential emigrants and to place posters on the
walls of boarding houses in seaport cities. He secured the help of
Irishmen who had been involved in the Young Ireland Movement
of 1848, which had agitated for Irish independence from Great
Britain, and sought out John Mitchell, an Irish Protestant leader
of the '48 uprising who had two sons fighting for the Confederacy.
Mitchell had recently written an article for *The Nation* in which
he encouraged his countrymen not to insert themselves in a war
against a young nation, like their own, fighting for its freedom.

Bannon also undertook a lengthy speaking tour throughout his
native land, emphasizing several key points:

The men of the South, Bannon claimed, were friends of
the foreigner, and many were Catholics, descendants of

[313]Faherty, *Exile in Erin*, 129.

Spanish who settled in Florida, French in Louisiana, and Irish in Maryland and Kentucky. In the South, one did not hear the Irish Catholics referred to as beggarly, ignorant papists and low foreigners, as one did in the North. It was the South that crushed Know-Nothingism in the election of 1856. Northerners reduced Catholics to a status lower than slaves in the South and then expected Catholics in the North to hazard their lives to improve the status of ones better respected than they. These were the only times Bannon ever referred to African Americans.[314]

The priest apparently met with considerable success in Ireland; he received many invitations from parish priests around the country to come and alert their congregations about the dangers of the New World. "In almost every place the parish priests were supporters of the Confederacy," Bannon's biographer writes, "and signs of their influence was [sic] clear."[315] In talking with these pastors, though, the Confederate agent ascertained that there had been more sympathy for the North at the war's outset, largely due to the influence of Archbishop Hughes and his praise for the Lincoln administration and the preservation of the Union. But Hughes had not followed up vigorously, probably owing to his declining health, and this may have given Bannon the opportunity to strongly influence Irish clerical opinion.

He appealed to the consciences of Catholics by pointing out that both St. Alphonsus Liguori and St. Thomas Aquinas, the greatest of all theologians, taught that a foreigner about to enter the military service of another country must, under pain of mortal sin, inquire as to the justice of the cause. As long as one continued to fight for an unjust cause, he could

[314] Ibid., 133.
[315] Ibid., 134.

not gain absolution unless he got his discharge as soon as possible. If one fought merely for pay in an unjust cause, he could not receive absolution.[316]

Bishop Patrick N. Lynch of Charleston, on his official mission for the Confederate government, arrived first in the city of Cork, Ireland, before proceeding to Rome. Here he met Father Bannon. The bishop traveled with his nephew, who was especially taken with the force and grandeur of Bannon's presence and the power of his eloquence in pleading the Southern cause. He noted the earnestness of Bannon's plea to the Irish to remain in their own land until the conflict in America had ceased. One could only imagine that the bishop was similarly impressed and grateful.

Once his mission was accomplished, Father Bannon's future was murky. St. Louis was the only city he had really known, but to return to a Union state risked, he feared, being jailed because of the legislation passed by Lincoln's "Black Republicans." The bishops of Richmond and Charleston would have happily welcomed him, but it would have been difficult to enter either city with the existing blockade. While in Rome after leaving Ireland, he made the Spiritual Exercises of St. Ignatius Loyola and determined that he was called to be a Jesuit. This seemed strange to some of his contemporaries because he had had little contact with the Society up to that point in his life. Nevertheless, he applied, and he was warmly received by the Jesuit superior general. He began his novitiate at Milltown Park, in Dublin's south end, and eventually professed vows in the Society. Father Bannon would spend the rest of his life as an Irish Jesuit—a renowned preacher, who left his former life in the background. He died in 1913 and is buried in the Jesuit plot in Glasnevin Cemetery, Dublin.

[316] Ibid., 135.

The War Years: 1861–1865

The Irreplaceable Contributions of Women Religious

Very close to Saint Matthew's Cathedral in our nation's capital is a monument to all the religious Sisters who served as nurses in the Civil War. This fitting tribute allows one to reflect on the various religious orders whose women of mercy did immeasurable good—bringing lapsed Catholics back to the practice of the Faith, winning many converts to the fullness of truth, and significantly contributing to breaking down barriers of hostility that had been erected so long ago, and under which so many Americans, not to mention America's soldiers, operated all their lives.

The human cost of the war, which these women were called in some small way to ameliorate, was astounding. One historian has estimated that 1.5 million men were actively engaged in the Northern armies.

> Of this number 56,000 died on the field of battle, 35,000 expired in the hospitals from the effects of wounds received in action, and 184,000 perished by disease. It is probable that those who died of disease after their discharge from the army would swell the total to 300,000. If inferior hospital service and poor sanitary arrangements are added to the other results of war, it is safe to assume that the loss of the South was greater than that of the North. But, considering the Southern loss equal to that of the North, the aggregate is 600,000. Add to this 400,000 men crippled or permanently disabled by disease, and the total subtraction from the productive force of the nation reaches the stupendous total of 1,000,000 men. These figures seem almost incredible, but they come from what, in this particular at least, must be regarded as a trustworthy source.[317]

[317] George Barton, *Angels of the Battlefield: A History of the Labors of the Catholic Sisterhoods in the Late Civil War* (Philadelphia: Catholic

Faith and Fury

The four major communities of women religious found on Civil War battlefields were the Sisters of Charity, the Sisters of Mercy, the Sisters of Saint Joseph, and the Sisters of the Holy Cross. There were three distinct branches of the Sisters of Charity: the "black caps," who had establishments in New York, Cincinnati, and other cities; the "white caps," or Cornette Sisters of Mother Seton of Emmitsburg, Maryland; and the Sisters of Charity of Nazareth, Kentucky, who did not have a colorful nickname. The Nazareth community was founded by a few devout women in Kentucky under Bishop Flaget of Bardstown, with Mother Catherine Spalding as their first superior. She was a cousin of Baltimore's archbishop, Martin J. Spalding, and his nephew John Lancaster Spalding, first bishop of Peoria.

The Sisters of Mercy were founded in Dublin, Ireland, by Mother Catharine McCauley. Seven original Sisters came to the United States to establish their order in Pittsburgh, Pennsylvania. The Sisters of Saint Joseph were founded in France in 1650. Many of their houses had been destroyed at the time of the French Revolution, but they reorganized in Lyon, and from there, at the request of Bishop Joseph Rosati, six Sisters came to St. Louis, where they founded a house at Carondelet, Missouri. This became their first motherhouse, and from there they established a number of independent houses, most notably at Chestnut Hill, Pennsylvania. The Sisters of the Holy Cross, meanwhile, were founded at Notre Dame, Indiana, out of the Congregation of Holy Cross.

There are innumerable stories of heroism on the part of the Sisters, but some were especially noteworthy. The area around the

---

Art Publishing Company, 1897), 2. The source to which the author makes reference is footnoted merely as Greely's American Conflict. Another source taking up this same material is to be found in Norah Smaridge and Albert Micale, *Hands Of Mercy: The Story of Sister Nurses in the Civil War* (New York: Benziger Brothers, 1960.)

Confederate capitol of Richmond saw much work on the part of
the Emmitsburg Sisters of Charity, but amid the difficulties there,
all the Sisters who could be spared were sent to a military hospital
in Harpers Ferry after a telegraph was received asking for help for
the wounded and sick soldiers. Here they labored for the physical
and spiritual health of the suffering men.

In St. Louis, the Sisters took charge of a military hospital to
remarkable effect. Some of the workers, at first, not knowing what to
make of the habited women, inquired "if they were Free Masons."[318]
The hospital was visited by the Ladies of the Union Aid Society,
who "could not understand the influence the Sisters exercised over
the patients, both sick and convalescent, who were as submissive
as children."[319] One of the Sisters especially remembered for her
heroism here was Sister Juliana, whose brother was Bishop Silas
Chatard of Vincennes, Indiana. Another story goes like this:

> A Sister was passing through the streets of Boston with
> downcast eyes and noiseless steps when she was suddenly
> addressed in a language that made her pale cheeks flush. The
> insult came from a young man standing on a street corner.
> The Sister uttered no word of protest, but raising her eyes
> gave one swift, penetrating look at the brutal offender. Time
> passed on; the war intervened. The scene changed to a ward
> in a military hospital in Missouri. A wounded soldier, once
> powerful but now as helpless as an infant, was brought in
> and placed under the care of the Sisters of Charity. It was
> soon evident that the man's hour had arrived; that he was
> not long for this world. The Sister urged the man to die
> in the friendship of God, to ask pardon for his sins, and
> to be sorry for whatever evil he might have done. "I have

[318] Ibid., 28.
[319] Ibid.

committed many sins in my life," he said to the Sister, "and
I am sorry for them all and hope to be forgiven; but there is
one thing which weighs heavy on my mind at this moment.
I once insulted a Sister of Charity in the streets of Boston.
Her glance of reproach has haunted me ever since. I knew
nothing of the Sisters then. But now I know how good and
disinterested you are and how mean I was. Oh! If that Sister
were only here, weak and dying as I am, I would go down
upon my knees and ask her pardon." The Sister turned to
him with a look of tenderness and compassion, saying: "If
that is all you desire to set your mind at ease, you can have
it. I am the Sister you insulted, and I grant you pardon freely
and from my heart."[320]

By 1862, approximately 450,000 troops were in the Union
Army, half of whom were in General George B. McClellan's Army
of the Potomac. Virginia had become one of the principal areas
of hostilities; with the confederate capital at Richmond, only a
sliver of land south of the Potomac separated the governments of
both nations. A disastrous defeat for the Union forces at Bull Run
in July 1862 forced much of the army to retreat to Washington.
Meanwhile, General Ulysses Grant had captured Fort Henry on the
Tennessee River and Fort Donaldson on the Cumberland River in
Kentucky. With casualties mounting on both sides, the need for the
nursing Sisters was growing rapidly — especially in the temporary
hospitals constructed around Washington.

Sisters of Charity were once again dispatched from their
motherhouse in Emmitsburg to act in the dual capacities of nurse
and doctor. One soldier in a Sisters-staffed hospital converted to

[320] Ibid., 33–34. The story was related by Archbishop Patrick J. Ryan
of Philadelphia, who, as a young priest, had ministered to many of
the soldiers in the St. Louis Military Hospital.

Catholicism and spent much time going from one bed to another, Bible in one hand and Catholic catechism in the other, trying to explain Catholic beliefs and bring others to the truth he had accepted. Some argued with him, but they could not help but be impressed with the conviction of the convert. This was just a small example of the effect of these saintly women.

The work of Sister Anthony at the Battle of Shiloh has been well documented. Born in County Tipperary of devout Catholic parents, she came to this country at a young age and entered the Sisters of Charity at Emmitsburg. After profession, she was placed in charge of a community in Cincinnati, where she displayed "unusual devotion, business talent and self-sacrifice."[321] When war commenced, a call came from the Governor of Ohio for volunteer nurses. Sister Anthony and a band of her Sisters responded; their work would keep them mostly in the South, in places such as Nashville, Richmond, New Creek, Cumberland, and Shiloh.

Sister Anthony wrote a series of recollections of her experiences, but the best account comes from an observer who witnessed her in action:

> Amid this sea of blood she performed the most revolting duties for those poor soldiers. Let us follow her as she gropes her way through the wounded, dead and dying. She seemed to me like a ministering angel, and many a young soldier owes his life to her care and charity. Let us gaze at her again as she stands attentive ... and assists Dr. Blackman while the surgeon is amputating limbs and consigning them to a watery grave, or as she picks her steps in the blood of these brave boys, administering cordial or dressing wounds.[322]

[321] Ibid., 46.
[322] Ibid., 43–44.

Faith and Fury

"Her person was reverenced by Blue and Gray, Protestant and Catholic alike," another observer said, "and the love for her became so strong that the title of the 'Florence Nightingale' of America was conferred upon her, and soon her name became a household word in every section of the North and South."[323] Sister Anthony returned to Cincinnati after the war and lived to a venerable age.

Gettysburg, the site of three of the bloodiest days of the war, where 140,000 men fought, was a town, as we have seen steeped in anti-Catholicism. And yet the Sisters of Charity became respected figures on the streets; everywhere they went, they were beacons of hope to the wounded and the dying.

> The Catholic Church in Gettysburg was filled with sick and wounded. The stations of the cross hung around the walls, with a very large oil painting of St. Francis Xavier holding in his hand a crucifix. The first man put in the sanctuary was baptized, expressing truly Christian sentiments. His pain was excruciating and when sympathy was offered him he said: "Oh, what are the pains I suffer compared with those of my Redeemer." Thus disposed he died. The soldiers lay on the pew seats, under them and in every aisle. They were also in the sanctuary and in the gallery, so close together that there was scarcely room to move about. Many of them lay in their own blood and the water used for bathing their wounds, but no word of complaint escaped from their lips.[324]

A young woman named Mary Agnes Grace from Baltimore entered the Sisters of Charity at Emmitsburg in the 1820s. In religious life she was known as Sister Gonzaga. Shortly after her reception into the community, she, with two other Sisters, opened a school

[323] Ibid., 47.
[324] Ibid., 97.

in Harrisburg. In 1830, she was reassigned to Saint Joseph's Orphan Asylum in Philadelphia, where she was anchored until her death in 1897. One biographer wrote of her that "if nobility of character, earnestness and purity of purpose, great natural executive ability, together with unaffected piety and humility tell for anything, this Sister will rank high in the bright galaxy of self-sacrificing women whose lives have illuminated the history of Catholic Sisterhoods in the United States."[325]

Much of her work in the war years was accomplished at the Satterlee Military Hospital in Philadelphia, where she was aided by forty other Sisters. One example of many involved events of August 16, 1862, when more than fifteen hundred sick and wounded men were brought to the hospital. Many had died from exhaustion on the way, and others were about to die. With care, compassion, and efficiency, the Sisters nursed and prepared these men to meet the Lord.

Mother Gonzaga was honored by the City of Philadelphia on the golden jubilee of her religious profession. Her enormous funeral was a fitting final tribute to her outstanding service to God and country.

Convert Commanders

The number of Catholic generals in both armies was impressive, though two examples of conversion to the Faith are of special interest: Confederate General James Longstreet and Union General William S. Rosecrans. Both were roommates at West Point in the class of 1842: Rosecrans had tutored Longstreet in mathematics.

James Longstreet was born in South Carolina in 1821, served in the Mexican War, and, in June 1861, joined the Confederate Army. He played a minor role at the First Battle of Bull Run and made

[325] Ibid., 104.

significant contributions as one of Lee's subordinates in the Army
of Northern Virginia. He led a devastating counterattack at Second
Bull Run but disagreed with some of Lee's tactics at Gettysburg. At
his own request, he was sent to the Western theater to fight under
General Braxton Bragg, and his troops led a grand assault against the
federals at Chickamauga. He was seriously wounded in the Wilder-
ness Campaign and later returned to Lee's command, serving at the
siege of Petersburg and at Appomattox. After the war, he and his
family settled in New Orleans, a city popular with a number of former
Confederate Generals, where he became active in the Republican
Party—remarkable for a soldier of the south. In his memoirs, he
wrote a number of critical comments about General Lee's wartime
performance. His friends and admirers in the South dwindled.

Neither did Longstreet have many friends in the North. He
was refused a formal pardon by President Andrew Johnson, who
believed that neither Jefferson Davis, Robert E. Lee, nor Longstreet
were deserving. Even Longstreet's Episcopalian church, which was
deeply divided about the war and its aftermath, did not welcome
him with open arms. This treatment accounted, at least in part,
for his conversion to Catholicism.

> He became religious in his declining years. In early life he
> was an Episcopalian, but in New Orleans, in the stress of the
> Reconstruction, he found himself to be intensely disliked
> by the members of his church. Consolation for this came
> in his union with the Roman Catholic Church, which he
> joined under the ministrations of the noted Confederate
> poet, Father Ryan. He remained a consistent member of
> the fold until the end.[326]

[326] H. J. Eckenrode and Byran Conrad, *James Longstreet: Lee's War
Horse* (Chapel Hill: University of North Carolina Press, 1936),
377.

Father Abram Ryan rarely mentioned Longstreet's conversion, given the circumstances. It is true that the general's second wife, several decades his junior, may have been a catalyst, but more than likely the priest poet instructed and encouraged him, albeit privately.[327]

William Starke Rosecrans was born in Ohio in 1819. After West Point, he left the army to pursue a career in civil engineering. He returned to the army after Fort Sumter, and in the war's early stages, he served under the command of General Grant. His victories over Confederate General Braxton Bragg at Stones River, and later in the Tullahoma Campaign, forced the Southern Army from Middle Tennessee, and eventually forced Bragg to abandon Chattanooga. Unfortunately, his pursuit of Bragg ended during the Battle of Chickamauga, where an order he had written mistakenly opened a gap in the Union line, and Rosecrans and one-third of

---

[327] "Longstreet remains the most reviled Scalawag in Lost Cause annals, where he roasts with Sherman. By the time Longstreet died, his Lost Cause demonization was so complete, and his military accomplishments so widely misunderstood, that many Confederate veteran groups declined to send flowers to his funeral.... One account has it that the poet-priest took Longstreet when no one else would have him. Unreconstructed Confederates literally emptied the pews when the General showed up at his Episcopalian church in New Orleans, according to Longstreet's second wife, a devout Catholic. She wrote that he was 'cut to the quick by such treatment,' and 'began to wonder if there was any church broad enough to withstand differences caused by the political and sectional feeling. He discovered that the Roman Catholic priests extended him the treatment he longed for. He began to attend that church, and said that its atmosphere from the first appealed to him as the church of the sorrow-laden of earth.' Obviously, he had been talking to Father Ryan, under whose ministration, Helen Longstreet avers, he converted on 7 March 1877." Beagle and Giemza, *Poet of the Lost Cause*, 179–180.

his army were driven from the field. For this, Grant relieved him of his command.

He was reassigned to command the Department of Missouri and was briefly considered as a running mate for Abraham Lincoln in the 1864 campaign—a most unusual, and probably unrealistic, thought for a Catholic at this point in the nineteenth century. After the war, he served in diplomatic and other appointed political positions and was approached on several occasions to run for Congress. In 1880, he was elected to Congress from California, where he had purchased sixteen thousand acres of land in Rancho San Pedro in the Los Angeles basin. He and his wife of forty years, Anna Elizabeth Hegeman, were the parents of eight children.

Rosecrans converted to Catholicism in 1845 and apparently convinced his brother, Sylvester, to do the same: Sylvester went on to study for the priesthood and became the first bishop of Columbus, Ohio. The family were of Dutch origin and Methodist in religion. William and Sylvester were great-grandsons of Stephen Hopkins, the colonial governor of Rhode Island and a signer of the Declaration of Independence.

The general's conversion seems to have been somewhat of an intellectual one, and, by all accounts, he presented himself as someone adept at defending the Faith. One friend did not think him the proper person to be placed in command of an army:

At that time he seemed to be a great enthusiast in regard to the Catholic Church; seemed to want to think of nothing else, and in fact do nothing else, except to proselyte for it and attend upon its ministrations. No night was ever so dark and tempestuous, that he would not brave the boisterous seas of Newport harbor to attend Mass, and no occasion, however inappropriate, was ever lost sight of to advocate its cause; in fact, he was what nowadays would be called most emphatically a crank on that subject, and might not inappropriately be considered a one-ideaed man lacking in the breadth and poise, so necessary to success in the commander of an army in the field.[328]

A newspaperman commenting on Rosecrans remembered that he "took an argument and carried it, often into the realms of Mother Church, where the vehemence of his intellect and his zealous temper developed themselves thoroughly." The journalist added that the general "had the Fathers of the Church at his tongue's end, and exhibited a familiarity with controversial theology that made him a formidable antagonist to the best read, even of the clerical profession."[329]

James A. Garfield, a close friend and future president, had long discussions with Rosecrans on religion. Garfield, a member of the Disciples of Christ, called Rosecrans "the intensest religionist I ever saw," though after observing his piety and listening to the reasoning behind his theology, Garfield wrote to his mother, stating he had no doubt that "the Catholics have been slandered."[330] Decades later, following Rosecrans's death, a Methodist bishop who had fought under him said "a devouter Christian there was not," adding that "all must admit that, though wholly a Romanist, he was catholic in his charity to those from whom he differed. He believed in God with all his heart."[331]

If anything good might be said to have come from war for American Catholics, it might be that it was an opportunity to show their patriotism in impressive numbers, and that they fought and

---

[328] David G. Moore, *William S. Rosecrans and the Union Victory* (Jefferson, NC: McFarland and Company, 2014), 79.
[329] Ibid.
[330] Ibid., 80.
[331] Ibid., 196.

died alongside their fellow countrymen with just as much devotion to the cause, be it Union or Confederate, as any Presbyterian or Episcopalian or secularist. And indeed, many false impressions and prejudices about Catholics dissipated, at least a bit and for a time. But the period of Reconstruction[332] brought with it another spike in anti-Catholicism, which has been present in this nation since colonial days, as the country again wrestled angrily and sometimes violently with questions of loyalty and faith and American-ness. It could well be argued, though, that the Church emerged all the stronger for the test.

---

[332] Historians are generally in agreement that Reconstruction began with the close of the war in 1865 and concluded, officially, with the withdrawal of the last federal troops of occupation from the former Confederate States in 1877.

Chapter 5

∞

The Irish Contribution

Irish Catholic Immigration

At the outbreak of the war, the Irish were, by far, the largest group of Catholic immigrants in the United States; by their sheer strength of numbers they made a substantial contribution to both the Union and Confederate armies.[333]

Irish immigration to America began in the colonial era, though the majority of those who came in the seventeenth and early eighteenth centuries were Ulstermen—that is, Protestant Irish from the North of Ireland. These are usually given the name Scotch-Irish Presbyterians; the families had often migrated from Scotland to Northern Ireland, lived there for some generations, then sailed to the American colonies.

When the Ulster Irish arrived in America, large numbers of them settled in New England, especially in the growing town of Boston, where they soon became the focus of hostility. Puritan city leaders resented the Ulster Irish loyalty to Presbyterianism while other Bostonians focused on economic

---

[333] Concentrating on the Irish in no way lessens the contributions of each Catholic ethnic group then represented in the United States. German Catholics, for example, rendered exemplary service, and have been the subject of several scholarly studies.

issues, primarily the number of destitute immigrants de-
pleting the town's limited charitable resources that, many
believed, should not be wasted on noncitizens.... Ulstermen
who settled in Pennsylvania and areas farther south found
more success, usually due to their ability to dominate sparsely
populated areas or to their settling in colonies with greater
religious tolerance.... [The] number of Irish Catholics entering America was limited during the "Great Migration" of
Presbyterian Ulstermen. Most Catholics lacked the money
for the journey from Ireland and the majority of those who
did come arrived as indentured servants or convicts.[334]

That would change significantly as the nineteenth century progressed, especially during the period from 1847 to 1851. The failure
of one of Ireland's leading crops, the potato, led to starvation,
death, and eventually mass emigration unparalleled in Irish history—mostly to the United States. In those five years,

850,000 Irish men, women, and children left Europe rather
than die on what remained of their tenant farmland. Even
if the estimate is accurate that 55 percent of these people
eventually left New York to make a new life elsewhere in
smaller cities, villages, and in the countryside, by 1860 there
were more Irish born people living in New York City than
lived in Dublin, Cork or Belfast.[335]

By the time the famine ended in the 1850s, estimates of the
death toll in Ireland ranged from 1.1 to 1.5 million people. In the
decade between 1845 and 1855, nearly 1.5 million Catholic Irish

[334]Susannah Ural Bruce, *The Harp and the Eagle: Irish-American Volunteers and the Union Army, 1861–1865* (New York: New York
University Press, 2006), 8–9.
[335]Loughery, *Dagger John*, 185.

traveled to the United States, substantially more than 300,000 to British North America (Canada), about that many to various parts of Great Britain, and thousands more to Australia. One historical estimate held that only one in three Irish males born around 1830 died in Ireland of old age.[336]

After less than a decade on America's shores, nativist sentiment spiked, politically in the form of the Native American Party of the 1840s and the Know-Nothings of the 1850s. As we've seen, the East Coast especially was full of acrimonious journalistic reaction to the newest arrivals, but the Midwest was hardly to be outdone, as this Chicago paper made clear:

> The great majority of members of the Roman Catholic Church in this country are Irishmen. The fact is peculiarly true in this city.... Who does not know that the most depraved, debased, worthless and irredeemable drunkards and sots which curse the community, are Irish Catholics? Who does not know that five eighths of cases brought up every day before the Mayor for drunkenness and consequent crime, are Irish Catholics? [337]

The Democratic Party, especially since the time of Andrew Jackson, had done everything in its power to attract Irish immigrants to its ranks. Although some did join the alternative—the Whigs and later the Republicans—strains of political anti-Catholicism fostered in both parties were usually enough to turn immigrants in the direction of the Democrats.

A curious complication in Irish-American politics was the figure of Daniel O'Connell, often called the "Liberator" in Ireland, who

[336] Bruce, *The Harp and the Eagle*, 15.
[337] *Chicago Tribune*, February 26, 1855, cited in Bruce, *The Harp and the Eagle*, 15.

was at the height of his political stardom. His peaceful approach to the topic of home rule for Ireland had been very successful; he had also achieved fame and success in the 1830s by securing Catholic emancipation in Ireland. O'Connell, however, was a known opponent of slavery and had strongly criticized the United States for retaining for so long a system of bondage that the rest of the civilized world had abandoned. He promised never to visit the United States until slavery was abolished, and so he became a favorite of many in the abolitionist movement, including its founder, William Lloyd Garrison. This put the celebrated Irish leader at odds with the vast majority of Irish Americans, and organized attempts to capitalize on O'Connell's views to persuade the Irish to join the abolitionist cause met with little success. Archbishop Hughes in New York can be credited with quashing such recruitment with his statement that, while he was no friend to slavery, "I am still less friendly to any attempt of foreign origin to abolish it."[338]

Another factor shaping the Irish consciousness in this country was the Young Ireland Movement. Described by one writer as a "disparate, fractious group of journalists, poets, politicians, firebrands,"[339] it included prominent Catholics such as Thomas D'Arcy McGee, Thomas Francis Meagher, Charles Gavan Duffy, and several others; Protestants included William Smith O'Brien and John Mitchell.

What they had in common, inspired by developments in France, was a sense that their time had come. Unfortunately they had a poor grasp of timing and seriously underestimated the willingness of a famine-starved population to see 1848 as the year in which to take on the might of the British

[338]Cited in Bruce, *The Harp and the Eagle*, 25.
[339]Loughery, *Dagger John*, 197.

Empire.... The group envisioned an uprising across the island.... Nothing of the kind happened.[340]

Irish Americans, though, were generally not distracted by the happenings back on their old island. They knew the names and heroes but were frantically busy maintaining themselves and their families here in the new world by backbreaking work on the railroads, on the canals, or in the mines. As one writer has put it "they sought a door that would open and give them access to hope."[341]

Irish Influencers in the Union Cause

Simple numerical superiority accounted for the greater number of Irish Catholics to be found in the Union Army. Though they readily answered Lincoln's call, it is doubtful that large numbers supported him in the 1860 presidential election. They were deeply suspicious of the elements making up the new Republican Party—though Stephen A. Douglas, Lincoln's Democrat opponent, whose wife was Catholic, was himself no great friend of the Church. A story was widely spread that he was once in Rome watching a procession of seminarians and bemoaned that "they are being trained to defend dogmas and superstitions contrary to the progress and enlightenment of the age."[342] What Douglas did do, however, was offer the Irish "all-out support and attention at a time when they were reviled."[343]

But, once Lincoln had been elected and was faced with the crisis of secession, many Irish immigrants warmed to him. In

[340] Ibid., 198.
[341] Shannon, *The American Irish*, 26.
[342] Niall O'Dowd, *Lincoln and the Irish: The Untold Story of How the Irish Helped Abraham Lincoln Save the Union* (New York: Skyhorse Publishing, 2018), 36.
[343] Ibid., 37.

addition to Archbishop Hughes, who was extremely pro-Lincoln, two other prominent Irishmen helped sway Irish thinking in favor of the Union cause: Thomas Francis Meagher and Michael Corcoran.

Meagher had been born in Waterford in 1823, the son of a prominent businessman who had been elected to the British Parliament. As a young man, Meagher reacted against his privileged background and threw in his lot with the rebels of Young Ireland. They had built on the vision of Theobald Wolfe Tone, a leader in the 1798 rebellion against Britain but clearly favored a more violent approach to achieve their ends. After his participation in the abortive 1848 uprising, Meagher was imprisoned in the penal colony of Australia. By the time he arrived in New York Harbor in May 1852, he was known as a national hero who had spent years fighting for the cause of Irish freedom.

Meagher was one of the prime movers behind the famed Irish Brigade and, following the death of Senator Douglas in 1861, became, at least in some minds, the most prominent political hero among Irish Americans. He threw his considerable influence behind President Lincoln and became an outspoken opponent of slavery. He was taking a dangerous position among his fellow Irish, the majority of whom did not want to fight a war for the freedom of African slaves. He also found himself at odds with Union generals Sherman and Grant. The former, a baptized but nonpracticing Catholic, strongly criticized the discipline of the Irish Brigade, while the latter had never been a friend of Catholicism.

This all notwithstanding, Meagher made great strides for the Irish, including visiting President Lincoln on the president's fifty-fourth birthday. He described Lincoln as looking "terrible, [with] the relentless onslaught of war and personal tragedy taking its toll," but he convinced the chief executive of the need to reinvigorate the Irish Brigade with more manpower and provisions.[344] Meagher died in 1867 while serving as territorial governor of Montana, under mysterious circumstances: He either fell or was pushed off a ship. His body was never found.

Michael Corcoran, another Celtic hero, is remembered in Irish American annals as a tremendous recruiter for Lincoln. He was the leading Fenian[345] in the United States, and his most famous act, for which he was arrested and held for court-martial, was his refusal to have his Irish unit parade before the Prince of Wales when he visited the United States in 1860. One Know-Nothing publication reacted: "What an insult to the monarch; those dreadful Irish, see, they have no intention of showing loyalty to the US."[346] Immediately after the bombardment of Fort Sumter, Corcoran was released and placed in charge of raising an army to go south. He was no defender of slavery and became an early friend of President Lincoln, who realized the political importance of having the Irishman as an ally.

Corcoran was captured at the First Battle of Bull Run but was released as part of a prisoner exchange in 1862. He drew one of the largest Irish crowds in New York City at a rally in his honor; shortly thereafter he was invited to dine at the White House with Lincoln, and, with the president's approval, he formed Corcoran's Legion, which consisted of six regiments who fought successfully in several key battles. He died at the early age of thirty-six after falling off a horse in Fairfax, Virginia, where he was the commanding general. It is estimated that five thousand recruits answered his call for service, so great was his popularity and skillfulness.

---

[344] Ibid., 69.
[345] The Fenians were a secret Irish American militia, only too happy to use the American Civil War experience for an eventual invasion of Ireland to drive the British out.
[346] Cited in O'Dowd, *Lincoln and the Irish*, 84.

Faith and Fury

On Staff at the White House

Irish influence on Lincoln included immigrants employed in the White House, beginning with one Edward McManus, an elderly gentleman who had served as doorman for several presidents. He was described as "the short, thin, smiling, humorous-looking elderly Irishman, the all-but-historic doorkeeper who has been so great a favorite through so many administrations."[347] He was also, apparently, a good keeper of secrets; he was often the only person on staff who knew the whereabouts of Abraham Lincoln when he left the White House. McManus was joined by another native Irishman, Thomas Burns, who guarded the second floor of the presidential home, making certain that the many assassination threats made against Lincoln did not materialize. Yet another fixture was Charles Forbes, whom Lincoln called Charlie, a valet who often accompanied the president, including to the secret peace talks with Confederate leaders at Fort Monroe in February 1865. These personalities compelled one journalist, Noah Brooks, to write that "the President has succeeded in getting about him a corps of attachés of Hibernian descent whose manner and style [were] about as disagreeable as can be."[348]

One writer has also noted that Lincoln was fond of the writings of Private Miles O'Reilly, a pseudonym for an Irish immigrant named Charles Halpine, who was an officer in the Union Army. He used his writing to criticize those insufficiently loyal to the president, and the account goes that "Lincoln would sometimes wake one of his personal secretaries late at night and read gobs of O'Reilly to him as he battled his own insomnia."[349]

The Old Soldiers Home, located in the present-day Rock Creek Cemetery, three miles from Lincoln's home, was one of Lincoln's

---

[347] Cited in ibid., 41.
[348] Cited in ibid., 42–43.
[349] Ibid., 44.

favorite getaways from the White House. He would often ride out alone on horseback, stopping to chat with residents, including Walt Whitman. Much of the Emancipation Proclamation was written in the thirty-four-room Gothic cottage where he stayed. One-third of the residents in the main house were Irish soldiers who had fought for the Union Army and were disabled, and Lincoln made the acquaintance of many of them, gathering many Irish stories for his repertoire. From such friendships, it is not difficult to see how he could write, "I regard our emigrants as one of the principal replenishing streams provided by Providence to repair the ravages of internal war and the waste of national strength and health."[350]

Edward McManus was replaced as doorkeeper at the White House by a native of Tipperary, Cornelius O'Leary. According to one opposition newspaper, he was placed in the job by Mrs. Lincoln, "where he would solicit bribes for access to the president and share the rewards with her."[351] This could be plausible, given Mary Todd Lincoln's well-documented excessive spending. O'Leary had served in the Irish Papal Brigade, which helped restore the pope in Rome after a rebellion led by Garibaldi. He later fought in the Irish Brigade in the Civil War but was wounded in battle and secured an appointment as postmaster of Lincoln Hospital in the District of Columbia. Later, he would return to his native land to take a part in the abortive Fenian uprising of 1867. McManus had been fired by Mary Lincoln for unexplained reasons, and O'Leary replaced him. For his part, McManus circulated stories to the press about Mary's spending habits, and even possible infidelities. Enraged, she described the Irishman as a "discarded menial" and convinced at least one writer that she "never did share her husband's fondness for the Irish."[352]

[350] Ibid., 45.
[351] Ibid.
[352] Ibid., 47.

Faith and Fury

Serving with Distinction

The contributions of Irish-Americans to the war were complicated. While Lincoln, especially given his close contact with so many Irishmen, was generally well disposed toward them, it was also the case that some of the most strident opposition to his administration, as we have seen, came from Irish-Americans in New York:

> The Irish-American conduct in the Civil war presents a picture of decided contrasts. On the one hand, the fighting men and their families who supported them had written a proud chapter of sacrifice and patriotic loyalty to their new nation. On the other hand, the mob who had let themselves be led by the politicians into the draft riots had brought down on the heads of their fellow nationals extensive criticism and unpopularity in [New York] City. The bulk of the Irish population had an unshakable loyalty to the Union and while they might follow politicians in a carping policy against the administration, they remained true to the United States throughout the war.[353]

Far less ambiguous, however, were the contributions of the group traditionally dubbed the "Fighting 69th," or the Irish Brigade. They originally had been New York State's second regiment of Irish volunteers, organized in 1851 from military companies begun by Irish immigrants who were members of, or at least sympathized with, the Young Ireland Movement. Six years later, two additional Hibernian outfits, the Ninth and Seventy-Fourth New York militia, were also merged into the Sixty-Ninth.

On April 23, 1861, amid "deafening cheers" the 69th, the first Irish regiment to enter the service of the Union, marched

---

[353] Gibson, *Attitudes of the New York Irish*, 173.

from Great James Street down Broadway to Pier #4. The regiment's color party proudly bore a United States flag and an emerald color embroidered with a sunburst and red ribbons. The latter flag was presented to the 69th on March 16, 1861, by a group of Irish American citizens "In Commemoration of the 11th Oct. 1860," when Colonel Corcoran's regiment snubbed the Prince of Wales. The regiment was preceded to the docks by a four horse wagon bedecked with the motto "Sixty Ninth Remember Fontenoy." The banner recalled the triumph of the French General Maurice de Saxe over the British in 1745, a victory owed to an unstoppable bayonet charge by the French army's brigade of Irish exiles.[354]

One of the more telling stories of the Brigade came from Father William Corby, who was with them in one of their best, and worst, moments:

The Irish Brigade had very many advantages over other organizations as it was at no time during the war without a chaplain; but I was the only one at the battle of Gettysburg. Often in camp and sometimes on the march we held very impressive religious services, but the one at Gettysburg was more public, and was witnessed by many who had not, perhaps, seen the others. The surroundings there, too, made a vast difference, for really the situation reminded one of the day of judgment, when shall be seen "men withering away for fear and expectation of what shall come upon the whole world," so great were the whirlwinds of war then in motion.

About a week after the battle, while on the march, a non-Catholic, rode up to me, and after an introduction

[354]Joseph G. Bilby, *The Irish Brigade in the Civil War* (Cambridge, MA: Da Capo Press, 1995), 5.

by a friend, said: "Chaplain, I would like to know more about your religion. I was present on that awful day, July 2, when you 'made a prayer,' and while I have often witnessed ministers make prayers I never witnessed one so powerful as the one you made that day in front of Hancock's corps just as the ball opened with one hundred twenty guns blazing at us." Just then I found use for my handkerchief to hide a smile which stole to my countenance caused by the, to me, peculiar phraseology in which the good captain expressed his mind. I could not but admire his candid, outspoken manner, though, and I gave him an invitation to call on me in camp, when I would take pleasure in giving him all the information in my power. One good result of the Civil War was the removing of a great amount of prejudice. When men stand in common danger, a fraternal feeling springs up between them and generates a Christian, charitable sentiment that often leads to most excellent results.[355]

On the other hand, Gettysburg was a battle that cost the Irish Brigade much:

The 69th New York went into the fight at Gettysburg with six officers and sixty-nine enlisted men, out of the 107 men carried on the regimental rolls. Twenty-five men, more than a third of those engaged, became casualties. Almost fifty percent of the men in the 28th Massachusetts, the brigade's largest regiment, were killed, wounded or missing in action.[356]

Saint Patrick's Day, as one might imagine, was dutifully observed, especially by the 69th. Father Corby recounts one such celebration at the Brigade's winter quarters at Camp Falmouth, to

[355] Corby, *Memoirs of Chaplain Life*, 185–186.
[356] Bilby, *The Irish Brigade*, 91.

which officers and enlisted men came from New York, New Jersey, Philadelphia, Boston, and elsewhere. Preparation began well in advance, especially on the part of General Meagher, "well instructed in his religion," who directed the military bands when and how to play during the Mass. General Hooker, then commander of the Army of the Potomac, attended, along with "many other distinguished officers." After Mass celebrated by Father Corby, Meagher brought all the guests to inspect the rustic chapel and to admire the "beautiful vestment of water-colored silk, richly embroidered with gold" that had been presented to Corby by the officers and men of the Brigade. The priest noted the devotion with which so many of the men had entered into the sacrifice of the Mass, each knowing it might well be the last Saint Patrick's Day they would live to celebrate.

The Irish Confederates

One of the most interesting facts of Ireland's participation in the Civil War was the similar enthusiasm and devotion with which Irish Confederates joined the Southern cause. In the South, Protestant Irish tended to predominate, though even they, with their brogues, were initially not made to feel terribly welcome. While generally the proportion of Protestants was due to migration patterns, many Irish Catholics, it is true, lost the Faith in the Southern states, particularly in those areas where no priests were present to minister to or instruct them. They often drifted into other denominations, mostly through intermarriage. Many did remain loyal, however, and aside from early studies on Charleston's Bishops John England and Patrick Lynch, only in recent years have Catholics in the South received significant historical attention.

Once assimilated, they usually took on the prevailing modes of thought among their fellow Southerners:

Faith and Fury

The Irish supported African slavery in the South.... They realized that its existence was the key to their survival and prosperity. Slavery provided economic opportunity for Irish immigrants, but more important, it made them members of the "ruling race." Their white skin and their acceptance of slavery automatically elevated them from the bottom of Southern society.... [Although] most of the Irish were not virulent "fire-eaters," they virulently opposed any attack on the "peculiar institution" and often contrasted the paternalism of slaveholders with the callousness of Anglo-Irish landlords.[357]

Southern Irish ignored pleas by Daniel O'Connell for an end to slavery. "They had found success in a slave economy," one historian has noted, "that they could never have found in Ireland."[358] One Catholic priest from Mobile, Father James McGarahan, went to Dublin to present O'Connell with a generous check for the Irish Repeal Movement and, in the course of the presentation, publicly defended slavery, asserting that slaves were "well fed, well taken care of, and sleek in their appearance."[359] Yet another cleric, Father Jeremiah O'Neill of Savannah, visited his native land and "reportedly scolded O'Connell for going out of [his] way to cast a nettle on the grave of the father [slaveholder George Washington] of my adopted country."[360]

Irish Southerners in 1861 were quick to rally to the Confederate cause by enlisting in the Army of the Confederacy, and many of the Irish formed their own ethnic companies.

[357] David T. Gleeson, The Irish in the South: 1815–1877 (Chapel Hill: University of North Carolina Press, 2001), 121.
[358] Ibid., 129.
[359] Ibid., 130.
[360] Ibid.

Although much smaller in total number than their compatriots who fought for the North, a greater proportion of Southern Irish served in the Confederate army. These men fought in every theatre of the war. Difficult in camp, they were nevertheless good fighters who impressed their native born officers. Their memories of Britain's treatment of Ireland influenced their decision-making in the South. By volunteering for Confederate units, Irish men hoped to halt the interference of a powerful central government in their affairs. The Irish also fought because they saw themselves as adopted southerners who had to protect their homes and loved ones from "foreign" invasion.... The Irish became caught up in what they and others in the South saw as the birth of a new nation. In Jackson, Mississippi, when that state passed its secession ordinance in January 1861, Harry McCarthy, a touring Irish comedian, reveled in the cause. Exhilarated by the festivity in the streets, McCarthy composed the first three verses of "The Bonnie Blue Flag," which Irish born John Logan Power, who later served in a Mississippi regiment, published in the *Jackson Mississippian*. In New Orleans, the Irish chose the St. Patrick's Day after secession to celebrate both their heritage and their loyalty to the Southern cause.[361]

Shortly after the bombardment of Fort Sumter, when President Lincoln called for seventy-five thousand volunteers to put down the rebellion, an Irish-born Protestant lawyer from Helena, Arkansas, named Patrick Ronayne Cleburne joined his state's first volunteer company and eventually rose to the rank of major general, one of only two foreign-born Southerners to do so. In Mobile, the

[361] Ibid., 141.

Irish formed the Emerald Guards and hoisted their banner displaying the Confederate flag on one side, and a harp and wreath of shamrocks on the other. The flag was blessed by the Irish-born bishop of Mobile, John Quinlan, an action that, in the minds of many Catholic Irish, bestowed the Church's official blessing on the cause. In Vicksburg, Irish soldiers set up the "Sarsfield Southrons" in honor of Patrick Sarsfield, an Irish cavalry hero who had fought against William of Orange's Protestant invasion of Ireland in the seventeenth century. They were led by an Irish farmer, Felix Hughes, and, like their compatriots in Mobile, unfurled a banner that displayed both their Southern and Irish heritage. Passion for the Southern cause among these men went deep:

> A North Carolina Irish man who identified himself only as
> "E. G.," hoped that "an over-ruling Providence [would] save"
> his fellow Irish men in the North "from the guilt of raising
> their hands against the Southern people." He ... wondered
> how "the Irish Catholics of the North side by side with the
> black-hearted Puritan, the enemy of their race and creed,"
> could oppose the South's attempt "to withdraw from the
> Union."[362]

Outspoken priests such as Jeremiah O'Neill were distinguished, revered figures among the Southern Irish; the Savannah Hibernians celebrated Saint Patrick's Day 1861 with toasts to Jefferson Davis and the Confederate government; and the Charleston Hibernian Society, a prestigious group of both Catholic and Protestant Irish, played a major role in the social life of that most beautiful Southern city.[363]

---

[362] Ibid., 156.

[363] For more on the work of Irish priest chaplains in the Civil War, as well as other Irish who distinguished themselves, see John O'Dea,

The Irish Contribution

The Irish Catholic contribution during the Civil War era displays a certain independence of mind. While there was some consistency in political sympathies — certainly for the Democrats before the war — in the end the Irish contribution defies easy categorization, with some leaders, such as Thomas Francis Meagher and Michael Corcoran, bucking trends in interesting and often courageous ways. On the one hand, their statesmen and foot soldiers often adopted the prevailing attitudes of their surrounding culture, but on the other, they universally maintained and often created subcultures of their own. All of this makes the study of the Irish in America, in this and every era, endlessly fascinating.

History of the Ancient Order of Hibernians and Ladies Auxiliary (St. Louis: National Board of the A.O.H., 1923), 11, 932–948; 949–969.

Chapter 6

∞

Reconstruction: 1865–1877

Political Wrangling

The argument over who should control Reconstruction—the executive or legislative branch of the federal government—emerged because the Constitution didn't foresee stitching the country back together. Each branch of the government was free to interpret the Constitution to its liking. Presidents Lincoln and Andrew Johnson felt that the war powers allocated to the executive to suppress insurrection and to pardon individuals gave the chief executive the upper hand. All that was needed, each man felt, was the restoration of legal governments in the seceded states, which was the proper prerogative of the president.

Southerners, on the other hand, felt there was no need for Reconstruction. In their mind, in spite of everything, the antebellum political situation hadn't been substantially changed: There was nothing to reconstruct. The view, however, was never taken seriously by the authorities in Washington.

During the war, President Lincoln was in a stronger position than Congress and made the most of it. All of Lincoln's plans were ordered around advancing and winning the war event. After Lee's surrender, he thought that it was his prerogative to marshal the Unionist sentiment in the country toward a central idea: that the government was not interested in punishment, but forgiveness. He

offered an amnesty to all Confederates who would take an oath
of allegiance to the federal government, support the Constitution
of the United States, and observe the changes in the slavery laws.
When 10 percent of a state's eligible voters had taken the oath,
those people could begin to establish a new government by forming a state Constitution.

The Radical Republicans were dissatisfied, feeling that the
president's plan ignored Congress and did little for the freedmen.
They especially rejected it for its lack of emphasis on civil rights,
fearing that the president intended to leave these concerns to the
individual states, whom these legislators did not trust to do right by
their former bondsmen. Congress, therefore, passed the Wade-Davis
Bill, which called not for 10 percent, but for a majority of White
voters taking what was described as an "ironclad oath," swearing
past and future loyalty, before they could be readmitted. Congress
was asserting its authority, telling Lincoln that they were going to
have the final say on Reconstruction. The president pocket vetoed
the bill, whose sponsors quickly followed with the Wade-Davis
Manifesto, a crude attack on the president's motives.

Lincoln's dealings with the Radicals in his own party were not
easy. Led by politicians such as Senator Charles Sumner of Massachusetts and Congressman Thaddeus Stevens of Pennsylvania,
their aim was to dispossess Southern aristocrats of their property
and replace them with a new ruling class of poor Whites and Blacks.
They felt rebels such as Jefferson Davis and Robert E. Lee should
all be hanged, and that Southern property seized during the war
should be sold off, with the proceeds placed in a pension fund for
retired Union officers. The president's assassination, though, was
to change the face of all that had gone before.

In the presidential campaign of 1864, Lincoln had chosen as
his running mate Andrew Johnson of Tennessee. He had been a
lifelong Democrat, and Lincoln felt that he could bring balance

to the ticket. A sensitive, proud, and argumentative man, self-conscious about his class, he was very opposed to Southern plantation aristocrats. He had been recognized as a representative of poor Whites in East Tennessee, where he was a tailor by profession; his wife had taught him to read and write. From there, he had served in the state legislature, then as governor of Tennessee, then in the U.S. Senate—both prior to and following his presidential term.

At the end of May 1865, the new president followed his predecessor's lead and issued amnesty to all who had participated in the rebellion, excepting fourteen specific categories, but pardons for those excepted were usually granted once applied for. That summer, he appointed provisional governors for the former Confederate states, mostly Southerners who had supported the Union. They, in turn, called state Constitutional conventions for the purpose of repealing the ordinance of secession, and all White males were eligible to vote unless they were excluded from Johnson's pardon. All voters had to take the oath of allegiance to the U.S. government, and the Constitutional conventions had to ratify the Thirteenth Amendment, recognizing the freedom of the former slaves. While Johnson was asserting strong executive powers, the Radicals in Congress felt he was entirely too lenient with the South and could not explain his change in attitude. Congress would not be in session until December, but already plans were being made to challenge the president seriously.

Meanwhile, Catholic and especially Irish opinion in the North tended toward supporting Johnson's leniency. The *Irish American* praised Johnson's pardon of Jefferson Davis and editorialized that, had Lincoln lived, the South would have been effectively reconstructed in far less time without so much Congressional interference. When General Grant was elected in 1868, the paper argued that Reconstruction would be "smoothly and finally carried out, since the man who, at the head of the army, had received the surrender of the rebels without restriction would not enforce restrictive measures in his civic capacity."[364]

Having been given basically carte blanche by the Johnson administration, early in 1866 the Southern states began to enact Black Codes, which were vagrancy and apprenticeship laws binding freed Blacks to the land. Often with the explicit support of Irish and Catholic interests, White supremacy was further entrenched as Black involvement in politics was functionally prohibited. In response, Congress passed a bill creating the Freedmen's Bureau, a temporary agency to care for the former slaves by placing them in jobs and homes. Congress sought to empower the bureau to try in military courts anyone accused of depriving freedmen of civil rights, but Johnson vetoed the bill, arguing that Congress had no right to negotiate with eleven states as yet unrepresented, and that the military trials would have been violations of the Fifth Amendment of the Constitution.

From December 1865 until December 1867, the Thirty-Ninth Congress was in session, and the stage was set for a conflict with Johnson. In March 1866, Congress passed a Civil Rights Act granting equal rights to all citizens, with the assumption that freed slaves were citizens. Johnson vetoed the bill, but Congress overrode his veto. The following month, the Fourteenth Amendment to the Constitution was introduced, formulated at least in part by the Radical Republicans; it defined citizenship, made Blacks U.S. citizens, penalized any area of the country refusing adult males the right to vote (a provision never enforced), and called for a complete repudiation of all debts of the former Confederate government by the U.S. Government. Since the Southern states were occupied by the U.S. Army, they were considered to be in the Union; to have the troops withdrawn, they had to pass the amendment.

[364]Gibson, *Attitudes of the New York Irish*, 231.

In March 1867, Johnson vetoed three bills, and in each case his veto was overridden. The First Reconstruction Act divided the South into five military districts presided over by military governors who could set aside civil law, close courts, and try cases by military tribunal. (This shift in policy, away from the priorities of the floundering Johnson, came to be known as Military Reconstruction.) The Tenure of Office Act, passed the same day, affirmed that the president could not remove, without the consent of the Senate, a civil office holder who had been appointed by the president and confirmed by the Senate. Finally, the Command of the Army Act defined that military orders must be issued by the general of the army rather than by the president of the United States.

Johnson's secretary of war, whom he inherited from Lincoln, was Edwin McMasters Stanton. He was constantly at odds with the president and would leak confidential news to the press from Cabinet meetings. Johnson wanted to get rid of him, and he also felt the Tenure of Office Act was unconstitutional. To get a test case into court, Johnson sent a letter to Stanton, dismissing him. (Rather than leave quietly, Stanton decided to barricade himself inside his office.) Ulysses S. Grant refused the appointment, with his eyes on the Republican nomination for president in 1868. Johnson's next pick, General Lorenzo Thomas, accepted and informed Stanton that if he did not evacuate his office within twenty-four hours, federal guards would remove him. Thomas was subsequently charged with breaking and entering in a violation of the Tenure of Office Act, but this would bring the new law to the courts. To avoid this, the Radicals persuaded Stanton to drop the charges.

Shortly after this drama, a Pennsylvania congressman introduced a resolution to impeach Johnson, which passed 126 to 47. Of the eleven indictments brought against Johnson, the only one of substance was an alleged violation of the Tenure of Office Act.

Faith and Fury

Johnson was acquitted by one vote and quietly served out the remainder of his term.

Amid this turbulence, Catholics would again take a role in the national story. But this role was not one of protagonist, and many of the gains Catholics had made in the national culture during the war quickly dissipated.

Booth's Boarding House

Mrs. Mary Surratt was a Catholic who ran a boardinghouse at 604 H Street NW in the nation's capital. It was here that John Wilkes Booth and several accomplices met often to draw up plans to murder the president, the vice president, and the secretary of state. Booth tried to enlist the help of Mary's son, John, as well. Of the conspirators, George Atzerodt was to kill Andrew Johnson, though he never got around to attempting it; Louis Powell was to murder Seward, which he nearly succeeded in doing, stabbing the secretary several times in his bedroom. And, of course, Booth was to kill the president.

The entire conspiracy, and especially the degree of involvement of Mrs. Surrat and her son, has been the subject of exhaustive historical studies. In the immediate aftermath, Mary was charged with abetting, aiding, concealing, counseling, and harboring her co-defendants. The federal government initially tried to find legal counsel for her and the others, but almost no attorneys were willing to take on the case, for fear they would be thought disloyal to the Union. After finally securing the services of Reverdy Johnson of Maryland, the military trial proceeded, and on June 30, 1865, it found her guilty on all but two charges. A week later, she became the first woman executed by the federal government. The mood of the country was one of revenge, though several historical inquires have concluded that Mrs. Surratt was the victim of a gross miscarriage of justice.

Mary Elizabeth Jenkins was born in 1823 into an English Protestant family in Prince George's County, Maryland. At age twelve, she was enrolled in a Catholic school for young ladies attached to Saint Mary's Church in Alexandria, Virginia, operated by Mother Seton's Sisters of Charity from Emmitsburg. While there, Mary converted to Catholicism, taking the Confirmation name Eugenia. In 1840, she married John H. Surratt, of a French Protestant family, though no record of a Catholic marriage has been discovered in the churches nearest their homes. At least one biographer does, however, think it likely she was married in the Faith.[365]

The Surratts initially lived on a farm near Oxon Hill, Maryland. Mary attended Mass regularly, made contributions toward the building of a new parish church, and saw to it that her children received Catholic educations—including her son John, who began at Saint Thomas Manor Jesuit school at Chapel Point in Southern Maryland, and continued at Saint Charles College near Ellicott City. Though Saint Charles was a minor seminary, day students like John were accepted; he studied there until his father's sudden death in 1862.

By October 1864, Mary had decided to lease the farm to a fellow Catholic named John Lloyd, and to move to the city, where she hoped to make a livelihood running a boardinghouse. Her boarders were almost exclusively Catholic, and the home was located just a few blocks from Ford's Theatre.

From December 1864, John Surratt, Jr. was an integral part of a plot to kidnap Abraham Lincoln. John Jr. was working with John Wilkes Booth, who often visited John at his mother's boardinghouse. Other members of the conspiracy also called, and stayed there at different times. In addition

[365] Kenneth J. Zanca, *The Catholics and Mrs. Mary Surratt* (Lanham, MD: University Press of America, 2008), 18.

it appears that John Jr., deeply involved in the Confederate underground, let it be known that his mother's residence was a safe house for agents and blockade runners passing through Washington. Mrs. Surratt entertained these people in her home on many occasions, conversed with them (often in private), fed them, and gave them beds. On the day of the assassination, she ran an errand for Booth, delivering supplies he would need on his escape (and maybe a message) to Lloyd at the Surrattsville tavern. Whether she knew Booth's business or the existence of a conspiracy under her very roof is not clear, even to this day. She also entertained priests and Sisters of Charity. This being said, while living in the capital, the Surratts and their boarders attended both St. Patrick's Church (F Street and 10th) and St. Aloysius's (north of the Capitol). Chilling evidence of the Surratts' involvement in St. Aloysius parish was found by D.C. police while they searched the boardinghouse after the assassination. On a slip of paper in the handwriting of Anna Surratt is written: "Those who have made contributions to benefit of St. A's Church: J. Wilkes Booth ... 5 —; J[ohn] H[arrison] S[urratt] — 3." Also, at this time, old friends, Father Stonestreet, pastor of that church, and Father Wiget, president of Gonzaga College, a secondary school, were in residence at St. Aloysius, on whose land the school was located.[366]

The response of the Catholic press in the United States was a study in contrasts. The *Pittsburgh Catholic* was favorable toward the trial and its verdicts, which was not surprising, given the extremely

---

[366] Ibid., 21. The Surrattsville tavern is a reference to the Oxon Hill location at which the Surratts had previously lived; Anna Surratt was Mary's daughter.

strong Unionist sentiment found in Pittsburgh, one of Lincoln's most loyal cities. The *Cincinnati Catholic Telegraph* criticized the trial but, in the end, accepted the verdict, while the Baltimore *Catholic Mirror*, publishing in a city where there had been mixed regional sympathies for decades, avoided all comment on both the trial and the verdict.[367]

Catholic Conspiracy?

What the sensationalism of the trial did do was bring America's ever-present anti-Catholicism back to the front of the national consciousness. Stories abounded that all the conspirators were Catholics, even taking their orders directly from the pope. Pius IX was clearly suspicious of American-style liberal regimes (the *Syllabus of Errors* against modern political arrangements had recently been promulgated), and it was said he had deputized scores, if not hundreds, of priests, especially Jesuits, to work tirelessly to destroy democracy. General Catholic support for the South's peculiar institution and Justice Taney's Catholic Faith were considered further evidence that the Church might have wanted to sabotage the healing of the county by killing Lincoln. How appropriate, then, that the conspirators met in the home of a Catholic woman, a home often frequented by priests and Jesuits—and all the boarders arrested on the evening of April 17, 1865, were Catholics.

After the murder, Booth escaped into Southern Maryland, where he was, indeed, aided by Catholics; John Surratt Jr., had escaped first to Elmira, New York, and later to Canada, where he was sheltered by Catholic priests with the approval of the local bishop, who, it was said, was a personal friend of Jefferson Davis. From there he fled to England, and then to Rome, where he assumed

[367] Ibid., 86.

the name Watson and was ultimately discovered among the papal guards. Other instances where Catholics, in fact, contributed to Mrs. Surratt's conviction, as well as the initiative of Pope Pius IX to have John Surratt arrested, were conveniently overlooked by the nativist-sympathizing press:

> Catholics had reasons "to feel the heat" from the assertion that a Catholic conspiracy had brought Lincoln down. Samuel Arnold, a convicted co-conspirator, attended Georgetown College. . . . David Herold, executed along with Mrs. Surratt, while not a Catholic, attended the same College for three years. Dr. Mudd, a convicted co-conspirator, from a prominent Maryland Catholic family, father of nine children (four of whom were baptized by father Peter Lenaghan, a witness on behalf of Mary Surratt at her trial), also attended Georgetown in 1851–1852. John Surratt, Jr. had attended a Catholic minor seminary, and *was* assisted by Canadian and English priests in his attempt to elude his pursuers. Mrs. Surratt, of course, had five Catholic priests testify on her behalf at her trial, and was accompanied by two clergymen to the scaffold. Thomas Ewing, a Catholic, did defend three of the co-conspirators (Arnold, Mudd, and O'Laughlin, and none of them received death sentences). John Lloyd, who gave Booth material aid and whiskey while he was fleeing Washington the night of April 14th, was a Catholic. Dr. William Queen, a friend of Dr. Mudd and a Confederate sympathizer, was a Catholic and a one time Jesuit scholastic from 1800 to 1806. His son-in-law, John C. Thompson, who had introduced Booth to Mudd, attended Georgetown from 1838 to 1842. Booth, Mudd, and Thompson had attended Mass together at St. Mary's Church, near Bryantown, Maryland in 1864. The air was foul with suspicion of Catholics.

Anti-Catholicism in the secular and Protestant papers advanced mistrust.[368]

The Doctor Mudd mentioned above was Samuel Mudd, who was
born in Charles County, Maryland, in 1833 and grew up on his father's tobacco plantation. After several years of private tutoring, he
went to Saint John's Catholic Prep School in Frederick, Maryland,
and from there to Georgetown, completing his education studying
medicine at the University of Maryland, Baltimore. Working as
a doctor and tobacco farmer in Southern Maryland, Mudd used
slaves and indeed believed that slavery was a God-given institution.

After shooting Lincoln, Booth rode with fellow conspirator
David Herold[369] to Mudd's home in the early hours of April 15,
1865. Mudd performed surgery on his fractured leg before the as-
sassin eventually made his way to Virginia, where he was killed
by Boston Corbett. It was not the first time Booth and Mudd had
met, though the doctor always maintained he did not recognize
Booth because of a disguise he was wearing. In all probability,
Mudd learned of the assassination of the president some time the
day after, but he did not report Booth's visit for twenty-four hours,
which seemed to link him to the crime. A military commission
found him guilty of aiding and conspiring in a murder, and he
was sentenced to life imprisonment at Fort Jefferson, in the Dry
Tortugas, about seventy miles west of Key West, Florida. He was
eventually pardoned by President Andrew Johnson for his heroic
efforts in a yellow fever epidemic and returned to live a quiet life
practicing medicine at his farm.

[368] Ibid., 85. The author has also considered the subject of Pope Pius
IX and the fate of the Lincoln conspirators. See Zanca, *Surratt*,
103–117.
[369] In Booth's original plan, Herold was to be assigned to kill Ulysses
S. Grant.

Faith and Fury

Some years after the assassination, Mudd's wife wrote a statement of the initial meeting between her husband and John Wilkes Booth:

> The first time I ever saw John Wilkes Booth was in November, 1864. My husband went to Bryantown Church, and was introduced to Booth by John Thompson, an old friend from Baltimore, who asked my husband if he knew of anyone who had a good riding-horse for sale; to which he replied, "My next neighbor has one." After this they made arrangements to have Booth come up to our home that evening to see about buying his horse. There was company in the house and supper was just over, when my husband came in and asked me to prepare for a stranger.... The conversation was on general topics. Nothing relative to the Administration or the war was spoken of by anyone present. After supper Booth joined the visitors and remained in general conversation until bedtime, which was about 9:30 o'clock. I did not see Booth again until at the breakfast table the next morning. After breakfast the horses were ordered, Booth tied his at the gate, and my husband threw the bridle rein of his horse over his arm and walked along with Booth across the field to Squire George Gardiner's. Booth soon returned, came in and got his overcoat which he had thrown over the back of a chair in the parlor, said good-by, and rode away.[370]

In the early hours of April 15, 1865, Mrs. Mudd wrote that she heard a rap on the door. Her husband was not feeling well and asked that she go see who it was—but she, being understandably apprehensive, asked him to go. He returned telling her a man with

---

[370]Nettie Mudd, *The Life of Dr. Samuel A. Mudd* (New York and Washington: Neale Publishing, 1906), 29.

a broken leg was downstairs, and she later heard her husband and a third man (Herold) assisting the injured man upstairs. The following morning after breakfast, the two men started to leave, but Mrs. Mudd noticed the whiskers on Herold (who called himself Tyson) becoming partially detached as he walked down the stairs and she became suspicious. She told "Tyson" to leave if he must, but to allow the injured man to remain, for his own safety. He assured her they would not travel far if the other man (Booth) were not able. Rather, he would "take him to my lady-love's, not far from here."

About an hour later, on Mrs. Mudd's telling, Dr. Mudd returned and told his wife of the president's assassination. "Those men were suspicious looking characters," he said, "I will go to Bryantown and tell the officers." She agreed with him about the men, but, being afraid to remain in the house alone, "as the next day was Sunday, I asked him to send word to the soldiers from church, which he did."[371]

Mary Surratt was interred in Mount Olivet Catholic Cemetery in Washington, and, in 1883, Dr. Mudd was buried in his parish cemetery, Saint Mary's, in Bryantown, Maryland.

A Black Catholic Church?

If Catholicism were being cast in a bad light in America, one would never have known it in Baltimore in 1866 as the Second Plenary Council closed — including among its observers President Andrew Johnson.

> Mulberry Street, alongside the Baltimore Cathedral, was lined with spectators, and people crowded windows and rooftops to watch the procession from Archbishop's House that opened the council. Forty-five Archbishops and Bishops

---

[371] Ibid., 32–33.

walked in the procession, attended by a phalanx of theological advisers and ceremonial assistants. As they turned the corner onto Cathedral Street and entered the Cathedral's main doors, a full orchestra welcomed them with the grand march from *Tannhauser*. For the music of the morning's liturgy the choir chose Mozart's Twelfth Mass. The bishops represented a church of nearly four million Americans in a national population of some thirty million. Since the last plenary council the number of churches and priests had doubled. The major reason for growth was evidenced by the council fathers themselves: of forty-seven mitred participants in the opening procession, thirty were foreign-born immigrants.[372]

While due concern was given to the creation of Catholic orphanages, protectories, and industrial schools, a great deal of discussion focused on the evangelization of the freed slaves, who numbered roughly four million. Baltimore's Archbishop Martin J. Spalding, writing to his episcopal colleague in New York, John McCloskey, was fully aware that if the current opportunity was lost, it would never present itself again. Even so, the rhetoric offered was vague, and little actual planning followed the formal statements of the participants. There was still a tendency to look on Lincoln's Emancipation Proclamation as too hasty an approach to eliminating a centuries-old institution that had become part of the social and economic fabric of the country:

> We could have wished that in accordance with the action of the Catholic Church in past ages, in regard to the serfs in Europe, a more gradual system of emancipation could have been adopted, so that they might have been in some measure

---

[372] Hennesey, *American Catholics*, 159–160. The previous plenary council had occurred in 1852.

prepared to make a better use of their freedom, than they are likely to do now. Still the evils which must necessarily attend upon the sudden liberation of so large a multitude, with their peculiar dispositions and habits, only make the appeal to our Christian charity and zeal, presented by their forlorn condition, the more forcible and imperative.[373]

Yet most outreach failed—both to succeed and to materialize at all. Some have advanced the argument that Catholic liturgical tradition lacked many of the characteristics of the traditional African understanding of worship—the "prayer meetings, shouting and spirituals which were an attractive feature of Black Protestantism, the bodily participation and ecstatic behavior … so reminiscent of African patterns of dance and possession."[374] There was, however, a deeper answer. The dean of American Catholic historians once posed the question of how much had been done by the Church for the freed bondsmen, and he just as quickly answered:

If one thinks in terms of the nearly 4,000,000 Negroes involved, relatively little. Catholics had indeed preserved organizational unity throughout the crisis more than any other religious body…. Facing the problem squarely the [second plenary] council decreed that every means be implemented for the religious care and instruction of Negroes. Anyone neglecting to provide these means for all, black and white, would, said the bishops, "merit the strongest reproach." But it was far easier to exhort than to win effective action, as the Archbishop of New Orleans learned when he returned from the council. His appeal to the religious orders within his jurisdiction to open schools for Negroes went unanswered for

[373]Cited in ibid., 162.
[374]Cited in ibid.

months. So intense was southern feeling against educating the Negroes that the religious orders, some of whose members as southerners shared the sentiment, shied away from the task for fear of alienating white patronage.... [Through] a combination of racial prejudice, timidity, and scarcity of manpower and resources, the chance for large scale conversion of the Negroes to Catholicism after the Civil War gradually slipped away.[375]

There were some bright spots, however, such as the stories of Henriette DeLille, discussed earlier, and Elizabeth Lange. Born in 1784 in a Haitian enclave in Santiago de Cuba, she left at an early age seeking the peace and security of the United States. She was directed to Baltimore, where there were a large number of French-speaking Haitians who had fled revolution in their native land. She quickly realized that the children of fellow immigrants needed education, and, though it was not illegal to teach Black children in the state of Maryland, there were no public schools for them. For several years, Elizabeth and a friend, Magdaleine Balas, offered free education to those children in their homes.

A meeting with a James Joubert, the Sulpician priest who served Black Americans, proved to be providential: He proposed opening a school for Black children, and, after the friends revealed their desire to consecrate their lives to God, Joubert decided to form a religious congregation for the Christian education of children. Baltimore's Archbishop James Whitfield approved, and it became a reality in July 1829, when Elizabeth (hereafter to be known as Sister and later Mother Mary) and three other women professed vows, forming the Oblate Sisters of Providence, dedicated to the Catholic education of children of color. Mother Mary would encounter many

[375] John Tracy Ellis, *American Catholicism* (Chicago: The University of Chicago Press, 1955), 99–100.

hardships, not the least of which was aggressive racial hostility; her unceasing faith persevered, however, and her cause for canonization has been opened.

The nation's first Black priest—whose cause is also under investigation—was Augustus Tolton, an ex-slave from Hannibal, Missouri, who was ordained in 1888 after years of study at Rome's North American College. The American apostolate to African Americans expanded with the arrival of the Mill Hill Fathers from England in 1871. Its American offshoot, the Josephites, was founded in 1891, with their first ordination of a Black priest, Father Charles Randolph Uncles, the same year. Their *Josephite Harvest* magazine would, for decades, chronicle the work of Black evangelization, which had been called for so strongly many years earlier, but, regrettably, had not been sufficiently acted upon.

Anti-Catholicism and Public Education

As Reconstruction proceeded, anti-Catholicism once again came into the spotlight, this time around Bible reading in public schools. The institutions of the Catholic Church in America had continued to be built up—especially in the form of parochial schools, where Catholics believed their children would be protected against Protestant indoctrination; this concern stemmed especially from the use of the King James Version of the Bible. Because Catholics felt unwelcome in and threatened by the public schools, they asked for government aid for their own school system.

In an effort to illustrate the growing threat of Catholicism, the celebrated cartoonist Thomas Nast depicted the pope and Jesuits firing on the White House. The threat that Catholics might become too strong, whether in the educational sphere or political life, and usurp "American values" was real and strong. Biblical translations became the battleground for this larger cultural war.

Faith and Fury

In Cincinnati, Archbishop John B. Purcell and his brother, Father Edward Purcell, editor of the *Catholic Telegraph*, tried to reach an accommodation between public and parochial schools, so that Catholic families could comfortably send their children to public schools and government support for Catholic ones would no longer be necessary—as long as readings from the King James Bible ceased. The local school board seemed amenable, but Protestant leaders immediately protested:

> Equating Catholicism with the Confederacy demonstrated how the Civil War, and the alleged disloyalty of many Northern Catholics symbolized by the New York City draft riots, directly shaped post war anti-Catholicism. But Nast's cartoons and criticism from Republican and Protestant leaders could not keep the Bible in Cincinnati's public school rooms. Such determined opposition ensued that a legal battle dragged on for years, but ultimately, in 1873 the Ohio State Supreme Court upheld the decision to remove the Bible from the state's public schools.[376]

The battle reached a fever pitch around the country, reminiscent of the Know-Nothing days. Ulysses S. Grant had been elected president in 1868, and effectively played the anti-Catholic card—especially when, after serving two terms, he was giving serious consideration to running again in the election of 1876:

> President Grant ... linked the Union's struggle from 1861–1865 to the debate over education in the 1870's. In October 1875, before a reunion of several thousand Union veterans in Des Moines, Iowa, the president called on Americans to

[376] William B. Kurtz, *Excommunicated from the Union: How the Civil War Created a Separate Catholic America* (New York: Fordham University Press, 2016), 137–138.

resist Catholic efforts to obtain public money for parochial schools. "If we are to have another contest in the near future of our national existence, I predict that the dividing line will not be Mason and Dixon's but between patriotism and intelligence on the one side, and superstition on the other." By "superstition" everyone in his audience knew he meant Roman Catholicism. By choosing to deliver his speech in front of a reunion of Union veterans, Grant had in the most powerful way possible linked the struggle for the Union to the struggle against Catholic influence in American society.[377]

Catholic editors were quick to respond to Grant; in particular, Paulist father Adrian Louis Rosecrans, son of the famed Union general, "mercilessly mocked Grant's Iowa speech in an unsigned editorial in the *Catholic World* which was so sarcastic that some obtuse observers mistook him for agreeing with Grant."[378]

---

[377] Ibid., 139. Though much of the Irish-American press turned against Grant as his administration progressed, the Republicans had made concerted efforts to win the Irish Catholic vote in the presidential election of 1868. The *Irish Republic*, a publication that had moved from Chicago to New York, edited by David Bell and Michael Scanlon, became the first such publication to endorse the Republican ticket. Later, the *Irish People*, originally an organ of the Fenians, edited by John O'Mahoney, joined in support. In June, 1868, an Irish Republican Campaign Club came into existence, castigating the Irish for their blind subservience to the Democrats, which, it argued, had alienated thousands of influential Americans who had the power to help Ireland. Gipson, op. cit., 218–220; 280–285.

[378] Kurtz, op. cit., 140. James A. McMaster, editor of the New York *Freemen's Journal*, predicted an onslaught against Catholics, while at the same time thanking the "Methodistic ass" President Grant for helping to reinforce the Catholic Church's unity by his persecution of it. Baltimore's *Catholic Mirror* also strongly hinted that Grant was under the control of the Methodists. Kurtz, op. cit., 140.

Faith and Fury

In December 1875, Republican Senator James G. Blaine introduced a constitutional amendment to forbid the use of public funds
for parochial schools.[379] Grant, in his annual message to Congress,
went even further, advocating "the taxation of church property,
forbidding religious instruction, and barring illiterate immigrants
from voting."[380] As it happened, Grant declined to run for a third
term, and Ohio's governor, Rutherford B. Hayes, was chosen as
the Republican nominee in 1876. After a seriously disputed election, Hayes was awarded the presidency. Blaine's amendment was
eventually modified in such a way that Congress was powerless to
enforce it. Democrats supported it; Catholic objections dwindled;
and the threat to Catholic institutions was temporarily diminished.

---

[379] This was curious, in that Blaine's mother was a Roman Catholic.
Blaine (1830–1893) represented Maine in the House of Representatives, serving as Speaker of the House from 1869–1875. He was
then U.S. Senator from Maine, 1876–1881. He served twice as
Secretary of State, and was the Republican candidate for President
in 1884.

[380] Kurtz, op. cit., 140.

∞

Conclusion

The three decades of American Catholic history around the Civil War were in many ways a positive story of the growing contribution of Catholics in American life. It was a period when the hierarchy was a source of guidance whom Catholics highly respected—even though their moral bearings were not always properly calibrated. It was a period of Catholic patriotism in both the North and the South, with significant episcopal and lay diplomatic and military contributions to both governments and unprecedented pastoral care on the part of chaplains and religious Sisters. Finally, though, it was a period in which many of these gains were quickly forgotten, as Catholics once again became the targets of bigotry and intolerance.

This is, perhaps, American Catholic history in microcosm, with important but complicated contributions from ragtag immigrants and sophisticated leaders being all too often overshadowed by ancient and reductionist prejudices. Let us venture to say, though, that the "melancholy strife" of this era was more endurable due to the faithful, tangible, and growing presence of so many members of Christ's Mystical Body.

Bibliography

Andrews, Wayne, ed. *Concise Dictionary of American History*. New York: Charles Scribner's Sons, 1962.

Barton, George. *Angels of the Battlefield*. Philadelphia: Catholic Art Publishing, 1897.

Beagle, Donald Robert, and Bryan Albin Giemza. *Poet of the Lost Cause: A Life of Father Ryan*. Knoxville: University of Tennessee Press, 2008.

Bilby, Joseph G. *The Irish Brigade in the Civil War*. Cambridge, MA: Da Capo Press, 1995.

Billington, Ray Allen. *The Protestant Crusade: 1800–1860*. Chicago: Quadrangle Books, 1938.

Boatner, Mark M. III. *The Civil War Dictionary*. New York: David McKay, 1959.

Boritt, Gabor. *The Gettysburg Gospel*. New York: Simon and Schuster, 2006.

Bruce, Susannah Ural. *The Harp and the Eagle: Irish-American Volunteers and the Union Army, 1861–1865*. New York: New York University Press, 2006.

Catton, Bruce. *The Civil War*. Boston: Houghton Mifflin, 1960.

Chesson, Michael Bedout, and Leslie Jean Roberts. *Exile in Richmond: The Confederate Journal of Henri Garidel*. Charlottesville: University Press of Virginia, 2001.

Faith and Fury

Connor, Charles P. "The American Catholic Political Position at Mid-Century: Archbishop Hughes as a Test Case. Ph.D." Dissertation, Fordham University, New York City, 1979.

Corby, William, C.S.C. *Memoirs of Chaplain Life*. New York: Fordham University Press, 1992.

Dangerfield, George. *The Awakening of American Nationalism*. New York: Harper and Row, 1965.

Dolan, Jay P. *The Irish Americans: A History*. New York: Bloomsbury Press, 2008.

Durkin, Joseph T. *Confederate Navy Chief: Stephen R. Mallory*. Columbia: University of South Carolina Press, 1987.

———. *General Sherman's Son*. New York: Farrar, Straus, and Cudahy, 1959.

Eaton, Clement. *A History of the Southern Confederacy*. London: Collier Macmillan, 1954.

Eckenrode, H. J., and Gary W. Gallagher. *James Longstreet: Lee's War Horse*. Chapel Hill: University of North Carolina Press, 1986.

Ellis, Edward Robb. *The Epic of New York City*. New York: Kondansha International, 1997.

Ellis, John Tracy. *American Catholicism*. Chicago: University of Chicago Press, 1956.

———. *Documents of American Catholic History*. Milwaukee: Bruce, 1956.

Faherty, William Barnaby, S.J. *Exile in Erin: A Confederate Chaplain's Story: The Life of Father John B. Bannon*. St. Louis: Missouri Historical Society Press, 2002.

Farrelly, Maura Jane. *Anti–Catholicism in America, 1620–1860*. Cambridge, UK: Cambridge University Press, 2018.

Foner, Eric. *The Fiery Trial: Abraham Lincoln and American Slavery*. New York: W. W. Norton, 2010.

Foote, Shelby. *The Civil War: A Narrative*. 3 vols. New York: Random House, 1974.

————. *Stars in Their Courses: The Gettysburg Campaign*. New York: Modern Library, 1994.

Garraty, John A. *The American Nation: A History of the United States*. 2 vols. New York: Harper and Row. 1966.

Gibson, Florence E. *The Attitudes of the New York Irish toward State and National Affairs: 1848–1892*. NewYork: AMS Press, 1968.

Glazier, Michael, and Thomas J. Shelley, eds. *The Encyclopedia of American Catholic History*. Collegeville, MN: Liturgical Press, 1997.

Gleeson, David T. *The Irish in the South: 1815–1877*. Chapel Hill: University of North Carolina Press, 2001.

Harwell, Richard B., ed. *The Confederate Reader: How the South Saw the War*. New York: Dover Publications, 1989.

Hassard, John R.G. *Life of the Most Rev. John Hughes, D.D.: First Archbishop of New York*. New York: D. Appleton, 1866.

Heisser, David C.R., and Stephen J. White Sr. *Patrick N. Lynch: 1817–1882: Third Catholic Bishop of Charleston*. Columbia: University of South Carolina Press, 2015.

Hennesey, James, S.J. *American Catholics: A History of the Roman Catholic Community in the United States*. New York: Oxford University Press, 1981.

Hueston, Robert F. *The Catholic Press and Nativism: 1840–1860*. New York: Arno Press, 1976.

Kehoe, Lawrence. *Complete Works of the Most Rev. John Hughes, D.D.: Archbishop of New York*. 2 vols. New York: Lawrence Kehoe, 1866.

Kurtz, William B. *Excommunicated from the Union: How the Civil War Created a Separate Catholic America*. New York: Fordham University Press, 2016.

Lankford, Nelson D., ed. *An Irishman in Dixie: Thomas Conolly's Diary of the Fall of the Confederacy*. Columbia: University of South Carolina Press, 1988.

Lockwood, Robert P., ed. *Anti–Catholicism in American Culture.* Huntington, IN: Our Sunday Visitor, 2000.

Longenecker, Steve. *Gettysburg Religion.* New York: Fordham University Press, 2014.

Loughery, John. *Dagger John: Archbishop John Hughes and the Making of Irish America.* Ithaca, NY: Cornell University Press, 2018.

Marlin, George J., and Brad Miner. *Sons of Saint Patrick: A History of the Archbishops of New York from Dagger John to Timmytown.* San Francisco: Ignatius Press, 2017.

McPherson, James. *Battle Cry of Freedom.* New York: Oxford University Press, 1988.

———. *Tried by War: Abraham Lincoln as Commander in Chief.* New York: Penguin Press, 2008.

McSweeny, Edward F. X. *The Story of the Mountain: Mount Saint Mary's College and Seminary, Emmitsburg, Maryland.* 2 vols. Emmitsburg, MD: Weekly Chronicle, 1911.

Merk, Frederick. *Manifest Destiny and Mission in American History.* New York: Vintage Books, 1966.

Moore, David G. *William S. Rosecrans and the Union Victory: A Civil War Biography.* Jefferson, NC: McFarland, 2014.

Morris, Richard B., ed. *Encyclopedia of American History.* New York: Harper and Row, 1965.

Mudd, Nettie. *The Life of Dr. Samuel A. Mudd.* LaPlata, Maryland: Dick Wildes Printing, 1983.

Noll, Mark A. *The Civil War as a Theological Crisis.* Chapel Hill: University of North Carolina Press, 2006.

O'Dea, John. *History of the Ancient Order of Hibernians and Ladies' Auxiliary.* 3 vols. St. Louis: National Board of the A.O.H., 1923.

O'Dowd, Niall. *Lincoln and the Irish.* New York: Skyhorse, 2018.

Panzer, Joel. S. *The Popes and Slavery.* New York: Alba House, 1996.

Peters, Dr. William G. *The Catholic Bishops in the Confederacy.* Chattanooga: C.S. Printing Office, 2016.

Bibliography

Pine, M. S. *John Bannister Tabb: The Priest-Poet*. Washington, D.C.: Georgetown Visitation Convent, 1915.

Rable, George C. *God's Almost Chosen Peoples: A Religious History of the American Civil War*. Chapel Hill: University of North Carolina Press, 2010.

Randall, James G. *The Civil War and Reconstruction*. Boston: D.C. Heath and Company, 1937.

Rice, Madeline Hooke. *American Catholic Opinion in the Slavery Controversy*. New York: Columbia University Press, 1944.

Roland, Charles P. *The Confederacy*. Chicago: University of Chicago Press, 1960.

Rubin, Anne Sarah. *A Shattered Nation: The Rise and Fall of the Confederacy, 1861–1868*. Chapel Hill: University of North Carolina Press, 2005.

Schauinger, J. Herman. *William J. Gaston, Carolinian*. Milwaukee: Bruce, 1949.

Shannon, William V. *The American Irish: A Political and Social Portrait*. New York: Collier Books, 1963.

Smaridge, Norah, and Albert Micale. *Hands of Mercy: The Story of Sister Nurses in the Civil War*. New York: Benziger Brothers, 1960.

Smith, Goldwin. *A History of England*. New York: Charles Scribner's Sons, 1966.

Stampp, Kenneth M., ed. *The Causes of the Civil War*. New York: Simon and Schuster, 1959.

———. *The Era of Reconstruction: 1865–1877*. New York: Alfred A. Knopf, 1966.

Swisher, Carl Brent. *Roger B. Taney*. Hamden, CT: Archon Books, 1961.

Thomas, Emory. M. *The Confederacy as a Revolutionary Experience*. Englewood Cliffs, NJ: Prentice-Hall, 1971.

Toomey, Daniel Carroll. *The Civil War in Maryland*. Baltimore: Toomey Press, 2009.

Tucker, Philip Thomas, Ph.D. *The Irish at Gettysburg.* Charleston, SC: History Press, 2018.

Van Deusen, Glyndon G. *The Jacksonian Era: 1828–1848.* New York: Harper and Row, 1959.

Varon, Elizabeth R. *Disunion! The Coming of the American Civil War: 1789–1859.* Chapel Hill: University of North Carolina Press, 2008.

Zanca, Kenneth J., Ph.D., ed. *American Catholics and Slavery: 1789–1866: An Anthology of Primary Documents.* Lanham, MD: University Press of America, 1994.

———. *The Catholics and Mrs. Mary Surratt: How They Responded to the Trial and Execution of the Lincoln Conspirator.* Lanham, MD: University Press of America, 2008.

∞

About the Author

Fr. Charles P. Connor, S.T.L., Ph.D., is a professor of systemic theology and Church history at Mount St. Mary's Seminary in Emmitsburg, Maryland. He has previously authored books on several topics, such as *Classic Catholic Converts*, *Defenders of the Faith in Word and Deed*, *Meditations on the Catholic Priesthood*, *The Saint for the Third Millennium: Thérèse of Lisieux*, *The Spiritual Legacy of Archbishop Fulton J. Sheen*, *John Cardinal O'Connor and the Culture of Life*, and *Pioneer Priests and Makeshift Altars: A History of Catholicism in the Thirteen Colonies*. He has co-produced dozens of series for EWTN and is actively engaged in preaching retreats for priests and laity throughout the United States. A priest of the Diocese of Scranton, Pennsylvania, he served in diocesan parishes for eighteen years, including as rector of St. Peter's Cathedral in Scranton. Fr. Connor holds a B.A. and an M.A. in U.S. history from the University of Scranton, a Ph.B. from the Institute of Philosophy at the Catholic University of Louvain in Belgium, a doctorate in U.S. history from Fordham University in New York City, an S.T.B. from the Gregorian University in Rome, an M.A. from the Angelicum University in Rome, and an S.T.L. from the Pontifical John Paul II Institute for Studies on Marriage and Family in Washington, D.C.